This is an important book. Why? It focuses on Africa, the "last frontier" in business, with insights for all BoPMs; as well it covers a lot of territory on brand positioning strategy, in contexts from retailing and social networks to corporate reputation and nation branding; and it is written by two eminent scholars who know both Africa and positioning better than most. Therefore it is a must-read for anyone interested in its theme.

— **Nicolas Papadopoulos**, *Chancellor's Professor of Marketing and International Business, Sprott School of Business, Carleton University, Ottawa, Canada*

A long overdue book, containing many rich insights of the peculiarities of branding and positioning in African markets. The scope of the content, from micro and small businesses to nation brands, from services brands to corporate brands, makes this book an invaluable resource for both brand managers and scholars.

— **Francesca Dall'Olmo Riley**, *Professor of Brand Management at Kingston Business School, UK*

T0382911

Branding and Positioning in Base of the Pyramid Markets in Africa

Brand management to sustain corporate reputation and customer loyalty is essential for both multinationals and indigenous firms in Africa. This book provides a practical overview of country branding and positioning activities in Africa, based on a broad definition of base of the pyramid (BoP) marketing, which includes both goods and services, as well as business–to–business marketing, corporate branding, and country branding.

The text highlights branding strategies that can be adopted in BoP markets, as well as marketing mix strategies appropriate for much of the continent. Taking into account the role of social networks, culture, and religion, the book explores avenues for developing and building competitive advantage, and how African countries can leverage country branding as part of the development process.

The book is ideal for researchers, educators and advanced students in international marketing, management, and brand strategy who are interested in the unique branding characteristics of the African continent.

Dr Charles Blankson (Ph.D. Kingston University, UK) is Professor of Marketing in the Department of Marketing, Logistics and Operations Management, G. Brint Ryan College of Business, University of North Texas, Denton, Texas, United States. Dr. Blankson's research interests include marketing strategy – positioning and brand management, advertising, industrial marketing, micro and small business marketing, and international/multicultural marketing. He co-edited *The Routledge Companion to Contemporary Brand Management*. Dr. Blankson is a visiting professor of marketing at the University of Ghana Business School and the Ghana Institute of Management and Public Administration (GIMPA).

Dr Stanley Coffie is Senior Lecturer in Marketing at the Ghana Institute of Management and Public Administration (GIMPA). Dr Coffie previously lectured at Birkbeck College, University of London where he obtained his Ph.D. His research interests include marketing strategy in emerging and developing economies, strategic positioning, and the relationship between positioning and branding, as well as services marketing. His recent publications include a contribution to *The Routledge Companion to Contemporary Brand Management*.

Routledge Studies in Marketing

This series welcomes proposals for original research projects that are either single or multi-authored or an edited collection from both established and emerging scholars working on any aspect of marketing theory and practice and provides an outlet for studies dealing with elements of marketing theory, thought, pedagogy and practice.

It aims to reflect the evolving role of marketing and bring together the most innovative work across all aspects of the marketing 'mix' – from product development, consumer behaviour, marketing analysis, branding, and customer relationships, to sustainability, ethics and the new opportunities and challenges presented by digital and online marketing.

Marketing and Mobile Financial Services
A Global Perspective on Digital Banking Consumer Behaviour
Edited by Aijaz A. Shaikh and Heikki Karjaluoto

Ethic Marketing
Theory, Practice and Entrepreneurship
Guilherme D. Pires and John Stanton

Relationship Marketing in the Digital Age
Robert W. Palmatier and Lena Steinhoff

Strategic Brand Management in Higher Education
Edited by Bang Nyugen, T.C Melewar and Jane Hemsley-Brown

Digital Disruption in Marketing and Communications
A Strategic and Organizational Approach
Edoardo Magnotta

Branding and Positioning in Base of the Pyramid Markets in Africa
Innovative Approaches
Charles Blankson and Stanley Coffie

For more information about the series, please visit https://www.routledge.com/ Routledge-Studies-in-Marketing/book-series/RMKT

Branding and Positioning in Base of the Pyramid Markets in Africa

Innovative Approaches

Charles Blankson and Stanley Coffie

LONDON AND NEW YORK

First published 2020 by Routledge

2 Park Square, Milton Park, Abingdon, Oxon, OX14 4RN

605 Third Avenue, New York, NY 10017

Routledge is an imprint of the Taylor & Francis Group, an informa business

First issued in paperback 2020

British Library Cataloguing-in-Publication Data
A catalogue record for this book is available from the British Library

Library of Congress Cataloging-in-Publication Data
A catalog record for this book has been requested

ISBN: 978-1-138-48933-2 (hbk)
ISBN: 978-0-367-77753-1 (pbk)

Typeset in Bembo
by Apex CoVantage, LLC

Contents

1 Introduction   1

2 Positioning strategies for branding services in BoP markets   6

3 Marketing mix strategies for service brands in BoPMs
   in Africa   22

4 Positioning strategies and positioning activities of
   upscale retailers in BoPMs in Africa   35

5 Social networks, relationships, and positioning of micro
   and small businesses in Africa   79

6 Branding nation-states: South Africa and Ghana   89

7 Corporate reputation, brand crisis, and customer
   loyalty in BoPMs and developed economies   102

8 Conclusion   143

   Index   146

1 Introduction

This book dwells on the contemporary topic of branding and positioning activities in base of the pyramid markets (BoPM) with Africa as the setting for the content. The book describes attempts by organizations and countries in Africa to branding with the view to achieving competitive advantage that emanates from strong brands. In addition, the book provides practitioners, researchers, and students with an overview of organizations' positioning activities in Africa. The text evaluates branding efforts by organizations operating in Africa, and countries within the continent and puts forward some managerial implications from empirical studies conducted in the study setting. There is virtue in doing business in the bottom of the pyramid marketplaces (see Agnihotri, 2013) in that there is a "win-win" situation in which organizations can make profits and poor people can benefit from products and services that enhance their living standards (Prahalad & Hammond, 2002, cited in Agnihotri, 2013, pp. 591).

For the purposes of this book, the setting of Africa is apt in the sense that most of the countries on the continent fall within the classification of BoPM as per the definition of Prahalad (2002, 2004) who first coined the terminology to describe low purchasing power markets with per capita income of less than US$2,000.00 per annum. There is a general lack of universal definition of base of the pyramid market. While most scholars derive their definitions from the foundational articles by Prahalad and his co-authors (e.g., Prahalad & Hammond, 2002; Prahalad, 2002, 2004), some scholars consider low-income populations in a general sense, which may extend well above poverty lines to include, for instance, people in a position to afford a US$3,000.00 car (Kolk, Rivera-Santos, & Rufin, 2014). The seeming divergence of definitions results in studies focusing on very different target populations and settings. To a degree, the lack of precision in definition has, in turn, fueled criticism of BoPM research, especially from Karnani (2007), who claims that most BoPM studies in the literature do not target the BoPM. Even though the quoted figure is expected to change with the passage of time, conceptually, the key indicator remains the strength of purchasing power comparative to economies where the populace on average are deemed to have stronger purchasing power (World Bank, 2015). Notwithstanding the variations in definitions, this text adopts Prahalad's (2002, 2004) definition and examines BoPM issues from the broader context of contemporary Africa, as opposed to anecdotal discussion or a focus on a single country in Africa. This means that, for the purposes of this book, even though a single country may be the context of discussion of a chapter, the country is discussed merely as an illustration of the broader African domain.

There is an increasing interest in matters relating to branding in the context of BoPM and Africa in particular (Abimbola, 2006; Opoku & Hinson, 2005; Wanjiru, 2005). This drive comes partly from the recognition of the importance of branding generally and its effect on the fortunes of organizations. Further, there is the need for firms operating in Africa to leverage on branding and positioning for the purpose of achieving competitive advantage within the markets and industries they operate (Mpoyi, Festervand, & Sokoya, 2006; Coffie & Darmoe, 2016). To that end, the chapters in the book take the perspective of the high levels of growth in African economies in the last decade, and the expectation that the pace of growth will continue. In this regard, there are growing calls for greater emphasis on business and management research – conceptually and empirically – on topics of interest and relevance to African economies (Georg, Corbishley, Khayesi, Haas, & Tihanyi, 2016; Nwankwo, 2012).

Contemporary branding relies on the immaterial and affective labor of stakeholders as resource to create competitive advantage for the brand. At the same time, globalization has allowed for similar practices at the base of the pyramid (BoPM), in spite of the unique conditions in these markets. Bonsu & Godefroit-Winkel (2016) write about a recent conceptualization of branding and illustrate their writing with a social reading of two pan-African advertisements by Guinness: *Michael Power* and *Made-of-Black*. Bonsu and Godefroit-Winkel find that branding in Africa (and BoPM) depends on immaterial labor to create affect and shared meanings. This approach to branding in Africa tends to over-promise emancipatory possibilities as it maintains certain emblems of colonialism.

Interestingly, many African countries including South Africa, Egypt, Nigeria, Ghana, and Kenya exhibit characteristics of pre-industrial, industrial, and post-industrial societies when it comes to branding (Abimbola, 2006). Specifically, in spite of the comparative underdevelopment in African BoPMs, branded products are well-accepted and accorded higher social prestige than unbranded products (Abimbola, 2006).

One experiences brands in all aspect of our lives – waking up every morning using branded products for our morning rituals, enjoying breakfast made of branded products, putting on branded clothes and hopping onto a branded automobile to our daily chores! Brands indeed have become so ubiquitous that most people are not consciously aware of its pervasive character. That branding is a capitalist tool that seeks to enhance product identities for competitive advantage toward improved profitability is not in doubt (Bonsu & Godefroit-Winkel, 2016).

Still, branding deliberations at the base of the pyramid – the poorest consumers in the world – has been overlooked in business and management discussion forums. Perhaps the reason for the lack of attention is that the poor who live on less than two dollars per day are deemed to be more focused on affordability and functionality than considering any other dimension (e.g., luxury) of the products they choose. However, this assertion has long been discounted by Aryee (1984) who observed that the poor in Ghana tended to prefer branded shoes that communicated quality and durability. Moreover, Bonsu and Belk (2003) find that, notably, in the Ashanti Region of Ghana, friends, colleagues, and extended family members donate cash, and in some cases donate expensive branded products and food products to bereaved families, and exhibit opulence in public during funeral celebrations. As Papadopoulos and Blankson (2018) put it, contrary to practices in many advanced countries, the poor in Africa tend to spend excessively, by comparison to their financial standing, on death rituals (see also Bonsu & Belk, 2003). Bonsu's (2008) research challenges the general view that people with little money would have less of an inclination to engage in materialism and other aspects of the global consumer culture and supports the argument that materialism is neither uniquely Western nor related only to an affluent existence. The search for product quality, often facilitated by branding (Aaker, 1996), thus seems to be a prudent way for the poor to manage their scarce resources. Branding, then, is a major source of distinction for poor consumers and that consumers at the base of the pyramid markets are brand-conscious. The marketing of tourist destinations such as Kenya, Morocco, Tanzania, The Gambia, and South Africa in Europe and North America clearly supports the importance of branding in BoPMs in Africa. The interested reader of BoPM research may see Singh and Bharadwaj's (2017) extensive discussion on base of the pyramid research in the context of macromarketing.

Increasingly, organizations face challenges in maintaining credible brand differentiation in view of imitation and homogenization of offerings within overcrowded and fragmented markets (Blankson, 2016). As a result, organizations can no longer pursue strategies based solely on operational efficiencies (Porter, 2001) and on stable and predictable customer markets. Rather, even with the strongest of brands, organizations are challenged to generate sufficient competitive advantages in order to remain competitive and superior among their rivals (Blankson, 2016). To achieve such competitive superiority, the organization must possess a distinct and difficult-to-imitate position in the minds of customers (i.e., reflecting favorable perceptions) which complements its offering(s) (i.e., product[s], service[s], or brand[s]). Thus, the firm enters the domain of positioning – the act of designing the firm's offering(s) and brand image to occupy a distinct place in the minds of the target market.

Although "doing business in Africa is not a tea party" (Onukwuba, 2019, p. 23), the markets in Africa are now gaining currency as a viable market in contemporary capitalism (see Amaeshi & Idemudia, 2015), paving the way for the development of a deeper understanding of branding in these markets. This is especially important in that a new wave of development effort – the BoPM strategy – is being touted as the way forward for poverty alleviation (Arnould & Mohr, 2005; Beninger & Robson, 2015; DeBerry-Spence & Elliot, 2012; Davies & Torrents, 2017; Blankson, Cowan, & Darley, 2018). The BoPM strategy references a market-based framework of cooperation, networking, and practices that affords profit-oriented organizations' significant involvement in the socioeconomic development for the billions of people who live at the bottom of the global economic pyramid (e.g., Prahalad, 2004). This strategy is intended to make the BoPM a core part of global capitalism, whereby tools of contemporary business may be applied for the mutual benefit of the organization and the poor (Bonsu & Godefroit-Winkel, 2016). Thus, branding – a potent capitalist tool – may be used to mobilize the large number of poor consumers toward emotional preference for the brand. In BoPMs in Africa, organizations and other stakeholders hope to inculcate creativity (e.g., co-creation) by providing localized input for brand development.

References

Aaker, D. A. (1996). *Building strong brands*. New York, NY: Free Press.

Abimbola, T. (2006). Market access for developing economies: Branding in Africa. *Place Branding, 2*(2), 108–117.

Agnihotri, A. (2013). Doing good and doing business at the bottom of the pyramid. *Business Horizons, 56*, 591–599.

Amaeshi, K., & Idemudia, U. (2015). Africapitalism: A management idea for business in Africa? *Africa Journal of Management, 1*(2), 210–223.

Arnould, E. J., & Mohr, J. J. (2005). Dynamic transformations for base-of-the-pyramid market clusters. *Journal of the Academy of Marketing Science, 33*(3), 254–274.

Aryee, G. A. (1984). Income distribution, technology and employment in the footwear industry in Ghana. In W. van Ginneken & C. Baron (Eds.), *Appropriate products, employment and technology* (pp. 120–147). London: Macmillan.

Beninger, S., & Robson, K. (2015). Marketing at the base of the pyramid: Perspectives for practitioners and academics. *Business Horizons, 58*, 509–516.

Blankson, C. (2016). Positioning a brand. In F. D. Riley, J. Singh, & C. Blankson (Eds.), *The Routledge companion to contemporary brand management* (pp. 164–185). Abingdon: Routledge.

Blankson, C., Cowan, K., & Darley, W. K. (2018). Marketing practices of rural micro and small businesses in Ghana: The role of public policy. *Journal of Macromarketing, 38*(1), 29–56.

Bonsu, S. K. (2008). Ghanaian attitudes towards money in consumer culture. *International Journal of Consumer Studies, 32*(2), 171–178.

Bonsu, S. K., & Belk, R. W. (2003). Do not go cheaply into that good night: Death-ritual consumption in Asante, Ghana. *Journal of Consumer Research, 30*(1), 41–45.

Bonsu, S. K., & Godefroit-Winkel, D. (2016). Guinness in Africa: Contemporary branding at the base of the pyramid. In F. D. Riley, J. Singh, & C. Blankson (Eds.), *The Routledge companion to contemporary brand management* (pp. 391–403). Abingdon: Routledge.

Coffie, S., & Darmoe, J. (2016). Branding in the base of the pyramid: Bases for country and organisations in Ghana. In F. D. Riley, J. Singh, & C. Blankson (Eds.), *The Routledge companion to contemporary brand management* (pp. 378–390). Abingdon: Routledge.

Davies, I. A., & Torrents, A. (2017). Overcoming institutional voids in subsistence marketplaces: A Zimbabwean entrepreneurial case. *Journal of Marcromarketing, 37*(3), 255–267.

DeBerry-Spence, B., & Elliot, E. A. (2012). African microentrepreneurship: The reality of everyday challenges. *Journal of Business Research, 65*, 1665–1673.

Georg, G., Corbishley, C., Khayesi, J. O., Haas, M. R., & Tihanyi, L. (2016). Bringing Africa in: Promising directions for management research. *Academy of Management Journal, 59*(2), 377–393. doi:10.5465/amj.2016.4002.

Karnani, A. (2007). Misfortune at the bottom of the pyramid. *Greener Management Journal, 51*, 99–110.

Kolk, A., Rivera-Santos, M., & Rufin, C. (2014). Reviewing a decade of research on the "Base/Bottom of the Pyramid" (BOP) concept. *Business & Society, 53*(3), 338–377.

Mpoyi, R. T., Festervand, T. A., & Sokoya, S. K. (2006). Creating a global competitive advantage for sub-Saharan African companies. *Journal of African Business, 7*, 119–137.

Nwankwo, S. (2012). Renascent Africa: Rescoping the landscape of international business. *Thunderbird International Business Review, 54*(4), 405–409.

Onukwuba, H. (2019, March/April). Manage volatility. *BizEd – AACSB International, 28*(2), 23–24.

Opoku, R., & Hinson, R. (2005). Online brand personalities: An exploratory analysis of selected African countries. *Place Branding, 2*(2), 118–129.

Papadopoulos, N., & Blankson, C. (2018). Managing culture and money: Some critical issues facing African management and managers. *Africa Journal of Management, 4*(1), 33–56.

Porter, M. E. (2001). Strategy and the internet. *Harvard Business Review, 79*(3), 62–78.

Prahalad, C. K. (2002). Strategies for the bottom of the economic pyramid: India as a source of innovation. *Society for Organizational Learning Reflections, 3*(4), 6–17.

Prahalad, C. K. (2004). *Fortune at the bottom of the pyramid: Eradicating poverty through profits.* Upper Saddle River, NJ: Pearson Education.

Prahalad, C. K., & Hammond, A. (2002). Serving the world's poor profitably. *Harvard Business Review, 89*(9), 48–58.

Singh, R., & Bharadwaj, A. (2017). BOP research meets macromarketing: Content analysis of BOP-related research in the journal of macromarketing. *Decision, 44*(1), 69–82.

Wanjiru, E. (2005). Branding African countries: A prospect for the future. *Place Branding, 2*(1), 84–95.

World Bank. (2015). *World development indicators.* Retrieved July 1, 2015 from http://data.worldbank.org/country/ghana

2 Positioning strategies for branding services in BoP markets

Introduction

Positioning and branding are key aspects of marketing strategy. Positioning is important in determining how an organization works and can be understood as the outcome of a strategic planning process that is often elaborate. When executed successfully, positioning requires managers to understand their target customers' preferences, their understanding of value, and their perceptions of the features of an offering in order to make decisions about attributes that are important to customers (Lovelock & Wirtz, 2011). An effective positioning strategy needs to resonate in communications with customers. Well-positioned products and services need to resonate with the target audience's preferences in order to meet the customer's needs. An effective positioning allows the organization to communicate to the target audience in a way that underscores its capabilities and competitive strengths whether in the form of a slogan or in advertisements (Aaker, 2005, 2011; Hooley, Piercy, Nicoulaud, & Rudd, 2017).

Consumers tend to prefer branded products to unbranded, since brands help them with their purchasing decisions once they develop an understanding and appreciation for the brand and its value, and are able to trust in the quality standard (Rajagopal, 2009) since knowledge of and familiarity with a given brand gives the product or service greater credibility. The benefits of strong brands are not only available to the consumer; they affect organizations as well. For organizations, strong and successful brands serve as vehicles for charging higher prices, often resulting in high profitability (Cravens & Piercy, 2013).

Romaniuk (2001) explained that a well-positioned brand strengthens brand associations through marketing communications. Not all brand positions will perform equally well, however, as some brand positions are "better" than others. Brand positioning that is particularly in sync with consumer-preferred attributes tends to achieve better outcomes since customers identify with the positioning and the attributes, and therefore consider them important in their decision making. According to Lovelock and Wirtz (2011), preferred attributes that inform customer decisions can be understood as positionings of products and services that are in line with managerial and customer expectations. Blankson (2016) notes that there are greater commonalities between the concept of positioning and branding (management) than researchers have alluded to. Successful positioning allows firms to draw on the strengths of a brand for improved performance and effective brand management (Esch, 2010; Hooley, Piercy, & Nicoulaud, 2012). In this regard, the chapter argues that the relationship between positioning and branding is not far-fetched. In fact, effective positioning can inform the branding that an organization undertakes (Blankson, 2016; Urde & Koch, 2014).

Urde and Koch (2014, p. 482) distinguish between two approaches in positioning – market-oriented and brand-oriented approaches. The market-oriented approach defines and implements the intended positioning through customer and stakeholder perceptions of brand image. In this regard, there is a strong link between the intended positioning and customer/stakeholder preferences. The brand-oriented approach to positioning operates from the perspective of the brand identity as a key point of reference, bearing in mind how the identity may be influenced by the mission, vision, and values of the organization. This chapter argues that positioning strategies based on consumer perceptions make significant contributions toward branding and its effects in the marketplace (Coffie, 2018; Coffie & Darmoe, 2016; Desarbo, Kim, Choi, & Spaulding, 2002; Knilans, 2009). The chapter emphasizes the feasibility for positioning as a basis for branding and adopts positioning strategies developed by Coffie and Owusu-Frimpong (2014) to illustrate the viability of the argument.

From the aforementioned perspective, this chapter aims to explore the linkages between positioning strategies for the purpose of branding, to assess the suitability of the positioning strategies adopted for the purpose of branding services in a bottom of the pyramid market (BoPM), and to illustrate the feasibility of using positioning strategies for branding in a BoPM in Africa. These purposes form the bases of the subsequent sections of the chapter.

The relationship between positioning and branding

Urde and Koch (2014, p. 479) observe that, in general, all established brands have a position:

> The actual position of a particular brand may be more or less clear in the market and for its key audiences, and it may be more or less matched with the brand owner's intentions. All of brand owner's activities and choices affect the brand's position.

The suggestion here is that there is a strong conceptual relationship between branding and positioning, whether intended or accidental. Branding and its associated activities affect positioning, and so does the intended or attained positioning affect branding. While that may be the case, the logic is that it is possible for a brand image or association to be in sync with the positioning of a product, and that may be intended or achieved accidentally.

Further, on positioning and branding, de Chernatony (2009) and Blankson (2016) assert that the effective employment of positioning strategies creates avenues for developing preference(s) for a firm's products and services over its competitors. Successfully positioning a brand creates a better opportunity for the success of that brand. Though the concepts of positioning and branding are accepted by scholars as being capable of individually enhancing the fortunes of an organization (Blankson, 2016; Hooley et al., 2012), this individual conceptual capability can be reinforced by exploring the potential linkages between the two, as they are conceptually closer than has generally been acknowledged in the literature (Fuchs & Diamantopoulos, 2010).

Commenting on the purpose of branding in positioning strategies, Romaniuk (2001) explains that managers tend to operate with the assumption that not all positions are appropriate to help achieve the optimum performance of a brand. This pre-supposes that some positionings are better than others at facilitating better market and competitive performance. The implication is that to apply a positioning type for branding, the synergy between the positioning strategies and the brand associations – along with consumer expectations – should closely align. Desarbo et al. (2002) expand on this notion, and argue that positioning models based on consumer perceptions offer strong avenues for success in the market. This results from additional opportunities for diagnosing the requirements and nature of the competition in the marketplace. Ghosh and Chakraborty (2004) note that brand uncertainty can arise where the positioning model informing branding has been contaminated by consumers' uncertainty about the brands they were asked to evaluate. Ghosh and Chakraborty (2004) further explain that managers need to take steps to limit the degree of uncertainty when using positioning models to measure and manage brand uncertainty in order to improve on the success of strategic branding and planning.

Kachersky and Carnevale (2015, p. 161) observed that brands positioned to offer personal benefits to consumers tend to have a better chance of success, as the benefits offered coincide with consumer preferences. Lovelock and Wirtz (2011) define positioning as the attributes of a product or service that are important to customers. The logic is that important attributes will serve as a strong basis for the choices the consumer makes. Further, in exploring the importance of branding, Dall'Olmo Riley (2016) distinguishes between "brand" with a small "b" and "Brand" with a big "B." The "brand" refers to the name, logo, or visual identifier of a brand; the "Brand" refers to all other associations of the brand, including its personality, equity, and other attributes that appeal to the consumer. The importance of branding for the purpose of marketing dwells more in "Brand" than in "brand" because the former points to the defining elements of the consumer's preferences. Such preferences (Dall'Olmo Riley, 2016) may be in sync with Lovelock and Wirtz's (2011) view of positioning as a group of attributes that are important to customers. This suggests that there is a point at which positioning and branding merge when and where the attributes for positioning and branding associations coincide and meet consumer preference(s).

Based on the foregoing arguments and observations (Blankson, 2016; Dall'Olmo Riley, 2016; Desarbo et al., 2002; Fuchs & Diamantopoulos, 2010; Ghosh & Chakraborty, 2004; Kachersky & Carnevale, 2015; Lovelock & Wirtz, 2011;

Urde & Koch, 2014) about the relationship between positioning and branding, it is inferable that positioning strategy is a viable ground for branding products and services. This provides the basis for this chapter's tentative derivation: Namely, that positioning strategies formed from consumer views and expectations offer a good chance of success when used for branding. Such coincidences of consumer preferences are more likely to occur in situations where the adopted positioning strategies were developed based on consumer perceptions. The key positioning types (see Appendix) were developed conceptually, based on managerial views or consumer views. Drawing on the key positioning types (Appendix), only Blankson and Kalafatis (2004) and Coffie and Owusu-Frimpong (2014) used consumer-based views. Blankson and Kalafatis' (2004) was developed from a developed country setting (UK), whilst that of Coffie and Owusu-Frimpong (2014) was from an emerging-country context (Ghana). Therefore, for the purpose of branding in BoPMs, Coffie and Owusu-Frimpong's (2014) typology has a better chance of success as it reflects the context and setting in which it is being applied.

In order to illustrate the logic and viability of using a positioning type for branding in a BoPM, the author adopts consumer-based positioning strategies (Table 2.1, Coffie & Owusu-Frimpong, 2014) for the purpose of branding services in a transitioning economy. The rest of this chapter explains how the adopted positioning strategies serve as a basis for branding, followed by discussion and conclusion.

Using positioning strategies to brand services: a BoPM illustration

A focused attempt to integrate positioning and branding efforts will achieve a more positive outcome (Esch, 2010; Knilans, 2009). Table 2.1 is a summary of the three positioning strategy options available to service firms adopted from Coffie (2018) for the purpose of branding. The strategies spelled out in the "service reliability" positioning option, such as customer relations, service quality, reliability, convenience, proximity, and trust appear to reflect the dominant expectations of consumers from products and services alike (Coffie & Owusu-Frimpong, 2014), as well as the expectations of consumers in terms of "good service" (Porter, 1985; Aaker, 1991; Owusu-Frimpong, Effah, & Osei-Frimpong, 2015; Zaichkowsky, 2010).

Quality and reliability remain key themes in the "service reliability" positioning strategy. Quality of service for branding for competitive advantage is an eloquent theme in the work of Porter (1985) who identifies that as one of the generic strategies available to the firm. The key strategies under the "service reliability" strategy may suit some organizations better than others, and therefore it is expected that organizations focused on "service reliability" will be selective as to which of the strategy's features on which to develop the brand. In the automobile industry, for example, Toyota is known for reliability while Volvo is noted for its safety (safe guarantees). The suggestion is that service firms in

Ghana will build on their brand strength in line with consumer expectations. For example, as a fast food restaurant in Ghana, Papaye will rely on speed as a key strength for its branding given the activity in which it is engaged.

Coffie and Darmoe (2016, p. 366) note that "it is important for managers to determine closely which attributes serve the branding purpose, and have the emotional attachment that reflects the experiences of customers with given products and services." If we interpret branding in the broader sense of its value and the associations that the consumer perceives (Dall'Olmo Riley, 2016, pp. 5–6), then there is a greater likelihood of fulfilling the attributes and benefits that may be sought by the target consumer group. Further, Gupta, Garg, and Sharma (2016) observe the need to brand on a best-fit basis by both international and local firms in emerging markets. This chapter argues that in using the "service reliability" strategy for branding, organizations need to be selective of the attributes that best reflect the values of that organization, and, most importantly take customer expectations into account.

Positioning strategies used for the purpose of branding is the second option available (Table 2.1), and focuses on corporate social responsibility (CSR) as a theme. Liu, Wong, Shi, Chu, and Brock (2014) examined the impact of customer preference for brands and uncovered that the performance of CSR activities has an enhancing effect on the environment, society, and stakeholders to different degrees. The study (Liu et al., 2014) showed that CSR activities had the most impact on stakeholders in terms of brand preference among other CSR domains: Environment, society, and stakeholder. Brand quality perception emerged as a positive moderator of the relationship between CSR performance and brand preference. CSR performance is, however, not the strongest predictor of branding outcomes. Perceived brand quality had a stronger influence on consumer preferences, with perceived brand quality mediating the relationship between CSR performance and brand preference. A similar study by Famiyeh, Kwarteng, and Dadzie (2016, p. 258) in Ghana concluded that a "CSR initiative by firms will have a positive relationship with firm's reputation in terms of product and service quality, management performance and attractiveness as well as overall performance." Thus, there appears to be a degree of consistency in the positive relationship between CSR activities on perceived service quality and performance. This relationship is further confirmed in the work of Agyemang and Ansong (2017) focusing on 423 small- to medium-sized enterprises (SMEs) in Ghana.

In examining the development of brands through CSR for the purpose of realizing the enhancing effects on performance and the influence customer preference, Lindgreen, Maon, and Vallaster (2016) make suggestions based on a number of cases of interviews with managers examined from both public and privately owned organizations. Key suggestions/findings for the purpose of consistency between corporate branding and CSR efforts include the following: Organizations should practice their beliefs by integrating the CSR policy as part of the strategic development or orientation of the brand such that the brand image aligns with the CSR activities; the strategic domain or policy must be clearly defined to the target market; resources need to be allocated such that the brand associations form a critical part of the overall positioning; and finally, one be prepared and react appropriately to failure.

The core emphasis of the "social responsibility strategy" (Table 2.1) suggests a community orientation, which affects national development cumulatively and results in trust among organizations that undertake such activities. Gupta et al. (2016) and Assimeng (2007) note that most emerging economies – including Ghana – are collectivist in nature. This may contradict the predominantly individualistic nature and culture of Western-developed economies. This difference is also reflected in the purposes for which CSR activities may be undertaken by firms in emerging economies.

Focusing on Ghana, Ofori and Hinson (2007) found that, in general, internationally connected firms in Ghana are more strategic in pursuing CSR activities than local firms dominated by SMEs. A study by Kuada and Hinson (2012) on CSR activities uncovered that foreign firms in Ghana undertake CSR activities for the purpose of building and/or enhancing their market image, suggesting that brand-strategic purpose applies more to foreign firms operating in Ghana, followed by internationally connected Ghanaian firms seeking or engaging in exporting activities (Kuada & Hinson, 2012; Ofori & Hinson, 2007). Some key factors limiting the practice of CSR activities of local and some internationally connected firms in Ghana include the presence of insufficient managerial commitment and leadership, corruption, and poor allocation of resources for CSR activities (Abugre, 2014). Local Ghanaian firms (predominantly SMEs) tend to invest in CSR for moral and ethical reasons, reflecting the cultural nuance. Vallaster, Lindgreen, and Maon (2012) observe that although there are benefits from branding on CSR, there may be challenges associated with potential conflict of interest between managers and other stakeholders of the firm and associated with the danger of the brand association contradicting some of the CSR activities. This can be avoided where CSR activities are carefully planned and developed as a unifying aspect of the brand. In general, the evidence from Ghana appears to support the collectivist social nature where CSR activities by firms are seen as part of a moral obligation (Assimeng, 2007). The foregoing discussion on branding via CSR and in the specific context of the Ghanaian society leads us to propose that organizations need to understand the social, moral, and ethical ideology of the Ghanaian environment so as to succeed with CSR as a branding strategy.

The key features of the "branding strategy" as shown in Table 2.1 point to successful firms that have a high level of brand recognition and are leaders in the markets in which they operate. Hooley et al. (2012, 2017) assert that in most cases, established brands with positive international reputations have a greater chance of selling products at higher prices and/or win high market share. Khojastehpoura and Johns (2015, p. 516) note that the success of multinational corporations in branding leans partly on establishing "multinational corporate branding . . . fashioned by three major success factors: the strategic role, organizational culture and structure, and knowledge." This means supporting and/or

Table 2.1 Summary of strategic positioning options

Service Reliability Strategy (option 1)	Social Responsibility Strategy (option 2)	Branding Strategy (option 3)
quality of service	national development-oriented	pioneer in market
customer relations	supports communities	internationally recognized
reliability	innovative	market leadership
comfort	technical and design efficiency	branding
convenience	trusted	dominant
flexibility		
availability		
speed		
trust		
proximity		
safe guarantees		

Source: Coffie and Owusu-Frimpong (2014).

relying on subsidiaries and viewing them as playing strategic roles in developing the brand; the culture and structure of the multinational corporation subsidiary should facilitate the development of the brand. The transfer of knowledge by multinationals is important in building successful brands through subsidiaries. This transfer could be dual directional from the multinational firm to the subsidiary and vice versa.

On whether pioneering advantage leads to branding and competitive advantage, Cleff and Rennings (2012) reviewed a number of theoretical and empirical studies in the area of business management and industrial economics to determine the effect of timing of entry on the strategic success of the organization. The successful firm with a strong brand and market leadership is not necessarily the first mover, but often the first mover is among the successful firms in the market. Factors influencing success often included timing strategy based on country-specific issues, lead market potentials, technology and market characteristics, the regime of the country-specific regulation, environment, and stage of innovation.

In the Ghanaian telecommunications industry, for example, MTN and Vodafone are the leading firms with the most market share and network coverage. The absolute leading firm is MTN, with about 47% market share mobile of voice subscriptions, while Vodafone had 24% in April 2017 (National Communications Authority Ghana, accessed 22nd July 2017). Ghana Telecom – the pioneering firm from which Vodafone acquired a 70% share in 2008 – was not profitable for decades due to poor management. Again, in the bottled water market in Ghana, the pioneering firm was Standard: A brand dominant in the 1990s. However, today the Voltic brand is the leader in market share. Thus, the logic is that while pioneering brands have a good chance of success (Cleff & Rennings, 2012), a strong start can't be taken as a guarantee of future success, as lasting presence depends upon a number of factors. It appears that the "branding strategy" best suits internationally recognized brands such as Samsung, Toyota,

Gillette, and Lucozade. It is important to note that such established firms have developed their brand strength over a long period of time, and the status they occupy possibly emanated with other attributes as the basis for their branding. In other words, their current status may be the outcome or evidence of success from pursuing and developing the brand from a range of measures and factors that define the brand success. The point remains that the "branding strategy" will be more suitable to established firms that are already exposed and known for what they stand for at the international level.

Discussion and conclusion

The chapter principally argues that among the positioning types – conceptual, managerial, and consumer-based (Appendix) – the consumer-based strategies have a better chance of success as they will most likely be in sync with the preferences of consumers regarding the desired features of brands. The chapter therefore builds on the feasibility of a consumer-based positioning typology for the purpose of branding and applies this as an illustrative case for services in Ghana reflecting literature support for branding based on positioning strategies (Coffie & Darmoe, 2016; Knilans, 2009; Urde & Koch, 2014).

Branding on positioning has its advantages if based on attributes important to customers (Lovelock & Wirtz, 2011). It is therefore logical to argue and expect that these important attributes as bases for branding will resonate with the customers due to the consonance between the brand associations and the attributes important to the customer. Knilans (2009) argues that not all product or service attributes may be appropriate for branding; it is important that there is an emotional linkage between the said attributes and the commonalities consumers expect.

The "service reliability" strategy may have features or attributes that appear prevalent and therefore will allow most service organizations in Ghana to identify strategies that fit with the nature of their product/service for the purpose of branding. Among the listed positioning strategies, service quality appears to have the most support in comparison with previous studies. The works of Blankson and Kalafatis (2007a, 2007b), focusing on positioning views of executives and experts from the United Kingdom, found that quality of service is important to managers. It appears that service quality remains an important attribute to consumers and managers alike in both developed and emerging economies. This suggests that service quality can serve as a dependable basis for branding as long as the attributes being provided to the consumers are in sync with their expectations. This also means that "service reliability" strategies need to be examined for their individual relevance to the particular service or product alongside customer preferences for the purpose of selecting what is preferred by the consumer in order achieve the best branding and competitive outcomes. Gilmore (2003) argued that service quality is central to a firm's activities both for core service organizations and as supplements to physical products. This underscores the importance of quality or perceived quality of service, which should not be taken for granted by organizations in view of the likely effect on reputation and profits. Some of the strategies such as reliability, comfort, convenience, flexibility, and speed of service could be treated as elements of quality of service; practically, each of them can serve as the basis of the consumer's decision, and cumulatively they contribute to the quality of the service on offer.

Customer service and relationships are important to customers, and customer relations are increasingly important in gaining and sustaining positioning advantage (Hooley et al., 2017). Over the last two decades, Ghana's economy has been on a path of growth. This trend is expected to continue over the next few years with an average growth rate of 7% per annum (World Bank, 2017). Along with that increase has come increased competition, and it will be expected that managers of organizations will seek avenues to develop long-term relationships with customers as a way of sustaining any competitive advantage they may have. This expectation is in conformity with earlier studies in Ghana (Appiah-Adu & Blankson, 1998; Kuada & Buatsi, 2005) which found that improving levels of marketing and market orientation makes it imperative for organizations to function more effectively to sustain customers' interest and satisfaction.

Availability of service (distribution) and proximity are among the dominant positioning strategies for the purpose of branding. Smithson, Devece, and Lapiedra (2011) found that visibility, particularly on the internet, can boost the performance of organizations – with a particular reference to SMEs. Given that majority of firms in Ghana are SMEs (Ofei, 2005), it is logical to argue that SMEs that are able to maintain an online presence will do better as internet usage continues to grow in BoPM and emerging economies. Distribution alone, however, may not be sustainable as a source of advantage: Any advantages obtained from distribution will be imitated by competitors, thereby reducing or removing the advantage over time. With the generally low level infrastructure in developing countries in much of sub-Saharan Africa (Mpoyi, Festervand, & Sokoya, 2006), managers from Ghana may be treating an organization's ability to effectively meet the needs of customers through availability and proximity as sources of competitive advantage. In exploring the role of trust in organizational settings, Dirks and Ferrin (2001, p. 451) argue that trust engenders a number of benefits and that "higher levels of trust are expected to result in more positive attitudes, higher levels of cooperation and other forms of workplace behavior, and superior levels of performance." The research confirmed these benefits in most cases: The ways in which organizations generate or develop trust might be through different pathways. Trust is unlikely to be a self-existing entity – instead, it is likely that organizations that are trusted have gained this favor through sustaining the high standard of service or product they offer. Once that trust has been developed, it will serve as an anchor for the organization to perform better. Service guarantees offer assurances to the consumer and give peace of mind that, should something go wrong, the organization will take responsibility. Service guarantees can also help organizations in service development through the service process, the recovery process, and the development process (Liden & Sanden, 2004). Thus, service guarantees benefit both the organization and the consumer.

The "social responsibility strategy" is probably the most easily applicable either on its own or as part of other associations for the purpose of branding. This follows from the knowledge that Ghanaian society is communal and expectant in nature (Assimeng, 2007). Not surprisingly, communication companies such as Vodafone Ghana and MTN all vigorously pursue CSR as part of their strategy, and reach out to customers, for example, through the provision of water to village communities and the support of some education initiatives. The key elements under this strategy – such as a focus on national development, community support, and trust – probably reflect the growing trend of the social and cultural expectations that consumers have of organizations. Some researchers (Ghauri & Cateora, 2010) consider the need for organizations to have an understanding of the cultural values of the settings in which they operate. As Ghanaians are seen as "extremely sociable" and show "appreciation for reciprocity" (Codjoe, 2003, p. 343), they almost certainly will react positively towards organizations that share such a philosophy and practice. The cohesive, inclusive, and expectant nature of Ghanaians is also corroborated by Assimeng (2007) and Nukunya (2003). The suggestion is that Ghanaians expect organizations doing business to undertake some CSR activities to contribute toward the progress and development of society. With the increasing importance of CSR and its impact on customer goodwill, organizations need to evaluate their policies in order to meet these growing customer expectations.

Innovation emerges as a positioning strategy for the purpose of branding in the Ghanaian context. The increased levels of competition in Ghana's service economy, and the general increase in growth and competition within the last decade (Bank of Ghana Statistics, 2008; Ghana Statistical Service, 2012; World Bank, 2017) might explain the growing importance of innovation. Previously state-owned organizations such as Ghana Telecom and the State Insurance Company (SIC) had to innovate in order to sustain their market leadership since they have lost their monopoly status due to government privatization policies and the government's desire to stimulate competition within the economy. In the case of technological advantage, it is possible that the increasing importance of innovation is part of the drive by organizations to improve their service provision through the use of technology. The use of mobile communication is also on the rise as the economy improves. The vast improvement in internet usage has been driven mainly by mobile phone usage in developing economies, automated cash machines, and other technological developments (Gilmore, 2003; Porter, 2001) which have provided opportunities for service organizations to improve on their service provision. This may explain the importance of technology application as part of the strategy for branding services. This suggests that those organizations that can make use of technologies, including the internet, to enhance their provision of services stand a better chance of gaining through strategic flexibility, which in turn influences competitive advantage positively (Celuch & Murphy, 2010; Porter, 2001). Celuch and Murphy (2010, p. 140) concluded that "small businesses can improve strategic flexibility through Internet use that facilitates communication and by aligning IT capabilities to a market orientation." This will enhance their level and quality of service provision, and this is particularly important in an SME-dominated BoPM such as Ghana.

The third option for the purpose of branding is the "branding strategy." A key element of branding as a means of differentiation is to exploit the associations of the brand for higher pricing in most cases (Cravens & Piercy, 2013; Hooley et al., 2017). The inclusive elements of the current "branding strategy" are market pioneers, international recognition, branding, market leadership, and dominance. Previous positioning strategies such as Ries and Trout (1986) and Kalafatis, Tsogas, and Blankson (2000) appear to suggest that the stage of the organization including market leadership can offer a basis for competitive advantage. Although Ries and Trout (1986) and Kalafatis et al. (2000) did not explicitly associate the stage of the organization with branding, evidence from the best-known brands such as BMW, Coca-Cola, Mercedes, and Nike are indications that their presence and their longevity in the market has significantly contributed to the brand status they occupy. Additionally, the best internationally recognized brands are also dominant in their markets (Coca-Cola with soft drinks), market leaders (BMW in car manufacturing), and pioneers (Ryanair in low-cost air travel). Branding on positioning strategies can offer a competitive advantage, and this is reinforced by other studies in the United Kingdom and in South Africa (Blankson, 2007; Blankson & Kalafatis, 2004, 2007a, 2007b). This implies that service organizations should seek avenues to effectively brand their offerings as a means of improving on their competitiveness in the marketplace. In the Ghanaian sense, some observe that the economy is "dual" in nature, meaning that there are people who have the resources to afford branded products and services ("Ghana – Special Report," 2009).

The challenge in branding on the "branding strategy" may apply more to international firms who also tend to be better established and seek to grow through international expansion. These firms have to confront the dilemma of either keeping their existing brand associations in the international market or modifying those associations to suit local market conditions. Ghauri and Cateora (2010) contend that this is not an easy decision, but the choice of the organization should be grounded in research findings based on the nature of the product or service.

The argument in this chapter that positioning strategies are appropriate for branding needs to be tested empirically to determine its applicability in different industries and products/services. It should be noted that while the use of positioning strategies for branding services as illustrated in this chapter is conceptually sound, different positioning strategies may be appropriate for different services. This again suggests that organizations need to test service attributes in each target market to arrive at the best branding decisions. It is expected that organizations will investigate the positioning strategies examined in the chapter to determine which option may be most appropriate and relevant to their ideology and consumer expectations. If this is done imaginatively, it should result in effective use of the positioning strategies for branding services in BoPM environments.

References

Aaker, D. A. (1991). *Measuring brand equity: Capitalizing on the value of a brand name.* New York, NY: Free Press.

Aaker, D. A. (2005). *Strategic market management* (7th ed.). Hoboken, NJ: Wiley.

Aaker, D. A. (2011). *Strategic market management* (9th ed.). Hoboken, NJ: Wiley.

Aaker, D. A., & Shansby, J. (1982). Positioning your product. *Business Horizons, 25,* 56–62.

Abugre, J. B. (2014). Managerial role in organizational CSR: Empirical lessons from Ghana. *Corporate Governance, 14*(1), 104–119. https://doi.org/10.1108/CG-10-2011-0076

Agyemang, O. S., & Ansong, A. (2017). Corporate social responsibility and firm performance of Ghanaian SMEs: Mediating role of access to capital and firm reputation. *Journal of Global Responsibility, 8*(1), 47–62. https://doi.org/10.1108/JGR-03-2016-0007

Appiah-Adu, K., & Blankson, C. (1998). Business strategy, organisational culture, and market orientation. *Thunderbird International Business Review, 40*(3), 235–256.

Arnott, D. C. (1992). *Bases of financial services positioning in the personal pension, life assurance and personal equity plan sectors.* PhD dissertation, University of Manchester, UK.

Assimeng, M. (2007). *Social structure of Ghana: A study in persistence and change* (2nd ed.). Tema: Ghana Publishing Corporation.

Bank of Ghana. (2008). *Statistical bulletin.* Accra: Bank of Ghana.

Berry, L. L. (1982). Retail positioning strategies for the 1980s. *Business Horizons, 25*(6), 45–50.

Blankson, C. (2007). Testing a newly developed typology of positioning strategies in South Africa. *Journal of African Business, 8*(1), 67–97.

Blankson, C. (2016). Positioning a brand. In F. D. Riley, J. Singh, & C. Blankson (Eds.), *The Routledge companion to contemporary brand management* (pp. 164–185). Abingdon: Routledge.

Blankson, C., & Kalafatis, S. P. (2004). The development and validation of a scale measuring customer derived generic typology of positioning strategies. *Journal of Marketing Management, 20,* 5–43.

Blankson, C., & Kalafatis, S. P. (2007a). Congruence between positioning and brand advertising. *Journal of Advertising Research, 47*(1), 1–16.

Blankson, C., & Kalafatis, S. P. (2007b). Positioning strategies of international and multicultural-oriented service brands. *Journal of Services Marketing, 21,* 435–450.

Brown, H. E., & Sims, J. T. (1976). Market segmentation, product differentiation and market positioning as alternative marketing strategies. In K. L. Bernhardt (Ed.), *Marketing: 1776–1976 and beyond* (pp. 483–487). Chicago, IL: Educators Conference Proceedings Series No. 39, American Marketing Association.

Buskirk, R. K. (1975). *Principles of marketing* (4th ed.). Hinsdale, IL: Dryden Press.

Celuch, K., & Murphy, G. (2010). SME internet use and strategic flexibility: The moderating effect of IT market orientation. *Journal of Marketing Management, 26*(1/2), 131–145.

Cleff, T., & Rennings, K. (2012). Are there any first-mover advantages for pioneering firms? Lead market orientated business strategies for environmental innovation. *European Journal of Innovation Management, 15*(4), 491–513. https://doi.org/10.1108/14601061211272394

Codjoe, H. M. (2003). Is culture the obstacle to development in Ghana? A critique of the culture-development thesis as it applies to Ghana and Korea. In W. J. Tettey, K. P. Puplampu, & B. J. Berman (Eds.), *Critical perspectives on politics and socio-economic development in Ghana* (pp. 335–363). Leiden, Netherlands: Brill.

Coffie, S. (2018). Positioning strategies for branding services in an emerging economy. *Journal of Strategic Marketing,* doi: 10.1080/0965254X.2018.1500626.

Coffie, S., & Darmoe, J. (2016). Branding in the base of the pyramid: Bases for country and organisations in Ghana. In F. D. Riley, J. Singh, & C. Blankson (Eds.), *The Routledge companion to contemporary brand management* (pp. 378–390). Abingdon: Routledge.

Coffie, S., & Owusu-Frimpong, N. (2014). Alternative positioning strategies for services in Ghana. *Thunderbird International Business Review, 56*(6), 531–546.

Cravens, D. W., & Piercy, N. F. (2013). *Strategic marketing*. New York, NY: McGraw-Hill.

Crawford, C. M. (1985). A new positioning typology. *Journal of Product Innovation Management, 4*, 243–253.

de Chernatony, L. (2009). Towards the holy grail of defining "brand". *Marketing Theory, 9*(1), 101–108.

Desarbo, W. S., Kim, J., Choi, S. C., & Spaulding, M. (2002). A gravity-based multidimensional scaling model for deriving spatial structures underlying consumer preferences/choice. *Journal of Consumer Research, 29*, 1–16.

Dirks, K. T., & Ferrin, D. L. (2001). The role of trust in organisational settings. *Organisation Science, 12*(4), 450–467.

Easingwood, C. J., & Mahajan, V. (1989). Positioning of financial services for competitive strategy. *Journal of Product Innovation Management, 6*, 207–219.

Esch, F. R. (2010). *Strategie und Technik der Markenfuhrung*. Munchen: Vahlen.

Famiyeh, S., Kwarteng, A., & Dadzie, S. A. (2016). Corporate social responsibility and reputation: Some empirical perspectives. *Journal of Global Responsibility, 7*(2), 258–274. https://doi.org/10.1108/JGR-04-2016-0009

Fuchs, C., & Diamantopoulos, A. (2010). Evaluating the effectiveness of brand-positioning strategies from a consumer perspective. *European Journal of Marketing, 44*(11/12), 1763–1786.

Ghana Statistical Service. (2012). *Statistics for development and progress*. Retrieved from www.statsghana.gov.gh

Ghana: Special Report. (2009). *Financial Times*, London, UK.

Ghauri, P. N., & Cateora, P. (2010). *International marketing* (3rd ed.). Maidenhead: McGraw-Hill.

Ghosh, A. K., & Chakraborty, G. (2004). Using positioning models to measure and manage brand uncertainty. *Journal of Product and Brand Management, 13*(5), 294–302.

Gilmore, A. (2003). *Services marketing and management*. London: Sage.

Gupta, S., Garg, S., & Sharma, K. (2016). Branding in emerging markets. In F. D. Riley, J. Singh, & C. Blankson (Eds.), *The Routledge companion to contemporary brand management* (pp. 366–377). Abingdon: Routledge.

Hooley, G., Broderick, A., & Möller, K. (1998). Competitive positioning and the resource-based view of the firm. *Journal of Strategic Marketing, 6*(2), 97–116.

Hooley, G., Piercy, N. F., & Nicoulaud, B. (2012). *Marketing strategy and competitive positioning* (5th ed.). Harlow: Pearson Education Limited.

Hooley, G., Piercy, N. F., Nicoulaud, B., & Rudd, J. M. (2017). *Marketing strategy and competitive positioning* (6th ed.). Harlow: Pearson Education Limited.

Kachersky, L., & Carnevale, M. (2015). Effects of pronoun brand name perspective and positioning on brand attitude. *Journal of Product and Brand Management, 24*(2), 157–164. https://doi.org/10.1108/JPBM-02-2014-0495

Kalafatis, S. P., Tsogas, M. H., & Blankson, C. (2000). Positioning strategies in business markets. *Journal of Business and Industrial Marketing, 15*(6), 416–437.

Khojastehpoura, M., & Johns, R. (2015). The role of MNC's subsidiaries in creating multinational corporate brand. *Journal of Strategic Marketing, 23*(6), 512–525. http://doi.org/10.1080/0965254X.2014.1001861

Knilans, G. (2009). When positioning and branding conflict. *U.S. Business Review*, 14–15.

Kuada, J., & Buatsi, N. (2005). Market orientation and management practices in Ghanaian firms: Revisiting the Jaworski and Kohli framework. *Journal of International Marketing, 13*(1), 58–88.

Kuada, J., & Hinson, R. E. (2012). Corporate social responsibility practices of foreign and local companies in Ghana. *Thunderbird International Business Review, 54*(4), 521–536.

Liden, S. B., & Sanden, B. (2004). The role of service guarantees in service development. *The Service Industries Journal*, 24(4), 1–20.

Lindgreen, A., Maon, F., & Vallaster, C. (2016). Building brands via corporate social responsibility. In F. D. Riley, J. Singh, & C. Blankson (Eds.), *The Routledge companion to contemporary brand management* (pp. 228–254). Abingdon: Routledge.

Liu, M. T., Wong, I. A., Shi, G., Chu, R., & Brock, J. L. (2014). The impact of Corporate Social Responsibility (CSR) performance and perceived brand quality on customer-based brand preference. *Journal of Services Marketing*, 28(3), 181–194. https://doi.org/10.1108/JSM-09-2012-0171

Lovelock, C., & Wirtz, J. (2011). *Services marketing: People, technology, and strategy* (7th ed.). Upper Saddle River, NJ: Pearson Prentice Hall.

Mpoyi, R. T., Festervand, T. A., & Sokoya, S. K. (2006). Creating a global competitive advantage for sub-Saharan African companies. *Journal of African Business*, 7, 119–137.

National Communications Authority Ghana. (2017). Retrieved from https://nca.org.gh/industry-data-2/market-share-statistics-2/voice-2/

Nukunya, G. K. (2003). *Tradition and change in Ghana: An introduction to sociology* (2nd ed.). Accra: Ghana University Press.

Ofei, K. A. (2005). Internationalisation and management of Ghanaian export firms. In J. Kuada (Ed.), *Internationalisation and enterprise development in Ghana* (pp. 76–128). London: Adonis and Abbey.

Ofori, D. F., & Hinson, R. E. (2007). Corporate Social Responsibility (CSR) perspectives of leading firms in Ghana. *Corporate Governance*, 7(2), 178–193. https://doi.org/10.1108/14720700710739813

Owusu-Frimpong, N., Effah, A., & Osei-Frimpong, K. (2015). Consumer-based brand equity as a differentiator in an emerging African economy. In S. Nwankwo & K. Ibeh (Eds.), *The Routledge companion to business in Africa* (pp. 421–438). New York, NY: Routledge.

Porter, M. E. (1985). *Competitive advantage: Creating and sustaining superior performance*. New York, NY: Free Press.

Porter, M. E. (2001). Strategy and the internet. *Harvard Business Review*, 79, 63–78.

Rajagopal. (2009). Branding paradigm for the bottom of the pyramid markets. *Measuring Business Excellence*, 13(4), 58–68.

Ries, A., & Trout, J. (1986). *Positioning, the battle for your mind* (revised 1st ed.). New York, NY: McGraw-Hill.

Riley, F. D. (2016). Brand definitions and conceptualisations: The debate. In F. D. Riley, J. Singh, & C. Blankson (Eds.), *The Routledge companion to contemporary brand management* (pp. 3–12). Abingdon: Routledge.

Romaniuk, J. (2001). Brand positioning in financial services: A longitudinal test to find the best brand position. *Journal of Financial Services Marketing*, 6(2), 111–121.

Smithson, S., Devece, C. A., & Lapiedra, R. (2011). Online visibility as a source of competitive advantage for small- and medium-sized tourism accommodation enterprises. *The Service Industries Journal*, 31(10), 1573–1587.

Urde, M., & Koch, C. (2014). Market and brand-oriented schools of positioning. *Journal of Product and Brand Management*, 23(7), 478–490.

Vallaster, C., Lindgreen, A., & Maon, F. (2012). Strategically leveraging corporate social responsibility: A corporate branding perspective. *California Management Review*, 54(3), 34–60.

Wind, Y. (1982). *Product policy: Concepts, methods and strategy*. Reading, MA: Addison-Wesley Publishing.

World Bank. (2017). Retrieved from http://data.worldbank.org/country/ghana

Zaichkowsky, J. L. (2010). Strategies for distinctive brands. *Journal of Brand Management*, 17(8), 548–560.

Appendix

Outline of key strategic positioning typologies

Author (s)	Positioning constructs and concepts
Buskirk (1975)	(1) features, (2) price, (3) advertising, (4) distribution
Brown and Sims (1976)	(1) problems solved, (2)usage situation, (3) users, (4) competitors
Berry (1982)	(1) value (warehouse, off-pricing), (2) time efficiency (superstores, catalogue stores, tele-shopping), (3) high contact (specialty, facilitating, advising, added value, resource usage), (4) sensory (sounds, smells and visuals)
Wind (1982)	(1) attributes, (2) benefits, (3) problem solutions or need, (4) usage occasions, (5) user, (6) against another product, (7) product class dissociation
Aaker and Shansby (1982)	(1) attributes, (2) price/quality, (3) use or application, (4) product/service usage, (5) product/service class, (6) competition
Crawford (1985)	(1) features, (2) benefits: Direct and indirect, (3) surrogates: Non-pareil, parentage (brand company, person), manufacture (process, ingredients, design), target (end use, demographic, psychographic behavioral), rank endorsements (expert, emulative), experience (other market, band wagon, years/time), predecessor, competitor
Ries and Trout (1986)	(1) market leader, (2) follower, (3) reposition the competition, (4) use the name, (5) line extension (use of house name)
Easingwood and Mahajan (1989)	(1) reputation/capabilities of organization: Expertise, reliability, innovativeness, and performance; (2) augmentation of product offering: Product augmentation, extra service; (3) people advantage;, (4) more attractive package offering; (5) a superior product through technology; (6) Accessibility; (7) extra attention given to individuals requirements through customization; (8) satisfaction of more user need within the sector, and through offering a complete product line
Arnott (1992)	(1) empathy, (2) solvency, (3) promotions, (4) administrative time, (5) helpfulness, (6) reliability, (7) attentiveness, (8) staff competence, (9) flexible products, (10) access to people, (11) reputation, (12) customization, (13) incentives, (14) social awareness, (15) security, (16) technology
Hooley, Broderick, and Möller (1998)	(1) low price–high price, (2) premium quality–basic quality, (3) innovation–imitation, (4) superior service–limited service, (5) differentiation benefits–undifferentiated features, (6) tailored offering-standard offering

Author (s)	Positioning constructs and concepts
Kalafatis et al. (2000)	(1) pricing, (2) easy to do business, (3) personal contact, (4) product performance, (5) range of offerings, (6) presence, (7) safety, (8) leadership, (9) distinct identity, (10) status, (11) country of identity, (12) differentiation, (13) attractiveness
Blankson and Kalafatis (2004)	(1) top of the range, (2) service, (3) value for money, (4) reliability, (5) attractive, (6) country of origin, (7) the brand name, (8) selectivity
Coffie and Owusu–Frimpong (2014)	(1) service reliability, (2) social responsibility, (3) branding

Source: Blankson and Kalafatis (2004), Coffie and Owusu-Frimpong (2014).

3 Marketing mix strategies for service brands in BoPMs in Africa

Introduction

The role of branding is important and recognized by both the organization and its customers. For the organization, an established and successful brand provides an avenue for charging higher prices resulting in higher performance. This is so because established brands have associations and a reputation that serve as magnets for the sale of the product or service (Cravens & Piercy, 2013). Such associations develop over a period of time, based on the levels of services delivered to the target customers. There is a tendency toward greater loyalty by customers of successful brands, which emanates from a combination of factors including increased market share due to penetration and frequency of purchase (Singh & Uncles, 2016). For customers, the benefits of successful brands accrue from confidence, values, and trust in the standards the brand offers (Rajagopal, 2009).

In bottom of the pyramid markets (BoPMs) however, branding to enable customers and organizations access to the associated benefits comes with its challenges. Such challenges include the often negative associations with products and services from BoPMs, resulting in mistrust in such products that consequently makes it difficult to successfully market products from BoPM-designated environments, particularly in international contexts (Zhou, Yang, & Hue, 2010). In addition, economic, sociocultural, and technological challenges associated with the practice of marketing in BoPM environments can inhibit the success of effective branding of products and services (Tesar & Kuada, 2013).

Much of Africa falls within the BoPM classification of Prahalad (2002, 2004): BoPMs have low purchasing power relative to developed- and advanced-economy markets. However, cumulatively, BoPMs constitute sufficient force to warrant the attention of organizations as an economic and market force to do business with. Specific to Africa, there is a strong expectation that the continent will be the next frontier of growth over the next decades as many of the economies register strong growth credentials (George, Corbishley, Khayesi, Haas, & Tihanyi, 2016). In this regard, BoP markets in Africa need research focus in order to uncover ways of advancing and/or developing strategies to enhance the progress of business activities on the continent. In that direction, branding of services plays a pivotal role in determining the value propositions of offerings from BoP markets in Africa. Further, among other things, brand marketing is an important competitive strategy through which Africa- and foreign-based firms could gain access to challenging BoP markets (Abimbola, 2006, p. 108) as well as international markets in general.

Branding services

The intangibility of service means that it poses its own challenges when it comes to branding. The success or strengths of a service business lies in its processes rather than in capital equipment. The intangibles and processes will include relationships with customers and the industry, competencies that are unique to the company, and branding (Gray, 2006). This position finds support in the work of Salzer-Mörling and Strannegård (2004), which holds that service branding should place greater emphasis on customer experience. According to de Chernatony and Segal-Horn (2003), the dominant factors that influence the success of service branding include clear positioning, consistency of delivery, and the value of the service delivered. There must be clear positioning that points to the benefits associated with the experience. Consistency is important to reassure the customers of what they are most likely to receive. For Lovelock and Wirtz (2011), organizations need to work hard to avert wide divergences in operational input and output, as well as to implement effective service recovery systems where a failure occurs. To attain higher levels of consistency, the behavior of the staff needs to be managed, as both internal and external communications are important in effecting stakeholder beliefs about the consistency of service delivery.

There is also an increase in the pace of the international expansion of firms and brands from developed to emerging economies. This expansion is largely driven by firms seeking to grow, and therefore naturally tends to consider developing and emerging economies as target markets. The drive particularly favors firms with leading market positions in mature domestic markets (Mullins & Walker, 2013) seeking avenues for expansion. It is expected that by 2025, close to 85% of global economic growth will be concentrated in developing BoP and emerging markets, of which much of Africa is part of (Gupta, Garg, & Sharma, 2016, p. 366). Given this expectation, established brands (particularly in matured markets) seek to expand to emerging and developing economies. The increasing competition resulting from this situation requires both domestic and international firms to adjust their marketing strategies – including branding – to meet the specific needs of their target customers in order to build trust and confidence in products and services among consumers – particularly in BoP markets (Gupta et al., 2016).

For organizations to brand successfully in BoP markets, they need to understand the key dynamics that shape and inform consumer decision making in such markets. The price-quality relationship has increasingly come under pressure in BoP markets, as some firms have artificially inflated prices to create a semblance of quality not commensurate with the performance of the product/service. Trust in strong brands offers an easier route for the consumer in making choice decisions. There is a tendency for the preference for Western products and services, partly due to a lack of trust in local products and the perception that they will not satisfactorily meet the needs of customers. There is also a trend towards blending the image of a local product by domestic firms with a foreign image; this practice is designed to defeat the lack of trust and confidence in some products from domestic firms (Zhou et al., 2010). The cumulative effect of these factors requires both domestic and international firms seeking to enter BoP markets to offer brands that consumers believe and see as credible in relation to what the brands acclaim to offer.

Gupta et al. (2016) examine the key dynamics of branding in emerging and BoP and find that they involve an understanding of familiarity and knowledge, personality, image, credibility, and marketing mix in relation to levels of economic development (e.g., infrastructure). This is because such dynamics may be different between developed and emerging economies. The evolving nature of markets and consumers means that standardized business and marketing strategies have been insufficient in meeting consumer needs. Therefore, the choice of branding strategy varies, as no single strategy will work for all firms (Gulati & Garino, 2000). In this context, marketing and branding strategy would be better to proceed on a best–fit basis.

The value of the service delivered is often embedded in the culture of the organization in motivating staff and supporting them to deliver the promised value. Other factors that influence the success of service brands included effective communication, innovation, relationships, emotion, added value, commitments, and competitive advantage (de Chernatony & Segal-Horn, 2003). Lovelock and Wirtz (2011) note that often it is the cumulative application of the identified factors that will make for successful branding and implementation of the service promise; this helps to limit the gap between the rhetoric from service providers and the reality in terms of what consumers get. In BoP markets in Africa, do these observations directly translate into practice in service branding? What are the dynamics of branding in BoP markets? This chapter aims to present the dynamics of branding in BoPMs in Africa. In particular, the focus is on branding services by organizations in BoPMs in Africa and how in the midst of challenges, effective branding can still be practiced successfully through the employment of marketing mix strategies. Consequently, the chapter is structured around the theme of branding services in BoP markets in Africa by examining issues of challenges, expectations, and the marketing mix strategies for branding by organizations (both foreign and local) operating in Africa.

Branding services in BoPMs in Africa

A wide range of factors might explain the dynamics and challenges of branding in BoP markets in Africa. Some of these factors are sociocultural, economic, political, perceptual, and attitudinal (Chikweche & Fletcher, 2011; Coffie & Darmoe, 2016). In this section, illustrative cases are introduced to help explore such dynamics.

The TinMan (Illustrative case 1) provides some pointers to the nature of life in a typical rural setting in Africa. Life largely focuses more on the practical and

Illustrative case 1   Developing and branding biomass energy products in rural Ghana

The TinMan project in rural Ghana was organized by a team of students and researchers in 2010 from Arizona State University with the key aim of developing a biomass energy brand relevant to the needs of rural Africa. Another purpose was to meet and validate a product concept that had been created: TinMan. TinMan relied on the leftover burning embers of village cook fires to generate electricity for rural usage as an alternative to solar power and rechargeable/disposable batteries. Michael Pugliese, a graduate student, invented this energy product and was accompanied by other researchers to test the suitability of the prototype in a rural area of Ghana in Domeabra and Biemso near Kumasi in the Ashanti Region. This research involved building trust and relationships with the inhabitants and obtaining their input for the development of the brand for the energy product.

The research relied on ethnographic observation and interviews of rural lifestyles in relation to energy usage in order to achieve the intended purpose. The researchers observed that the inhabitants used ingenuity in terms of their energy use. For example, they dismantled flashlights and reconfigured them into original lighting devices such that the flashlight worked on less expensive disposable Chinese batteries. The study uncovered that there was limited knowledge of branded products. In general, the emphasis for the inhabitants was the utilitarian role of products that they used as opposed to an emphasis on established or particular brands. It was challenging to get the inhabitants to suggest a realistic price for the TinMan: the original price for the object was about $20, and for the average income earner in the villages, this represented 60–70% of their monthly earnings. Asked what price they would sell the TinMan product for if they were to produce the item themselves was a more useful approach to questioning, and allowed responses from a producer's perspective rather than as a recipient of goods and services.

Source: Re-written based on Takamura (2011).

utilitarian aspects of products/services that will help meet basic needs. Therefore, the notion of branding in the sense of a wide range of choice(s) may not exist. This is also because of the low levels of income to the extent that the knowledge of the inhabitants on a realistic price of some products may be far-fetched. Here, there may be some known products/brands that meet basic needs. While there may exist some alternative brands of services that provide for the needs of people, branding in the competitive sense of higher priced products that will generate higher profitability (as in the Western sense) is often impracticable to the majority.

In this specific context, the development of a brand that will meet the needs of the people will require the marketer to study and engage the community in its development and take into consideration cultural and environmental sensitivities in order to arrive at what is relevant and beneficial to the community under consideration. This raises questions about the financial feasibility of developing such brands and what the sales prospects might be. This point simply goes back to the classic problem of whether BoP markets are worth the effort and investment. Again, in the specific context of a rural African setting, the answer is "yes" in the sense that if the organization can develop and market such products across many such communities (a numbers game), then the cumulative effect of sales is likely to justify the effort (Prahalad, 2002, 2004). The key point is that brands might still be profitable in the African rural context when viewed on a wider scale across many communities of a similar nature.

In Illustrative case 2, we witness a shift toward interest in branded products, which is partly explainable by the demographic make-up in improved

---

Illustrative case 2   Brands among the Tshwanes in South Africa

The predominantly black inhabitants of the urban Tshwane region of South Africa were known for their lack of interest in branded products. In apartheid South Africa, the townships – the poor urban areas – were mainly served with limited products by small, informal businesses. Consequently, in the Tshwane region of South Africa, exposure of the population to branding and branded products and services was rather limited.

There has been a change in attitude towards branded products and services in the Tshwane region in post-apartheid South Africa (since 1994). A number of reasons account for the changing interest and attitude towards brands. In apartheid South Africa, a majority of black people in the Tshwane region were on relatively low income. In post-apartheid South Africa, a sizeable middle class emerged, accounting for the increased interest in branded products and services. There was also a prior failure among organizations in understanding the needs of the population in these areas in order to meet such needs commensurate with the population's ability to pay.

The change in interest in branded products reflects in the growth of retailers setting up shops to serve areas that were previously ignored in order to grow their businesses and to seek competitive advantage. Research suggests that consumers now largely perceive advertised retail brands and branding in a positive manner. The majority of respondents to a survey disagreed that they only bought branded products, suggesting that people in the region now "mix" their purchasing of branded and unbranded products.

Source: Based on Cant and Manley (2013).

incomes, and the increasing middle class among the Tshwanes in South Africa. As the well-being of the population in the area increased, so has the interest in branded products increased. Not surprisingly, retail shops that usually sold branded products elsewhere now operate in the region by selling both branded and unbranded products. In the case of the Tshwanes, economic and political reasons account for the challenges of selling branded products and services before and after apartheid. The case also supports the general notion that branded products tend to be higher priced, and as the economic fortunes of the population increase, people want to be associated with some established brands.

The successful branding and profitability of M–Pesa in Kenya in Illustrative case 3 is intriguing. The key difference between this case and those of cases 1 and 2 is that this affects a branded service that is national in character and also draws the interest of the majority of the population. It is worthy of note that mobile technology is important in this case, and aids the transfer of money to relatives around the country. The success of M–Pesa may be largely attributed to the participation of most middle-class people who are also likely to be the senders of mobile money to their rural relatives who are often the recipients. In other words, mobile money transfer in Kenya met a specific need, as most well-off relatives in cities initiate transfers to their rural relatives in Africa.

Why did Safaricom not achieve the same level of success when it attempted to do so in South Africa? South Africa's banking service was much more developed in comparison with that of Kenya. Additionally, the dominant market share of Safaricom – the communication firm behind M–Pesa – was a key factor, as it already had access to the majority of mobile phone subscribers (quora.com, 2017). A key learning point is that a brand has a good chance of success in the African context when the product or service meets an important need and when the service is simplified and presented to the relevant people and communities. In this context, the utilitarian purpose of M–Pesa played a key part in the success of the brand in Kenya.

Illustrative case 3   The success of M–Pesa's mobile money service in Kenya

M–Pesa is, without doubt, the most successful money transfer service brand in Kenya. The money transfer service was a concept introduced by M–Pesa in Kenya in 2007. This was unprecedented for the purpose of transferring money via non–bank outlets through the use of mobile phones. The concept is now well accepted, and service usage has since skyrocketed along with consumer participation and interest in using the services of the company. Consequently, the communication firm Safaricom – the owners of the M–Pesa brand in Kenya – now controls 70–80% of all mobile money transfers based on 2017 figures.

What accounts for the phenomenal success of the M–Pesa money transfer service and its brand? Mobile phone penetration was high in Kenya when the concept was launched, which means the key medium to facilitate the service was in place. The service was an advanced form of what Kenyans used to do in the past (townsfolk sending money to their rural relatives), but made easier through the use of mobile technology. In this regard, there was little cultural disturbance, if any, and it was easier for recipients in rural areas to manage the technology involved than through formal banking accounts which most did not have. Safaricom was also already the market leader in mobile communications in Kenya; again, that provided a useful springboard for introducing a concept that married well with existing cultural and traditional practices. The service was instant and available to the recipient as soon as it was sent – in effect, it amounted to sending cash, as Kenyans had known it, but now at a greater speed.

To develop and successfully market the M–Pesa brand, there was a heavy initial investment in order to build awareness. The message emphasized person-to-person transfers and the utility for families in slogans such as "send money home." Following a national launch, it was able to achieve higher-than-expected levels of awareness within the first few months. This integrated application of the marketing communication mix is relevant to both area and location. There was consistency in the logo used in store outlets to represent the brand, and customer experience also bolstered the service and its success. The M–Pesa brand developed trust as it leveraged on the already trusted Safaricom name.

Source: Based on: Markovich and Snyder (2017); Olopade (2014); quora.com (2017).

Illustrative case 4   Developing the Watatu Brand in Tanzania

Watatu Company Limited was founded by three tertiary-level students who met and discussed how they could register a company. They were drawn together by a common interest of improving their economic well-being and religion. They were located in Dar es Salaam, Tanzania in central Africa. To build a viable business, the three friends with technical degrees needed to register the company and find a location to operate from. Additionally, a memorandum, articles of association, and other requirements were important to register the building and construction company. In the early years, finding start-up capital was no easy matter. Most banks the students approached required collateral due to the high risk associated with giving out loans. The owners of Watatu Co. Ltd. resorted to selling food crops, supervising residential building construction, and little monies they could individually raise for start-up capital. After a long period of financial uncertainty, including a time when the trio had to undertake unrelated activities, they raised enough money and Watatu Co. Ltd. became a reality.

The most pressing demand for the young entrepreneurs was the location of an office; they preferred the city and ideally the city center. As beginners, the rent was expensive for them, and there was the cost of furniture and other materials. One of the three partners, Muona, had a full-time job with another company and contributed towards running the business mainly in terms of ideas – he was the Marketing and Planning Director on a part-time basis. Muona felt that the ideas and programs he generated were not effectively implemented by the two other partners. This soon became a source of frustration for him.

The other two, Nguvu and Mpole, worked on a full-time basis for the joint venture as Managing Director and Finance Director, respectively. Nguvu felt that his strengths and his contribution to the enterprise resided in his "action man" approach. His action-oriented approach was sometimes a disadvantage where and when diplomacy was required. Pre-occupation with pushing and getting things done in situations requiring diplomacy caused problems for the business, as he sometimes found it difficult to accept alternative ideas. In the process, Nguvu also took up an additional role in a society of life – this was a religious role. As Managing Director, implementation of programs substantially depended on his efforts, and he needed to be available for that purpose. He soon mixed family issues with running the Watatu business, which led to rather poor supervision and accountability, an insufficient level of transparency, and poor communication.

Mpole, the Director of Finance who generally played a nominal role, saw his strength in the flexibility he brought to the business. He worked well with people to accomplish set missions, winning deals for the company. In challenging situations, Mpole was able to suggest workable solutions as a reflection of his tolerant and democratic nature. Nguvu somehow interpreted Mpole's negotiated approach to finding solutions to problems to mean a lack of transparency. In the circumstance, Mpole considered dissolving the joint venture since there were challenges facing the company, and he could not clearly see the way forward for the business.

Source: Adapted from Tumsifu (2013) and Tesar and Kuada (2013).

In many ways, the development of the Watatu brand echoes what happens in the establishment and development of an indigenous (local businesses) brand from scratch. Ofei (2005) and Tesar and Kuada (2013) explain that most businesses in BoPM Africa are small- to medium-sized enterprises (SMEs), and while some SMEs are well structured, others are not. To be structured to develop the business, the Watatu Co. Ltd. partners needed to build a consensus on business activities. This didn't appear to be the case with Muona, Nguvu, and Mpole. While one may not expect that the trio would necessarily think alike, the three needed to agree on the strategies and their implementation in order to develop a brand that started from nothing. As observed by Tesar and Kuada (2013), in many African cultures, a structured approach to running an SME is not easy. This is because the businesses are often family-owned or led by an owner-manager. In large families, there is a tendency for a family member to offer unsolicited advice when they may not fully understand the nature of the business. In the case of Watatu Co. Ltd. the issue was not the size of the family members involved; instead, it had more to do with building and developing a common understanding for the activities of the company to function well. When such African businesses grow and mature, they tend to develop structures at strategic and operational levels that help run the business, by which time the brand will be better established. In smaller businesses, the strategic and operational decisions tend to be made by the same people and can be said to be intertwined.

Another difficulty encountered by Watatu Co. Ltd. at the beginning was finding finance to start the business. This forced the entrepreneurs to engage in activities including those unrelated to the intended building and construction business. In small businesses, start-up finance is often a problem; in general, these tend to be mostly financial as well as human from African business and cultural perspective (Tesar & Kuada, 2013). These are critical issues for consideration at the start, if the business and an effective brand are to be developed.

Marketing mix strategies for service brands in BoPMs in Africa

The discussion thus far leads us to suggestions on marketing mix strategies for branding services in BoP markets in Africa, given the eccentricities of branding products and services in the environment. Ireland (2008) distinguishes between the urban poor and rural poor and argues that the two categories of customer groups may not necessarily require uniform strategies by organizations in order to successfully market a brand. Equally, the urban well off and the rural well-off persons may not require the same level of marketing mix in order to satisfy customers. Bearing in mind that this may be the case, we make suggestions for broad marketing and branding services in the African context with the majority as the target.

The evidence from the illustrative cases suggests that for service brands (products) to be successful in African BoP markets, the service should be socially and culturally embedded (Assimeng, 2007; Rajagopal, 2009). This means the nature of the service or product should meet or enhance the provision for the social and cultural needs of the majority. In the case of M-Pesa in Kenya, the phenomenal success of mobile money transfers was mainly tied to social and cultural factors. Many Kenyans living in major cities needed to send money to relatives in rural areas, and therefore the avenue offered by Safaricom met this social and cultural expectation. In other words, there was solid demand for the service. As most Kenyans did not have bank accounts – particularly in rural areas – money transfer became a perfect opportunity to meet the support needs of relatives in rural communities. The communal nature of most African societies creates expectations for the better-off individuals to support the needy, and therefore a service that provides such an opportunity also has a good chance of success. This point is further supported in the work of Ghauri, Tasavori, and Zaefarian (2014, p. 590): Namely, that organizations should "engage in activities such as addressing the neglected needs of the BoP people and offering sustainable solutions and empowerment opportunities." This provides a better chance of success in BoPMs.

The sociocultural values and "expectant" nature of the Africans (Assimeng, 2007) also suggests that corporate social responsibility (CSR) activities will usually resonate with communities and will help to develop an affinity with a given brand. For example, in developing positioning strategies for service firms in Ghana, Coffie and Owusu-Frimpong (2014) found that CSR was a major positioning strategy and resonated with consumer expectations. Such positioning strategy expectations can be adapted for the purpose of branding services. MTN Ghana and Vodafone Ghana are the two most successful service communication firms in terms of market share. These two companies owe their success in part to the many educational and community-based CSR activities they undertake. These help to build goodwill among the users of the service. The point must be made here that CSR activities should not and cannot be a replacement for the quality of service the organization has to deliver to its customers. CSR activities will augment the quality of service provision and help create a positive perception of the brand, and consequently the use of the service. The benefits of organizations engaging in CSR and entrepreneurial activities apply to both local and international firms seeking to operate in BoP markets. For multinationals, such benefits are more noticeable when these multinationals link up with the NGOs who tend to have a better understanding of the social and economic needs of the locals, and thereby such linkages and networks will afford a better provision of what is required. This, then, has a positive effect on the nature of service provision and helps to build a positive image and performance of the multinational firm (Ghauri et al., 2014).

Pricing of services in BoP markets has always been a challenging issue, given the affordability factor (Payaud, 2014). Service providers need to bear in mind that demographics roughly allow for the urban and rural poor on one hand and the urban and rural well-off on the other. In general, however, and for the majority (urban and rural poor) organizations should aim at low cost and low margin pricing in African BoP markets. Low cost can be achieved through a number of initiatives including low margins and high volumes/consumption of the service. Credit facilities may also be offered to credible, registered, and trusted networks and associations (Chikweche & Fletcher, 2012). The low-margin and high-volume strategy has been successfully exploited by telecommunication firms for mobile money transfers in Kenya by Safaricom, and in Ghana by MTN Ghana and Vodafone Ghana. In Kenya in 2017 (see Illustrative case 3), M–Pesa, owned and controlled by Safaricom, had about 70% of the share of the mobile money transfer market. It may not be feasible, however, for organizations to control such a large market share in most service situations at the country level. Nevertheless, working towards low cost, low margin, and high volume remains an attractive proposition for pricing services used by the majority.

In BoP and emerging markets, distribution is a critical factor in ensuring the success of services. Often, poor logistical and transport infrastructure challenges, as well as cultural influence on local channels, can inhibit organizations from accessing BoP markets. In this regard, accessibility and proximity of the service product are vital elements in keeping the consumer's cost of accessing the product low (Payaud, 2014). Further, the employment of multi-level channels serves as a means of targeting the urban poor and the rural poor (Ireland, 2008). For example, the spread of thousands of mobile money agents using a combination of existing and new outlets in both Kenya and Ghana makes the use of the service easily accessible to customers in both cities and rural areas. With over 80% of roads unpaved in Gabon (Payaud, 2014), for example, expecting the poor consumer to travel long distances to obtain a relatively minimal but needed service is unhelpful, and in some cases unrealistic. The availability of products/services in kiosks spread out in low–income areas in Kenya, as well as the use of bicycles, can be useful in providing the service in small pieces that are easily available to the consumer (Schupbach, 2013). In Illustrative case 2, the proximity of retail outlets in the Tshwane areas worked in unison with improving economic conditions to result in the Tshwanes of South Africa patronizing branded products/services.

To promote services in African BoP markets, there are challenges to do with accessibility and affordability of promotional media (Chikweche & Fletcher, 2012). In a study in Zimbabwe, it was found that access to television and radio, for example, limited organizations' ability to easily communicate their message to the intended target audience, particularly in rural areas. In such circumstances, below–the–line forms of communication through communities and associations such as women's groups, churches, road shows, and word of mouth work better. Consumer education through social networks, one–to–one interactions, and word of mouth are important in developing both the awareness and interest of consumers in services needed (Payaud, 2014).

Conclusion

It is generally acknowledged that well–branded services offer benefits to both the consumer and the service provider. To the consumer, such benefits may include an assurance of the quality and dependability of the service, while to the organization, successful branding results in customer loyalty and higher profitability. In BoP markets in Africa, and as those denoted in the illustrative cases, there is a range of economic, sociocultural, technological, and infrastructural challenges in the successful development, introduction, and growth of brands.

In order to develop successful service brands, organizations need to be more imaginative in addressing the environmental challenges posed in the context of BoPM consumers in Africa. Services that meet the needs of the majority may have a good chance of success, as in the case of M-Pesa in the telecommunications market in Kenya. In this regard, the targeting, positioning, and development of an imaginative marketing mix become very important. CSR as a strategy and working with NGOs will augment the efforts of the organization in identifying core social and service needs and will help organizations both local and foreign to meet the needs of the majority. Pricing to meet the target audience – urban or rural – is important. In general, low-margin, high-volume pricing for the majority will improve the chances of successful branding and marketing. Distribution through multi-level channels, with proximity and small volumes as key principles for most services used by the majority, may provide the answers to success. Promotion – predominantly via below-the-line methods – emphasizing word of mouth through community groups and associations might be the key for reaching out to the majority in BoP service markets in Africa.

References

Abimbola, T. (2006). Market access for developing economies: Branding in Africa. *Place Branding, 2*(2), 108–117.

Assimeng, M. (2007). *Social structure of Ghana: A study in persistence and change* (2nd ed.). Tema: Ghana Publishing Corporation.

Cant, M. C., & Manley, L. L. (2013). Investigating South African black urban area consumers perceptions of advertised retail brands. *3rd Annual International Conference on Enterprise Marketing and Globalisation*, 8–13. Retrieved from https://doi.org/10.5176/2251-2098_EMG13.02

Chikweche, T., & Fletcher, R. (2011). Branding at the base of the pyramid: A Zimbabwean perspective. *Marketing Intelligence and Planning, 29*(3), 247–263.

Chikweche, T., & Fletcher, R. (2012). Revisiting the marketing mix at the Bottom of Pyramid (BoP): From theoretical considerations to practical realities. *Journal of Consumer Marketing, 29*(7), 507–520. https://doi.org/10.1108/07363761211275018

Coffie, S., & Darmoe, J. (2016). Branding in the base of the pyramid: Bases for country and organizations in Ghana. In F. D. Riley, J. Singh, & C. Blankson (Eds.), *The Routledge companion to contemporary brand management* (pp. 378–390). Abingdon: Routledge.

Cravens, D. W., & Piercy, N. F. (2013). *Strategic marketing*. New York, NY: McGraw-Hill.

de Chernatony, L., & Segal-Horn, S. (2003). The criteria for successful services brands. *European Journal of Marketing, 37*(7/8), 1095–1118. https://doi.org/10.1108/03090560310477681

George, G., Corbishley, C., Khayesi, J. O., Haas, M. R., & Tihanyi, L. (2016). From the editors, bringing Africa in: Promising directions for management research. *Academy of Management Journal, 2*, 377–393.

Ghauri, P., Tasavori, M., & Zaefarian, R. (2014). Internationalisation of service firms through corporate social entrepreneurship and networking. *International Marketing Review, 31*(6), 576–600. https://doi.org/10.1108/IMR-09-2013-0196

Gray, B. J. (2006). Benchmarking services branding practices. *Journal of Marketing Management, 22*(7/8), 717–758.

Gulati, R., & Garino, J. (2000, May/June). Get the right mix of bricks and clicks. *Harvard Business Review*, 107–114.

Gupta, S., Garg, S., & Sharma, K. (2016). Branding in emerging markets. In F. D. Riley, J. Singh, & C. Blankson (Eds.), *The Routledge companion to contemporary brand management* (pp. 366–377). Abingdon: Routledge.

Ireland, J. (2008). Lessons for successful BoP marketing from Caracas' slums. *Journal of Consumer Marketing, 25*(7), 430–438. https://doi.org/10.1108/07363760810915644

Lovelock, C., & Wirtz, J. (2011). *Services marketing: People, technology, and strategy* (7th ed.). Upper Saddle River, NJ: Pearson Prentice Hall.

Markovich, S., & Snyder, C. (2017). *M-Pesa and mobile money in Kenya: Pricing for success.* Kellogg School of Management Cases. Retrieved from https://doi.org/10.1108/case.kellogg.2016.000221

Mullins, J. W., & Walker Jr., O. C. (2013). *Marketing management: A strategic decision-making approach* (8th ed.). New York, NY: McGraw-Hill Irwin.

Ofei, K. A. (2005). Internationalisation and management of Ghanaian export firms. In J. Kuada (Ed.), *Internationalisation and enterprise development in Ghana* (pp. 76–128). London: Adonis and Abbey.

Olopade, D. (2014). Africa's tech edge. *The Atlantic.* 10727825, 313, 82–86.

Payaud, M. A. (2014, January/February). Marketing strategies at the bottom of the pyramid: Examples from Nestle, Danone, and Proctor and Gamble. *Global Business and Organisational Excellence,* 51–63. https://doi.org/10.1002/joe.21533

Prahalad, C. K. (2002). Strategies for the bottom of the economic pyramid: India as a source of innovation. *Society for Organisational Learning Reflections, 3*(4), 6–17.

Prahalad, C. K. (2004). *Fortune at the bottom of the pyramid: Eradicating poverty through profits.* Upper Saddle River, NJ: Pearson Education.

Quora.com. (2017). *Why was MPesa so successful in Kenya, when comparable products are not as successful in South Africa or India?* Retrieved from www.quora.com/Why-was-MPesa-so-successful-in-Kenya-when-comparable-products-are-not-as-successful-in-South-Africa-or-India

Rajagopal. (2009). Branding paradigm for the bottom of the pyramid markets. *Measuring Business Excellence, 13*(4), 58–68. https://doi.org/10.1108/13683040911006792

Salzer-Mörling, M., & Strannegård, L. (2004). Silence of the brands. *European Journal of Marketing, 38*(1), 224–238.

Schupbach, L. (2013). KasKazi Network Ltd: Distributing to the bottom of the pyramid. In G. Tesar & J. Kuada (Eds.), *Marketing management and strategy: An African casebook* (pp. 212–224). London: Routledge.

Singh, J., & Uncles, M. (2016). Measuring the market performance of brands: Applications in brand management. In F. D. Riley, J. Singh, & C. Blankson (Eds.), *The Routledge companion to contemporary brand management* (pp. 13–31). Abingdon: Routledge.

Takamura, J. H. (2011). Branding for the BoP: Design collaboration with rural villagers in Ghana. *Design Management Review, 22*(1), 86–91. https://doi.org/10.1111/j.1948-7169.2011.00114.x

Tesar, G., & Kuada, J. (2013). *Marketing management and strategy: An African casebook.* London: Routledge.

Tumsifu, E. (2013). Watatu Co. Ltd – Managing growth: Entrepreneurs' tendencies and their impact on a joint venture. In G. Tesar & J. Kuada (Eds.), *Marketing management and strategy: An African casebook* (pp. 83–88). London: Routledge.

Zhou, L., Yang, Z., & Hue, M. K. (2010). Non-local or local brands? A multi-level investigation into confidence in brand origin identification and its strategic implications. *Journal of the Academy of Marketing Science, 38,* 202–218.

4 Positioning strategies and positioning activities of upscale retailers in BoPMs in Africa

Introduction

As shown by Blankson, Nkrumah, Opare, and Ketron (2018), the last few decades have witnessed retailers exploiting competitive advantages by focusing on strong brand identity as well as strong store and corporate images (Burt & Carralero-Encinas, 2000) in the internationalization process. Burt and Carralero-Encinas (2000) highlight that store image and the associated positioning of the firm are important sources of competitive advantage, and positioning is one of the fundamental components of marketing strategy in both domestic and international retailing (McGoldrick & Ho, 1992; McGoldrick & Blair, 1995; Kara, Kaynak, & Kucukemiroglu, 1996). Arnott (1992) claims that positioning encapsulates the deliberate, proactive, and iterative process of defining, measuring, modifying, and monitoring consumer perceptions of a marketable offering.

In international retailing, context matters for sampling purposes, and the examination of actual case studies of firms' activities is important (see Burt, Mellahi, Jackson, & Sparks, 2002; Poulis, Poulis, & Plakoyiannaki, 2013; Blankson et al., 2018). Additionally, even though qualitative case methodology plays an important role in the study of congruence in positioning research (Yin, 2009; Liu & Zhang, 2014; Galperin & Lituchy, 1999), international retailing and positioning scholars have overlooked such methodology in base of the pyramid markets (BoPMs) in Africa. The qualitative case method and purposeful sampling method presented in this chapter were inspired by Blankson et al. (2018) and were chosen because of the exploratory nature of the study and to allow for the exploration of the complexity surrounding retailers' positioning strategies and congruence in positioning activities in Africa, and specifically in a BoPM economy such as Ghana. The socio-cultural, economic, and political conditions under which international marketing strategies are made in Africa are unique and challenging (Babarinde, 2009), yet the environment is a reservoir of profitable business and investment ventures for creative and long-term–oriented international firms (Mmieh & Owusu-Frimpong, 2009). Across the region, cross-border firms are successful and are investing in stock exchanges in other African countries (see Mmieh & Owusu-Frimpong, 2009). Other successful firms such as Kenya Airways' business and marketing strategies are reported by Debrah and Toroitich (2005).

Similar to Blankson et al. (2018), the central purpose of this exploratory study has been to examine the employment of positioning strategies through the lens of international retailing for the purpose of assessing positioning congruence among both indigenous and foreign retailers in Africa, using Ghana as an illustration. To that end, this chapter contributes to the literature by studying an untapped yet potentially viable context for testing the theory of fit/congruence and the concept of positioning (Coffie, 2018). The scant knowledge on the positioning activities of retailers in Ghana is particularly critical for international marketing research (Appiah-Adu, 1999; Coffie, 2014, 2018; Coffie & Owusu-Frimpong, 2014).

Four major contributions to international retailing, international marketing, and positioning literatures are established in this study (see also Blankson et al., 2018). First, the concomitant examination of the growing middle-class perceptions of retailers' positioning strategies and activities will generate theoretical and practical value for researchers and practitioners currently engaged (or considering engagement) in assessing congruence research and, more specifically, in positioning research in BoPM African countries, with a particular focus on Ghana (Coffie & Owusu-Frimpong, 2014; Coffie, 2018). Second, this research responds to calls for more empirical research in positioning by firms operating in Ghana's post- Structural Adjustment Program (SAP) market environment (see Appiah-Adu, 1999; Kuada & Buatsi, 2005; Coffie & Owusu-Frimpong, 2014). While Appiah-Adu (1999) examines the impact of economic reform on business performance using foreign and domestic firms in Ghana, the author's study is wholly based not only on the assessment of economic reforms on business performance rather than firms' positioning activities but also on the context of manufacturers of consumer and industrial products and industrial services. Appiah-Adu (1999) did not examine actual retailers' positioning strategies in spite of calls for such research by Kara et al. (1996). Third, the results of this research add to ongoing discussion related to the efficacy of Western-derived marketing strategy and business practices of firms in emerging sub-Saharan African economies – a region that has, to date, received meager attention in discourse regarding global business activities (Owhoso, Gleason, Mathur, & Malgwi, 2002; Yang, Wang, & Su, 2006; Manwa & Manwa, 2007; Babarinde, 2009). Fourth, the complex and dysfunctional environment characterizing marketing practices in BoPMs in African countries, and Ghana in particular, is best appreciated by evaluating firm-specific positioning strategies (Wiig & Kolstad, 2010; Yang et al., 2006; Coffie & Owusu-Frimpong, 2014; Coffie, 2018; Liu & Zhang, 2014).

Literature background

International retailing and positioning

Interestingly, while internationalization of retailing in regard to entry mode strategies (Gielens & DeKimpe, 2001; Gripsrud & Benito, 2005), internationalization motives, retail format (Swoboda & Elsner, 2013; Swoboda, Berg, & Dan-Cristian,

2014), retail divestment (Cairns, Doherty, Alexander, & Quinn, 2008), store image (Burt & Carralero-Encinas, 2000), psychic distance (Evans & Mavondo, 2002), and retail failure (Burt, Dawson, & Sparks, 2003; Burt et al., 2002) receive much interest and attention in the literature, international retail positioning and congruence in strategies appear to have been overlooked by marketing scholars. Although Swoboda et al. (2014) conclude that retail format transfer and positioning decisions are important in retail internationalization, the authors do not indicate the actual positioning strategies used by the retailers, instead calling for future investigation of international retailers' positioning decisions. Additionally, Burt & Carralero-Encinas' (2000) research on store and corporate image does not deal with retail positioning *per se*, although the authors suggest that retailers should fully understand the importance of image in competitive positioning prior to image replication overseas. Given the pivotal role played by positioning in retail firms' marketing strategy formulation, the oversight of research in positioning and congruence in positioning activities – especially foreign and indigenous retailers' positioning strategies in the international retailing domain – is of concern to the success of the international retail venture (Burt & Carralero-Encinas, 2000; Blankson et al., 2018).

Moreover, not only has the literature shown little attention to the positioning strategies of retailers operating outside their home markets (McGoldrick & Ho, 1992; McGoldrick & Blair, 1995) but also there is a paucity of examination of how strong or well-positioned local/indigenous firms and brands benefit from high levels of local awareness (Schuiling & Kapferer, 2004). More specifically, while concern about foreign retailers in host countries continues to receive attention in the literature, there is a need to examine how indigenous retailers compete with foreign retailers in their countries (Coffie, 2014; Blankson et al., 2018). This is important for foreign and indigenous retail managers, as they must decide not only how to build their brands but also how to adjust their marketing strategies and benchmark best practices, respectively, in the local marketplace (Schuiling & Kapferer, 2004).

Table 4.1 shows a sample of studies dealing with retail internationalization. Content analysis of Table 4.1 shows that five main themes underpin international retailing literature. These include (1) entry mode decisions and strategies; (2) store image; (3) store format, type, location, and layout; (4) psychic distance; and (5) retail failure. Empirical studies (9 out of 15 papers) are dominant, followed by conceptual/literature review papers (5 out of 15 papers). Qualitative (five studies) and quantitative (four studies) data and analyses are prominent among utilized research methodology. Case study research is important in international retailing literature (four papers), followed by secondary data analysis (two studies). The majority of studies conducted in international retailing were carried out in the United Kingdom (eight papers) compared to Germany (two articles), Romania, Spain, Austria, Switzerland, the United States, and the Asia Pacific region (one article each). Two studies were carried out in Europe, and none took place in Australasia, South America, the Caribbean, the Middle East, or Africa.

Table 4.1 A sample of studies on international retailing

Author(s)	Objective/Research Question	Method of Study/ Study Setting	Sample/Variables	Method & Tool of Analysis	Findings/Conclusions
Vida and Fairhurstt (1998).	To offer a comprehensive assessment of the literature in the field of a firm's internationalization based on a behavioral paradigm and then to propose a model for the retail internationalization process.	Literature review	N/A	Synthesis of literature	A new model is put forward that discusses the antecedents, process, and outcomes of the international involvement of retail firms. The models answer two key questions: (1) what are the driving forces which lead a retail firm from a low to a substantial level of international involvement or possibly to a retreat from the process, and (2) how do intra-firm factors relate to the two critical strategic decisions: entry mode and market selection?
Doherty (1999).	To broaden the scope for potential theoretical development of retailer market entry mode strategy.	Literature review and conceptual development	N/A	Synthesis of literature and cases	The paper explains and adapts internationalization and agency theories and highlights the importance of information asymmetry in the entry mode context. The paper advocates the use of other economics-based theories in international retailing research.
Doherty (2000).	To address the deficiencies in international retailing research by attempting to ascertain the major issues influencing fashion retailers' choices of entry modes when entering an overseas market.	Empirical, qualitative/UK	Seven firms	Interpretive, in-depth, semi-structured interviews	Entry mode strategy in international fashion retailing is not predetermined. Rather, it emerges over time as a result of a combination of historical, experiential, financial, opportunistic, strategic, and company-specific factors such as changes in management structure.

Burt and Carralero–Encinas (2000).	To examine a set of pre-determined dimensions and associated attributes of store image chosen to represent tangible and intangible elements of image were perceived by customers in two different national markets.	Empirical, quantitative/ UK, Spain	150 consumers from the United Kingdom and 150 consumers from Spain/ Perceptions of store image attributes via survey	Descriptive statistics	Marks & Spencer was studied in domestic and non-domestic settings with respect to overall image. British respondents had an extremely positive impression of the Marks & Spencer's store image. Spanish respondents were less favorably disposed towards the attribute statements. Customer perceptions of store image are more positive and coherent in the domestic market than in the host market.
Gielens and Dekimpe (2001).	Simultaneously examines five strategic entry decisions: scale of entry, mode of entry, order of entry, the adaptation of the retail format to local market conditions, and the familiarity of the store format to the parent company.	Empirical/ secondary data/ Europe	75 European grocery retail firms, Dependent: Post-entry performance – sales performance, efficiency Independent: Entry decisions – scale of entry, mode of entry, order of entry, format adaptation, and format familiarity Control: retail mix – assortment size, pricing strategy (EDLP), loyalty card	Descriptive statistics/ Gompertz model for estimation results	Strategic decisions made at entry continue to influence the foreign operations' post-entry performance, both in terms of long-run sales and long-run efficiency.

(Continued)

Table 4.1 (Continued)

Author(s)	Objective/Research Question	Method of Study/ Study Setting	Sample/Variables	Method & Tool of Analysis	Findings/Conclusions
Evans and Mavondo (2002).	To develop a reconceptualization and operationalization of psychic distance.	Empirical/ Quantitative/ United States, UK, Western Europe, Asia Pacific region	Sample of 204 senior executives based in the United States, United Kingdom, Western Europe, and the Asia Pacific region via survey Dependent: Financial performance, strategic effectiveness. Independent: Cultural distance, business distance	Regression	Results support a broader conceptualization of psychic distance. Also, psychic distance explains a significant proportion of the variance for both financial performance and strategic effectiveness in distant markets but not in close markets. The study demonstrates that disaggregation of the dimensions of psychic distance significantly increases the explanatory power of the model in both close and distant markets. After disaggregation, significant predictors for the distant market were positive while those for the close market were largely negative. The overall results support the existence of a psychic distance paradox.
Burt et al. (2002).	To use Marks & Spencer as a case illustration to probe international retailing activity.	Literature review and case study of M&S/United Kingdom	One company: M&S	Secondary data analysis of M&S business performance, international business development and locations, export sales	To answer the question: why did the internationalization activity of M&S fail? The authors conclude that there has been no overall internationalization strategy. Some of the activities have been serendipitous and some were probably misguided. There was a lack of direction over a long period. Many of the elements that made M&S successful in the United Kingdom did not apply in the global arena. There was a lack of clear retail positioning. In addition to entry, there is a need to focus on activities and strategies after establishment.

Author (Year)	Objective	Methodology/Country	Sample	Analysis	Findings
Burt et al. (2003).	To conceptualize failure in international retailing and to provide research propositions for further research.	Literature review	N/A	N/A	Retailer internationalization is a process, not simply an event. Retailer internationalization is a very different process than that undertaken by manufacturers; established theoretical frameworks of international business require major modification if they are to be applied in a meaningful way to retailing.
Gripsrud and Benito (2005).	To develop a model of foreign market choice with a micro-foundation concerning human choice behavior.	Secondary data, spatial-interaction modeling/United Kingdom	Dependent: Early, intermediate, and late entries of investment Independent: GNP, urban population, geographical distance, cultural distance	Regression	The selection of which foreign markets to enter is influenced both by factors that make a particular market attractive and by the distance to that market. In agreement with the internationalization process model, distance factors are particularly important early on in companies' internationalization. Sizeable customer concentration is important at both the early and intermediate phases of internationalization but is less apparent at the more advanced stages of internationalization.
Hutchinson et al. (2007).	To explore the reasons small specialist retailers internationalize and the facilitating factors that help them overcome the obstacles to internationalization.	Empirical/qualitative/case studies/United Kingdom	9 companies	Content analysis/inductive approach	Smaller specialist retailers had a strong luxury or middle-market appeal to customers in domestic and international markets and are identified by their brands and range of merchandise. Brand identities of nearly all the specialist retailers are linked to the product, image, and market appeal of the company and feature a strong emphasis on luxury along with a distinct British/English image.

(Continued)

Table 4.1 (Continued)

Author(s)	Objective/Research Question	Method of Study/Study Setting	Sample/Variables	Method & Tool of Analysis	Findings/Conclusions
Cairns et al. (2008).	To explore how retailers manage and respond to the whole of the divestment process rather than only the decision to divest (which has dominated the literature to date).	Empirical/qualitative/case study/United Kingdom	32 senior managers of retail organizations in the United Kingdom	Content analysis of case study	Five fundamental issues impact on the process of divestment for the company studied: an inward-looking corporate culture, the need for stability in the domestic market, negative consequences of persevering with a failing strategy internationally, new management, and entry mode strategy. International retail divestment activity and processes are conceptualized in four stages: decision, process, strategic reorientation, and response.
Doherty (2009).	To explore how international retail franchisors select international markets and to identify the key factors influencing the process of market selection for international retail franchisors.	Empirical/qualitative/case studies/United Kingdom	Six retailers: senior managers and functional employees	Interviews, documentation, observation	There is a three-stage process of international market selection for retail firms: market screening, market attractiveness, and market selection culmination. Organizational learning is an important issue when choosing markets and particularly when choosing partners.
Alexander and Doherty (2010).	To examine the development of research in international retailing over the last 20 years and to propose a future research agenda within a conceptual framework.	Literature review	N/A	N/A	International retailing is reasonably well understood. The contribution international retailing studies has to make to the broader internationalization and globalization agenda has not been fully realized.

Author	Research question	Type/Data & Country	Sample	Method	Findings
Swoboda and Elsner (2013).	Which processes and marketing program elements are standardized or adapted, and how do these processes and offers interact?	Empirical/scale development comprising qualitative/quantitative data./Germany, Austria, Switzerland	126 executives comprising CEOs and managers	PLS-SEM	There are two types of marketing program elements that determine a firm's performance in a host country: the unchanged transfer of store types, store locations, and store layouts (core elements), and the adapted transfer of assortments, prices, and promotions (peripheral elements). The core elements should be well known and appropriately defined within each organization. These elements should be managed deliberately in a firm's home country. It is valuable to adapt peripheral elements even if their association with performance is weaker than the influence of core elements.
Swoboda et al. (2014).	Examines the role of core and country-specific attributes of particular formats in determining retailers' local positioning in inter-format competition.	Empirical/quantitative surveys/Germany, Romania	2,531 respondents	CFA	The successful internationalization of grocery retailers occurs through local responsiveness and through the adaptation of offers, but this adaptation occurs within the boundaries of core attributes that are specific to each format. Format-specific core attributes determine format transfer efforts and consumer-related market success. Format-specific perspective is useful for retailers and researchers who seek to analyze the foreign expansion of retail firms. When retailers transfer format elements abroad, they must consider both the level of adaptation of the different attributes and the perceptions of consumers.

Overall, the conclusions drawn from authors' studies as shown in Table 4.1 highlight the need for a concerted effort to research marketing strategy and brand positioning (Burt et al., 2002; Blankson et al., 2018) in international retailing. Burt et al. (2002) conclude that there is a need for clear positioning strategies, citing the lack of clear positioning on the part of Marks and Spencer, an upscale retailer in the United Kingdom. The findings of Cairns et al. (2008) corroborate the latter through research on 32 senior managers of UK retail organizations.

While Burt et al. (2003) believe that extant theoretical frameworks – most of which originate from the manufacturing domain – require major modification in the international retailing sector, Alexander and Doherty (2010) conclude that the contribution that international retailing studies have to make to the broader internationalization and globalization agenda has not been fully realized, confirming the assertion that there is a need for research that examines indigenous and foreign retailers within the global retail marketplace.

Hutchinson et al. (2007) conclude that well-positioned foreign retailers perform well in the international marketplace in that, as Swoboda et al. (2014) have found, successful internationalization of retailing is heavily dependent on how well the retailer is positioned. Notwithstanding the latter, firms should be well positioned in their home counties before going abroad (see Swoboda & Elsner, 2013). In sum, Table 4.1 confirms the need for positioning research in international retailing and the need to explore other global marketplaces, including Africa, as study settings.

As cultures become increasingly interconnected and familiar with one another, major retailing firms are afforded the opportunity to expand into new international markets that offer potentially fruitful opportunities for entry and/ or expansion. Opportunities for international retailing and international marketing have been recognized in many emerging world regions, including Latin America (D'Andrea, Silvestri, Costa, Fernandes, & Fossen, 2010), Southeast Asia (Coe & Bok, 2014), and, more recently, Africa (Hollander, 2000; Reardon, Timmer, Barrett, & Berdegue, 2003; de Bruyn & Freathy, 2011; Babarinde, 2014; Donaldson, 2015; A. T. Kearney Report, 2015).

As gathered from Table 4.1, there is a need to explore other international marketplaces, including Africa, as study settings for international retailing and positioning issues. In addition, given the current state of the literature (i.e., Table 4.1), assessments of managerial deliberations in the course of applications of retailer positioning strategies and observations of retailers' day-to-day positioning activities appear to be missing in positioning research (Hooley, & Greenley, 2005; Hooley, Piercy, & Nicoulaud, 2012), including the international retailing domain. This is unfortunate in that the ultimate objective of marketers of any firm is to achieve congruence in positioning activities (Coffie, 2014). Moreover, the quest for congruence and attempts at establishing and maintaining market positions for retailer offerings are among the most critical strategic marketing actions (Hooley & Greenley, 2005; Trout, 2012; Blankson et al., 2018). We now turn to an examination of the importance of congruence in retail positioning.

Congruence in retailer positioning

Congruence or *coherence/fit* refers to the quality of agreeing or coinciding (Webster Dictionary, 2004, p. 153). Nadler & Tushman (1980) define congruence as "the degree to which the needs, goals, objectives, and/or structure of one component are consistent with the needs, demands, goals, objectives, and/or structure of another component" (p. 40). Eckstein, Fleron, Hoffmann, and Reisinger (1998) clarify this relationship by adding that "congruence requires 'contiguous' or 'proximate' social units" (p. 11). Eckstein (1998) claims that congruence creates a condition of being in agreement and that congruence sometimes denotes the act of being in harmony with something or being fit/suitable for a condition. Concerning positioning, congruence refers to the magnitude of correlations in judgments brought about by activities that take place between intended and achieved brand positions.

In order to predict the direction of congruence, it is necessary for retailers to understand the existing scenario (e.g., strategies, phenomena) in question and the context within which congruity is being sought (Young, Meterko, Mohr, Shwartz, & Lin, 2009). Congruence in retailer positioning activities involves a degree of fit (Milliman, von Glinow, & Nathan, 1991), which ultimately results in improved corporate performance (Hooley et al., 2012). de Chernatony and McDonald (1994) write that a successful brand manager emphasizes *matching* products that the firm produces and sells with what the target audience actually wants. Therefore, positioning calls for distinctiveness and fit, because the more distinct an offering's position is, the less likelihood exists that a customer will accept a substitute.

Due to the massive investments required by international retailers to launch or expand operations in foreign markets, congruence in positioning strategies is paramount to the success of the firm (Fuchs & Diamantopoulos, 2010; Blankson, Nkrumah, Opare, & Ketron, 2018). Grounded on this rationale, although Blankson (2004) and Blankson & Kalafatis (2007) offer empirical insight into patterns of congruence between managerial decisions, communications, and target audience perceptions, they lack explanatory power in that they make no distinction in actual firm (i.e., case study) positioning practices and between foreign and indigenous retailers in BoPM African countries.

Based on these findings in the literature, international/foreign retailers that are able to achieve congruence to a greater degree than their indigenous counterparts are more likely to realize stronger performance. Likewise, indigenous retailers can buffer against the advancement of foreign retailer competition by enhancing the congruence of their own positioning activities. As such, congruence in positioning should be a foundational element of both foreign and indigenous retailer strategies and should be continuously evaluated to ensure that managerial intentions, customer perceptions, and actual practices – the three primary elements of positioning among which congruence is desired (Coffie, 2014) – remain aligned.

Interestingly, there exists a lack of research addressing these three elements of positioning congruence among foreign and indigenous retailers. Review of the literature reveals that with the exception of Blankson et al. (2018), only two related publications, both of which examine the positioning activities of brands in the UK financial services domain (Blankson, 2004; Blankson & Kalafatis, 2007). Both fail to tap into actual retailers' practices (i.e., a case study approach) and do not explore BoP African markets: A lacuna in the literature as noted by Yang et al. (2006) and Owhoso et al. (2002). As Yang et al. (2006) and Owhoso et al. (2002) confirm, sub-Saharan Africa is overlooked despite its market of over 700 million inhabitants and the unique challenges and opportunities it presents to foreign and indigenous firms alike (Reardon et al., 2003; de Bruyn & Freathy, 2011).

The study setting

Consistent with Blankson et al. (2018), this research centers on Africa as a study setting and uses Ghana, specifically, as an illustration. Africa – especially sub-Saharan Africa – has lagged behind other regions in terms of business competitiveness, productivity, and growth (Economist, 1997; Nwankwo, 2000) as well as in international business research (Yang et al. 2006; Owhoso et al., 2002) (see also Table 4.1). While the rationale motivating this comparative dearth of research on the sub-Saharan African marketplace may once have been reasonable, the associated reasons underlying the historical divisions between North American, Western European, Asian, and African markets are no longer clear, which renders the continued paucity of research indefensible (Mmieh & Owusu-Frimpong, 2004).

Namely, Africa is generally overlooked in global business and international marketing discourse, and empirical insights into African marketing practices is largely absent from the Western academic canon (Babarinde, 2009). This oversight not only hampers the efficacy of international marketing practices and research but also prevents international and multinational firms from taking advantage of the thriving inflow of capital (private equity, foreign direct investment, and remittances) to the continent and increased trade with the rest of the world (Babarinde, 2009). Specifically, Africa's global trade increased threefold from $230 billion in 2000 to $663 billion in 2007 (IMF, 2008). This surge in trade attests to the robust global demand for Africa's abundant commodities. What's more, foreign direct investment flow to the continent increased from about $10 billion in 2000 to $53 billion in 2007 (World Investment Report, 2008). In fact, according to the U.S. Overseas Private Investment Corporation (OPIC) and the United Nations Conference on Trade and Development (UNCTAD), the return on foreign direct investment in sub-Saharan Africa is the highest of any region in the world (Babarinde, 2009). The deficit in international business and international marketing naturally extends to executives' lack of appreciation of general marketing and positioning practices in Africa (Coffie & Owusu-Frimpong, 2014) and, more specifically, in Ghana (Coffie, 2018) – than they might otherwise be.

This research concentrates on Ghana as the study setting for several reasons. Referred to as an African trailblazer (Wrong & Holman, 1996), star pupil of the World Bank and IMF (Hawkins, 1989), and an African leader (see Holman, 1999), Ghana has a comparatively stable democratic governance, attractive economic growth rates (Economist, 2007), and growing numbers of joint ventures and foreign direct investment (Kuada, 2002). The country has ample natural resources and a recent discovery of oil in commercial quantity: Factors that combine to qualify the nation as a viable market for research in international marketing (i.e., positioning practices of firms operating in Ghana).

In addition, the Ghanaian marketplace offers a challenging but potentially fruitful domain in which academic research can be conducted, largely because Ghana's economy is representative of the growing business activities in Africa (Debrah, 2002; Mmieh & Owusu-Frimpong, 2009; Blankson et al., 2018). Ghana's post-1983 liberalized macroenvironment, the successful collaborative partnerships between Scandinavian and Ghanaian companies in recent years (Kuada, 2002), and the remarkable impact of economic reforms on both foreign and indigenous firms' performance (Appiah-Adu, 1999) are now well documented (Mmieh & Owusu-Frimpong, 2009; Debrah & Toroitich, 2005; Coffie & Owusu-Frimpong, 2014).

Despite a weak infrastructure and economic challenges, recent indicators show that the Ghanaian economy is growing on average at 5% per annum, and the level of inflation is now more manageable: Under 15% within the last decade (Blankson et al., 2018). Observation of the marketplace reveals an influx of foreign firms originating from China, France, India, Italy, the Netherlands, Turkey, the United Kingdom, and the United States, among others. The liberalization of the economy, the ease of doing business (Doing Business, 2014), and the Ghanaian government's policy of positioning the country as a gateway to West Africa (Republic of Ghana, 2014) appear to have paved the way for the influx of foreign firms into Ghana. The Ghanaian marketplace, a lower-middle-income economy, thus represents a challenging but potentially fruitful research domain (World Bank, 2018; Economist, 2007). The complexity and challenges that are routinely present in this transitional, liberalized environment means that marketers must address dynamic and dysfunctional (rather than functional) competition (Economist, 2007; Republic of Ghana, 2014), a growing middle class, expatriate communities (Bruner, 1996; Zachary, 2001), and low purchasing power, as well as socio-political challenges and unpredictable government interventions in the operations of firms (Ayitey, 2001). However, with a manageable population of 28 million, a GDP of $47.93 billion, GNI per capita $1,760.00, annual GDP growth of 7.1% (with projections of 7.3% in 2015, 7.5% in 2016, and 7% in 2018), and life expectancy at birth of 61 years (World Bank, 2018), Ghana remains an emerging sub-Saharan African economy and an important international business research setting, hence the selection of Ghana as study setting.

The increasing liberalization of the Ghanaian marketplace has seen a small but growing and affluent middle-class population with purchasing power comparable with other lower-middle-income economies (World Bank, 2018; Doing

Business, 2014; Blankson et al., 2018). A concomitant examination of middle-class and affluent customers' perceptions of upscale retailers' positioning activities in Ghana has obviously been overlooked in the extant literature. This gap in the literature further underscores the impetus for this research.

Within the Ghanaian marketplace, increased competition among indigenous and foreign firms (Appiah-Adu, 1999; Debrah, 2002) has exposed customers to Western and other foreign consumer products, marketing communications tactics, and upscale retail malls populated by retailers from advanced and emerging economies alike (Coffie & Owusu-Frimpong, 2014). Thus, the fast-growing economy, competitive marketplace, the relative peace and good governance acknowledged by the international community (IMF and World Bank), and the comparative ease of doing business in Ghana (Doing Business, 2014) show that the contemporary Ghanaian marketplace has changed and hence will benefit from empirical research inquiry. The environment is well-positioned to offer fresh insight into retailers' positioning strategies (Coffie, 2014, 2018). This research first probes whether indigenous and foreign retail firms in Ghana pursue similar positioning strategies in the competitive marketplace. Second, this study examines how congruence among managers' intentions, firms' actual positioning practices, and consumers' perceptions differs between indigenous and foreign retail firms. These are important retail internationalization challenges worthy of empirical research (see also Hutchinson et al., 2007; Swoboda et al., 2014; Blankson et al., 2018).

Research questions

Drawing upon the findings and gaps in the literature and using the Ghanaian retail domain as the context, we seek to address three research questions: (1) What positioning strategies do firms pursue? (2) What are the differences between indigenous and foreign firms' positioning strategies? and (3) Is there evidence of fit among managerial intentions about their positioning strategies, actual strategies employed, and target audience perceptions of firms' positioning strategies? For the purposes of this chapter, "congruence" denotes "fit" or "coherence" and is used interchangeably throughout the discussion in the chapter.

Methodology

PILOT STUDY

Following Dubois and Gadde (2002) and de Chernatony and Cottam (2009), active, incognito, and participant observations of positioning activities of two upscale apparel and wax print retail stores (i.e., Woodin [www.woodinfashion.com] and Vlisco [about.vlisco.com], respectively) in the Accra Mall formed the pilot study (see also Blankson et al., 2018). The store observations lasted 30 minutes each and involved assessments of internal and external layout, ambience, décor, the number of employees present, and how they interacted with customers, managers' interactions with customers, and employees, employee mannerisms, number of customers entering the shopping environment, purchases made by customers, the time it took for customers to make purchases, prices of products, the general arrangement of products on fixtures, and the assortment of products on offer. In addition, the authors purchased products as a form of participant observation. Knowing which positioning strategies are pursued in studies of this sort conveys credence about the relevance of the strategies (see Pieters, Wedel, & Batra, 2010).

MAIN STUDY

Study one

Study one involved covert, overt, and participant observation techniques. Following de Chernatony and Cottam (2009), estimates of the monies spent on purchases and meals were made. Prices and styles of clothing were checked, as were store promotions, pamphlets, and leaflets. The layout, attractiveness, and cleanliness of the store – including the restrooms – and the storefront, window displays, and overall ambiance were scrutinized (Jarratt & Fayed, 2001; Dubois & Gadde, 2002; Blankson et al., 2018). These observations provided subtle knowledge about the relevance of positioning strategies (see Pieters et al., 2010) in the marketplace. Supporting the use of observation techniques in international retail research, Alexander and Doherty (2010) show that the use of observation techniques and in-depth qualitative accounts of actual firm activity lead to more robust theory building.

Study one began with three indigenous stores (Life Healthcare Clinic, Accra Mall Pharmacy, and Galaxy Perfumery) operated under a "mini-mall" concept. Worthy of note is that the three stores are confined in the same space in the mall, and although all three are owned by a Ghanaian entrepreneur and run by a chief executive officer (CEO), each store is independently managed.

An overt observation followed each face-to-face interview and lasted 30 minutes, while each covert observation lasted 45 minutes. The authors took on the roles of customers in order to conduct participant observations that lasted 45 minutes in each store. For example, a member of the research team used covert and participant observation in the form of a "mystery shopper"; this lasted 30 minutes. Observation of a fourth case study (Spendstre Photo Store) was also carried out. The overt observation lasted 20 minutes following an interview with the manager. The fifth case study (Shoprite) was conducted with covert observation and lasted 30 minutes. The overt observation followed the interview with the managers and lasted 30 minutes. The sixth case study (Barcelos Restaurant) was undertaken with covert observation and lasted 40 minutes prior to meeting with the managers. The overt observation followed the interview with the managers and lasted 30 minutes (see also Blankson et al., 2018).

The vast majority of research on positioning adopts a quantitative perspective. This is, however, restrictive considering the pivotal role that day-to-day firm activities have on the operationalization of positioning strategies (Ries & Trout, 2001; Liu & Zhang, 2014). Unlike quantitative research, qualitative studies have a tendency to uncover the subtle, benign, and subterranean management drives and efforts that are important in the application of marketing and business strategies in the international retail domain (Hutchinson et al., 2007; Cairns et al., 2008; Doherty, 2009). As Doherty (2000) emphasizes, qualitative methodology is important in international retailing research which has, in the past, been largely positivistic and quantitative in nature. Moreover, given the minimal attention to positioning studies in the study setting, qualitative investigation is deemed appropriate (Cairns et al., 2008). According to Doherty (2000) and de Chernatony and Cottam (2009), qualitative research and the inductive process of data generation captures complexity and provides a thicker description of the process, meaning, and understanding of congruence in the positioning strategies of upscale retailers in Ghana. In addition, qualitative case studies are used to confirm and/or build theory (Burt & Carralero-Encinas, 2000; Doherty, 2000; Hutchinson et al., 2007; Yin, 2009). Despite incessant calls from practitioners (Ries & Trout, 2001) and scholars (Burt & Carralero-Encinas, 2000; Burt et al., 2002), qualitative case study research in positioning appears to have been overlooked in the international retail domain.

The current study concerns this neglected but potentially pivotal research method – qualitative case study research – in the operationalization of the concept of positioning. Case study research has the potential to capture the dynamics of the studied phenomenon within single settings (Doherty, 2009; Burt et al., 2002; Eisenhardt, 1989; Yin, 2009). This is important in view of the challenges encountered in the implementation of positioning strategies (Piercy, 2005), especially in the international retail domain (Burt et al., 2002), which necessitates an appreciation of in-depth qualitative examination of managerial actions in typical study settings (see Hutchinson et al., 2007; Doherty, 2009; Burt et al., 2002).

Study two

Sample and data collection

Following recommended best practices in case study research (Doherty, 2009; Burt et al., 2002; Yin, 2009) and purposeful sampling methods (Poulis et al., 2013), we surveyed six retailers at the Accra Mall. We randomly targeted three indigenous and three foreign retailers for this research, consistent with Blankson et al. (2018).

More specifically, study two involved face-to-face interviews with 15 managers across six stores, coupled with mall intercept surveys of target customers. The literature reveals an increasing pursuit of in-depth face-to-face interview methods in data collection and analysis in the international retailing domain and, as shown by Alexander and Doherty (2010), this development highlights a maturing domain in the literature. Face-to-face interviews were conducted for the present study. The retailers included three indigenous retailers: The Accra Mall Pharmacy, Life Healthcare Clinic, and Galaxy Perfumery. The three foreign retailers include Spendstre Photo Store, Shoprite, and Barcelos Restaurant. Our decision to compare indigenous and foreign retailers' efforts at targeting the middle-class and affluent customers in Ghana stems from Coffie (2014) and Coffie and Owusu-Frimpong's (2014) call for the need to understand the impact of the contemporary liberalized Ghanaian marketplace on retailers' positioning strategies.

The Ghanaian retail business domain has been growing since the opening of the Accra Mall in 2008. Since then, the Marina Mall, A&C Mall, and in October 2014 and October 2015, West Hills Mall and Achimota Retail Center, respectively, opened in Accra. However, the Accra Mall was ultimately selected due to its status as the first world-class shopping mall in Ghana, positioned toward middle-to upper-class customers. The Accra Mall (see www.accramall.info) houses 65 glamorous shops, 30% of which are operated by Ghanaian retailers and 70% of which are operated by foreign retailers. Retailers include international franchise stores, restaurants, and department stores from South Africa, the Netherlands, Italy, the United Kingdom, and Nigeria. Indigenous retailers include African-inspired apparel stores, African fabric boutiques, and upmarket bars and restaurants. To qualify for inclusion in the study, a retailer had to have a budget devoted to promotions, advertising, and training of staff to excel in customer service in the last two years. In addition, retailers had to have impressions about their target audiences, have been operating at the Accra Mall for at least two years, and be wholly owned by either indigenous or foreign entrepreneurs or organizations.

A semi-structured long interview approach characterized the discussions, which developed naturally; the interviewers ensured that the discussion centered on firms' positioning and marketing activities. The interviews with the managers lasted between 30 minutes and one hour and took place in the stores in non-contrived settings. With permission, we recorded and took notes of the interviews.

Interview with customers (mall intercept survey)

Interviews with customers centered on questions regarding their perceptions of and/or their experience with customer service, responsiveness to customer queries and problems, attractiveness of service, products, and fixtures in the stores, quality of products, perceptions about store brands, features of products and customer service, stores' promotions and sales (inducing tactics), and general impressions of the stores as well as perceptions of stores' marketing practices (Blankson & Crawford, 2012). The mall intercept was undertaken first in front of the selected stores as customers entered and exited the stores and second in the foyer and in the two main entrances to the mall. A random selection of 22 customers who patronized the selected stores participated in the survey. Interviews lasted between 35 and 45 minutes; notes were taken. The researchers ensured a balance in the gender of our sample; hence, 11 men and 11 women participated. All participants were assured of the confidentiality of their statements. Supporting face-to-face interviews and the observation method, Stewart (2009) writes that "surveys and experiments seldom produce really surprising outcomes . . . that is why observation and qualitative methods are important in marketing . . . these types of methods do not produce definitive outcomes but they often suggest interesting avenues for research" (p. 382).

Cases one, two, and three are grouped in the same vicinity of the mall and are described as a "mini-mall." As a professionally run, indigenous, family-owned retail business, the mini-mall offers medical services, a pharmacy, a dental clinic, and beauty and perfumery services (see www.mondialfamily.com). According to the Chief Executive Officer, the mini-mall concept was conceived in 1995 during the initial planning of the larger Accra Mall. It was opened alongside the Accra Mall in 2008.

The mini-mall's overall selling proposition is a luxurious retail outlet, built and designed to attract the middle- to upper-class target market of the Accra Mall. The mini-mall attracts busy business executives, expatriates, and families who shop and at the same time visit the clinic to have general medical check-ups with a gynecologist, internist, or dentist. In addition, the clinic serves as an emergency unit for the minor accidents that occasionally occur in and around the larger Accra Mall. The initial concept of the mini-mall was geared toward a dental clinic and community pharmacy. However, after a few months of successful operation and following customers' requests, a healthcare and beauty retail section – namely, the Galaxy Perfumery – was added. As previously mentioned, each of the indigenous businesses at the Accra Mall (the Accra Mall Pharmacy, the Life Healthcare Clinic, and the Galaxy Perfumery) is an autonomous business managed under a general chief executive officer.

Case one

The Accra Mall Pharmacy is an indigenous firm specializing in the supply of pharmaceutical items to meet customers' needs and is part of the "mini-mall" concept. The pharmacy offers efficient, reliable, and friendly service. The firm is dedicated to providing excellent service, quality products, and competitive prices. Other branches are located in prime areas of Accra, such as the five-star Mövenpick Hotel. The firm's services include a 24/7 helpline service and an online chat with a pharmacist: the first service of its kind in Ghana. Two managers from this firm participated in the study.

Case two

The Life Healthcare Clinic is an indigenous retailer and is part of the "mini-mall" concept. Recognizing a growing, diverse target audience (expatriates, upper-, middle-, and lower-middle-income groups), the clinic has expanded its services from its traditional general practice and dentistry to include gynecology, an eye and ear unit, a laboratory, and a physiotherapy unit. Three managers from this firm participated in the study.

Case three

The Galaxy perfumery is the last store in the "mini-mall" concept and is an indigenous firm. The Galaxy Perfumery carries only original designer fragrances at comparatively competitive "duty-free" prices as well as cosmetics and makeup booths for well-known brands. One manager from this firm participated in the study.

Case four

Introduced in Ghana in 2006, the Spendstre Photo Store is a fast-growing photo and image firm headquartered in Lagos, Nigeria. The store operates a photo studio that offers professional and digital photo services (see www.spendstre. com). The firm currently operates four branches in prime locations throughout Accra, with the store in the Accra Mall as the flagship store. The firm's primary objective is to provide the best quality photos and videos while offering first-class service for every customer and maintaining a stimulating and enjoyable working environment for all staff and customers. Three managers from this firm participated in the study.

Case five

Shoprite, a South African multinational retailer, has since 1979 remained the largest brand of the Shoprite group of companies and has become one of South Africa's most trusted brands, having been voted South Africa's number one supermarket in the annual *Sunday Times* Top Brands Survey in 2006. The Shoprite group of companies was founded in 1979 and is headquartered in Cape Town, South Africa. Shoprite is Africa's largest retail and fast food multinational firm. Operating over 1,200 corporate and 270 franchise stores in 16 countries across sub-Saharan Africa and the Indian Ocean islands, the company is listed on the Johannesburg Stock Exchange (JSE), the Namibia Stock Exchange, and the Zambian Stock Exchange. The company also owns franchising brands through its OK Franchise Division under the names OK Foods, OK Grocer, Megasave, OK Minimark, OK Value, and Sentra (see www.Shopriteholdings.co.za). Shoprite ventured into the Ghanaian market in 2003, starting with its flagship store in the Accra Mall. Shoprite offers a wide range of quality products imported from South Africa, Europe, and local Ghanaian regions. The retailer has a simple philosophy: Bringing customers lower prices they can trust in a convenient shopping environment. Three managers from this firm participated.

Case Six

Barcelos Restaurant is a Western fast food chain restaurant. Wolak, Kalafatis, and Harris (1998) place restaurants within the retail sector and at the mid-point in the goods-services continuum. Barcelos is named after a Portuguese town that is famous for an ancient legend of the Barcelos rooster. Barcelos opened its first store in Pretoria, South Africa in 1993, and since 1998, the firm has opened franchises in 16 countries, including South Africa, Lesotho, Botswana, Zambia, Namibia, Mozambique, Ghana, Nigeria, Sudan, Canada, United Kingdom, Dubai, Oman, Mauritius, and Singapore, and will soon operate in Pakistan, India, and Qatar (see www.barcelos.co.za). Using recipes mastered by the Portuguese hundreds of years ago, Barcelos Ghana's menu includes hamburgers, fries, "peri-peri" chicken pieces, and more traditional Ghanaian dishes, such as "jollof rice." Its flagship dish of four varieties of "peri-peri" chicken from very hot peri-chicken to tangy lemon peri-chicken is catered to meet the taste preferences of its culturally diverse customers; the restaurant also includes a pastry and ice cream parlor. As noted earlier, although Barcelos is a South African franchise, the brand name, menu, and condiments are Portuguese. Three managers from this firm participated in the study.

Measurement construct

In view of the criticisms leveled against extant typologies of positioning strategies (Kalafatis, Tsogas, & Blankson, 2000) because of the absence of empirically derived consumer-generated positioning strategies (Aaker & Shansby, 1982; Crawford, 1985), an empirically based generic (i.e., appropriate for services and goods) consumer-derived typology of positioning strategies was adopted (see Appendix I). Eisenhardt (1989) supports the adoption of *a priori* constructs for emerging theory as a means of shaping the initial design of theory-building research. The rationale for adopting a consumer-derived generic typology of positioning strategies stems from the fact that the typology has been applied in the managerial/corporate environment, and it exhibits reliability and explanatory power (Blankson, Kalafatis, Cheng, & Hadjicharalambous, 2008). In addition, a review of the literature reveals that some of the earliest and widely referenced typologies of positioning (e.g., Aaker & Shansby, 1982; Wind, 1982) are conceptual. As for the empirically based typologies (e.g., Crawford, 1985), these mainly reflect organizational practices as exhibited in advertisements.

Inductive reasoning was utilized to decipher the type of positioning strategies pursued and guided by the construct proposed by Blankson and Kalafatis (2004) (Appendix I). In addition, our method is consistent with Poulis et al. (2013), who developed a framework from an inductive process following an actual case study project in international marketing promoting the idea that context matters for sampling purposes. Above all, we followed best practices of case study research and analysis suggested by Yin (2009).

Validity and reliability

Validation and reliability tests were carried out before they were used in this present study because the adopted typology was developed in the United Kingdom. A robust and generalizable typology is one that is tested and refined using different sample groups and is assessed in other environments (see Peterson & Merunka, 2014). To this end, in order to enhance the typology's generalizability, continued operationalization and replication are necessary (Peterson & Merunka, 2014). Content and face validation involved assessment of the properties and meaning underpinning the typology in Ghana. This was carried out through focus group interviews with three convenience samples of 20 executives undertaking MBA marketing research and strategic marketing courses at a leading Ghanaian business school in Accra. The average MBA student at this business school is an executive or manager in a business entity in Ghana. The validation tests took place during sabbatical leave by one of the authors at the business school. This approach is consistent with Si and Bruton (2005), who conducted 50 face-to-face interviews in China with foreign and local international joint ventures (IJV) in a pilot study prior to adopting an extant framework for their main research. Moreover, due to the subjective nature of the study, validity was assessed by sending a summary of the findings to two academics with expertise in qualitative case study research and the research setting for their critical review and comments. Their suggestions were subsequently incorporated into the final version of this chapter. In addition, consistent with Sweeney and Chew's (2002) method and Dubois and Gadde's (2002) suggestions, three types of tests were conducted to establish reliability and validity; the results are shown in Appendix II.

Results

Case one: application of positioning strategies – the life and health clinic

Our observation through covert and overt techniques revealed that upon entering the "mini-mall," a customer could either turn right to the Galaxy Perfumery, left to the pharmacy, or continue straight ahead to the clinic. The wall of the reception area of the clinic showcased a captivating definition of health: "Health is a state of complete physical, mental and social wellbeing and not merely the absence of disease and infirmity." The positioning of mirrors in strategic locations of the store stimulated an enhanced visual effect and served as a means of monitoring movements of both customers and staff in the stores. A large mirror by the clinic's reception desk, aligned to face the entrance and walkway of the mini-mall, presented an illusion that the walkway extended and connected to other sections of the general mall. This semblance was confirmed in the interview with the CEO, who said that some customers entered the shop under the impression that the walkway led to other sections of the general mall. As such, in their quests to hide their disappointment, customers ended up browsing other stores in the mini mall.

Cameras were placed at various corners of the clinic, which, when combined with vaulted lighting and excellent ventilation, created an ambiance of safety. The interview with the CEO revealed that the mini-mall concept (three stores under one roof) is a strategy to provide customers with intertwined options and an integrated shopping experience. The location of the stores at the immediate right-hand side of the entrance of the mini–mall is also strategic in regards to patients seeking medical care and pharmaceutical products. According to the CEO, similar mini malls are located at the five-star Mövenpick Hotel and the A&C Mall in Accra. He reiterated that his motive for the mini–mall concept is to fit into the lifestyles of the contemporary, middle–class Ghanaian and the time-constrained expatriate.

An interview with the senior manager revealed that the general pricing for all products in the clinic was not excessive despite the target market; this was evident in the patronage of the clinical services. The manager emphasized that the pricing of clinical services was competitive and geared toward a "value for money" strategy. This was confirmed in an interview with one of the customers, who said that the pricing of consultation fees is reasonable compared to two other private clinics visited; this highlights the "value for money" positioning strategy. The CEO stated emphatically that the stores did not advertise through any media since he believed that such practices were indicative of a strategy targeting low–income customers. Thus, the stores preferred a word of mouth (traditional advertising) approach, which seemed to be working well for the clinic and was confirmed by six of the eight customers interviewed.

Case two: application of positioning strategies – the Accra Mall Pharmacy

An interview with a senior manager of the pharmacy showed that prices of products were in line with average market prices, highlighting a "value for money" strategy. This confirmed the number of customers purchasing their products for the period of time (two hours) spent there by the researchers. Interviews with the managers also revealed that the CEO emphasized good customer service (a "service" positioning strategy) and that from time to time each store had customer care training for staff.

Customers of the pharmacy were impressed with the wide variety of quality, brand name drugs available (a "brand" positioning strategy). Two customers were particularly impressed with the fact that they could find drug prescriptions, which they otherwise could not find in town. A customer hinted that "the drugs sold here are more likely to be found in Europe," drugs which he believed most local pharmacy shops did not carry. This is consistent with the CEO's remarks that all of the firm's pharmaceutical products were sourced from the United Kingdom and France. He noted that he also gets supplies from Ghana through Ernest Chemist Limited and Vicdorris, indigenous wholesale distributors of German pharmaceutical products. These findings are in sync with the quality of products sold to customers. Both the CEO and the managers confirmed that the layout of the pharmacy is reconfigured every five years.

Case three: application of positioning strategies – the Galaxy Perfumery

The orderly arrangement of perfumery gave a strong, high-end visual impression. A rather interesting feature at the perfumery shop was the fact that the fixtures had mirrors and white lights, which created an impression of a wider display of products. Price tags were not affixed to the products at the perfumery shop; hence, customers had to inquire about the prices from store representatives who were always waiting on customers. The covert observation particularly helped to reinforce this assertion. The manager stressed sound customer service. Staff had frequent but brief product knowledge training for new perfumes that were introduced into the shop's assortment. The CEO also hinted that the wood-paneled floor was recently installed in the store to prevent perfume bottles from breaking when accidentally dropped. He said that the layout of the perfume store is changed every five years. Customers indicated that the staff members were friendly, highlighting a "service" positioning strategy, and they considered the display of merchandise to be attractive. Two customers, however, lamented the fact that the prices were ridiculously high for an average consumer. The CEO emphatically stated that the perfumery store was experiencing lackluster sales and profits and as such needed a senior manager to take charge of the shop's operations.

**Case four: application of positioning strategies –
Spendstre Photo Store**

The covert observation revealed two medium-sized posters advertising the photo shop and its name. The colorful, bright yellow and white walls with chic colored benches, a slideshow of pictures of television stars and models, and shelves holding myriad pictures create a compelling visual impression for the customer. However, the small waiting area vis-a-vis the number of customers causes shop congestion during high-traffic time blocks, leaving some impatient customers stressed. Employees were casually dressed and had name tags. An interview with a senior manager revealed that the presence in the mall was a strategic choice to position the firm in the photography market in light of its domination among strong competitors. He further insisted that the "reliability" strategy is their strongest positioning strategy, indicating that the store "opens to customers as long as it takes in order to serve customers." An employee shift system is in place to meet the time constraints of busy customers.

In the interview, the senior manager stressed that a "service" strategy is key in marketing activities. He reiterated that personal attention to detail, endless sacrifice for clients, friendliness of staff, and impressive service are some of the elements of this strategy, which were corroborated by the interview with the junior manager. Our interviews also showed that not all customers thought of the service process as smooth, with nine customers intimating that the process was not orderly, thereby prolonging the turnaround time. Interestingly, all the customers gave credit to the photo editors' personal attention to detail and selection of pictures for printing.

The last strategy that the senior manager considered prominent was a "value for money" strategy. Thus, the firm ensures that it is competitively priced by finding a balance between its prices and those of competitors. The junior manager supported this assertion by stressing the fact that the quality of the final prints delivered to customers and the price value are much better than what competitors offer: 7 out of the 22 customers interviewed supported this assertion with the view that the quality offsets the price. However, three customers disagreed, providing the researchers with comparative price differentials from other photo stores in Accra.

Case five: application of positioning strategies – Shoprite

Our observations through covert and overt techniques revealed products arranged and grouped in an orderly manner, well labeled with prices; this made the purchase process easy and convenient. We observed that management had put in place overhead directional signs and fixture signage to facilitate easy navigation of the large selling space. The staff is friendly, well mannered, neatly dressed in Shoprite uniforms with name tags, and positioned at vantage points on the sales floor in order to be of assistance to customers that need help and to restock depleted merchandise. The sales floor is clean, and so are the washrooms. Walls are painted in bold colors, which, combined with a fine display of merchandise, provided a very attractive ambiance consistent with a strategy targeting the middle class and commensurate with experience in the Western large-store atmosphere. The expanse of the sales floor, aisles, and fixtures add to the store's beauty. The layout also provides easy monitoring of customer and staff activities, and a closed-circuit television (CCTV) camera increases customer confidence in safety.

Interviews with the managers confirmed our observations that Shoprite pursues a "service" positioning strategy. Apart from the arrangement of merchandise, the ambiance hints at a friendly and impressive service strategy. All customers interviewed were in agreement about the existence of this strategy. The interviews with the managers further revealed that they employ a "value for money" positioning strategy. All managers confirmed that "providing variety at the lowest prices is the hallmark of Shoprite's success."

Shoprite also pursues a "reliability" positioning strategy. The managers highlighted warranty policies on electrical products and stated that the firm rarely has complaints about the durability or safety of any of its products or food. The managers also opined that perpetuity of stocked merchandise ensures the reliability of service. The importance of a reliable, service-oriented business environment is evidenced in managers' claims of no thefts of customers' personal items or injuries, illustrating the safety of the shopping environment. This was corroborated by interviewed customers. Interviews, however, highlighted that there are occasions when the store is depleted of preferred sizes of merchandise, but when asked, managers claimed that in most cases, the items are in stock at the warehouse but had not yet reached store shelves. Six customers complained about the waiting times at point-of-sale terminals. However, our observation showed that the long waiting time did not discourage several customers from purchasing only single items and waiting in the queue. The orderly arrangement of merchandise, bright lighting, music, and busy yet quiet atmosphere create an ambiance consistent with targeting the middle class, commensurate with experience in the Western large-store atmosphere. This observation and interviews with the ten customers and managers give credence to Shoprite's employment of an "attractiveness" positioning strategy. As stated by a customer, "the general atmosphere and standard of this shop is excellent and similar to my experience with shopping in London and New York. . . . I love coming here."

Shoprite also pursues a "branding" positioning strategy. This is seen in a variety of foreign products and brands, giving customers a wide assortment and familiarity with foreign brands. Interviews with customers supported this assertion, with seven customers attributing their patronage of the store to the breadth and quality of products. A customer simply said that "Shoprite leaves the customer spoiled for choice."

Case six: application of positioning strategies – Barcelos Restaurant

Covert observation revealed that 50 people came into the restaurant during our observation. Some came in to have a casual lunch and spend time with friends and family. Others waited for business partners, meanwhile enjoying the pastries and ice cream sold by the restaurant.

We found the staff friendly, neat, well dressed in company uniforms, and in compliance with all restaurant protocols of covering hair when in the kitchen and wearing no jewelry (with the exception of a staff member wearing a wedding ring). The décor and furniture are excellent and fitting for a restaurant, with warm colors that the managers indicated were intended to create a cozy atmosphere in which business could be held and friends and family could meet. The layout is attractive, with complementary paintings congruent with the theme of the restaurant.

In regard to the positioning strategy employed, interviews with the managers hinted that the Barcelos at the Accra Mall was the flagship store and that the store was keen on the "branding" strategy as exemplified in the emphasis on the brand name. To that extent, the branding of all the items used by the customer – napkins, cutlery, condiments, bags, and even a flag of Barceló's logo – was emphasized.

Managers were also keen on the "attractiveness" strategy and stressed that that was considered in the layout of the restaurant. A junior manager revealed that the firm aggressively pursues a service strategy by trying to ensure friendly, personal attention to customers and a hygienic environment in which to eat. This was corroborated by a senior manager, who stressed attention to detail and an open communication channel between management and employees in order to engender a culture of friendliness. Most of the customers interviewed shared the same sentiment of a neat, hygienic, and friendly environment. All managers interviewed hinted at employing a "reliability" strategy. They claimed consistency in the flavor of the food, especially the *peri-peri* chicken, and that menus were set with no day-to-day fluctuation in order to prevent a shortage. Regarding the "value for money" strategy, managers opined that the quality of the food matched its pricing, which creates value for the customer. Two out of ten customers said that the quality and ambiance compensated for the prices of the food. Three customers intimated that the prices were high compared to the other fast food restaurants in the Accra Mall food court. Meanwhile, five customers said that the food was averagely priced; this was consistent with the views of three managers.

Although managers said that the restaurant did not employ "selectivity" or "top-of-the-range" positioning strategies, interestingly, one said, "we rather target the middle- to upper-income clientele that the mall attracted." Customers, however, believe that the restaurant is not selective in the choice of its target audience. In terms of a "country of origin" strategy, managers hinted that the restaurant was not pursuing this strategy, even though they did admit that customers became confused about its Portuguese menu and South African origin.

Discussion and congruence in positioning deliberations

The findings show that three key positioning strategies are consistently employed by the six retailers surveyed in this research – namely, "service," "reliability," and "attractiveness." This reflects firms' targeting of lower-to-middle-class customer groups. With the exception of Galaxy Perfumery, no other retailer pursues "top of the range" or "selectivity." In addition, none of the retailers uses a "country of origin" positioning strategy. Incidentally, a comparison between indigenous firms (Life Healthcare Clinic, Accra Mall Pharmacy, and Galaxy Perfumery) and foreign firms (Spendstre Photostore, Shoprite, and Barcelos Restaurant) show that while all indigenous firms employ "brand name," foreign firms lead in the pursuit of "value for money." This shows that competitive activities of indigenous and foreign firms both serve the purpose of reaching the broader market and consequently achieving greater market share (Blankson et al., 2018). Further evidence of this competition is seen in the case of Galaxy Perfumery, an indigenous firm, which is the only retailer specifically targeting the middle class (see Table 4.2). This is supported by the Galaxy Perfumery manager, who stressed that "we provide durable, widely recognized brand name products, excellent customer service and constantly remodel our store's aesthetics to position ourselves as the best perfumery store in Accra . . . we focus on middle and upper-class purchasing group and expatriates."

All 15 managers emphasized their attention to serving customers to the highest level and believe "service" is their key positioning strategy, even though other strategies including "reliability" and "attractiveness" are prominently featured

Table 4.2 Summary of firms' positioning strategies

Positioning Strategies	Selected Retailers					
	Indigenous Firms			Foreign Firms		
	Life Healthcare Clinic	Accra Mall Pharmacy	Galaxy Perfumery	Spendstre Photo Store	Shoprite	Barcelos Restaurant
Top of the range			*			
Service	*	*	*	*	*	*
Value for money	*	*		*	*	*
Reliability	*	*	*	*	*	*
Attractiveness	*	*	*	*	*	*
Country of origin						
Brand name	*	*	*		*	*
Selectivity			*			

Note: * Denotes the employment of a positioning strategy.

in some retailers' quests for competitive advantages and positions in the marketplace. The growing number of expatriates and middle- and high-income consumers in Accra, coupled with an increase in disposable income among Ghanaians as a whole, support these findings (Debrah, 2002). As shown in Table 4.2, an asterisk (*) implies that a certain strategy is employed by a retailer. The determination of strategy follows an inductive reasoning approach as elaborated by Dubois & Gadde (2002), de Chernatony & Cottam (2009), and Poulis et al. (2013).

Accra Mall Pharmacy

Data collected from each population (managers, customers, and researchers' observations) were subjected to content analysis (de Chernatony & Cottam, 2009), with a summary of the results presented in Appendix III. Five strategies ("service," "value for money," "reliability," "attractiveness," and "branding") are congruent across all three populations and are dominant in the positioning activities of the Accra Mall Pharmacy. The managers' intended strategy of "country of origin" is neither perceived by customers of the shop nor observed by the researchers. This is because visibility or communication of the strategy is non-existent in print media (posters), which are accessible to most consumers. The "mall effect" perhaps clouds the judgment of most of the customers interviewed, preventing them from being attentive to the origin of the drugs.

Furthermore, examination of fit/congruence shows seven out of eight (87.5%) cases consistent among the three populations.

Life Health Care Clinic

Data collected from managers, customers, and researchers' observations were subjected to content analysis. Four strategies, namely "service," "value for money," "reliability," and "attractiveness" are dominant and fit all three populations. The "top of the range" and "branding" strategies were judged to be employed through covert and overt observation techniques but were neither intended by managers nor perceived by customers (Appendix IV). Moreover, congruence occurs in six out of eight cases (75%).

Galaxy Perfumery

"Attractiveness" is the only strategy that achieves congruence (one out of eight, or 13%) among the three populations. On the basis of an interview with the CEO, this may be attributable to the fact that the layout and flooring of the store are changed every five years. However, some variations exist in the strategies intended by management, perceived by customers, or observed by researchers. Specifically, while managers intend to employ six strategies, customers only perceive four strategies, two of which ("reliability" and "attractiveness") are congruent with intentions of managers (Appendix V). The other two, "top of the range" and "selectivity," are perceived by customers due to the prices of the products which they claim are too high but which the CEO claims to be stemming from "duty-free prices," which allow a markup of about 10%. Researcher observation, however, is consistent with the "top of the range" strategy perceived by customers, which may be due to the elegance in design and layout of the shop.

Spendstre Photo Store

Analysis of results from the three populations shows coherence in the employment of three strategies ("service," "reliability," and "attractiveness"). This is consistent with how retailers operating in the Accra Mall aim to position themselves in order to win market share (Miles & Mangold, 2005). Researcher observation, however, is not consistent with that of managers' intentions and customers' perceptions of a "value for money" strategy, because in the view of the researchers, prices for soft copy prints and multiple copies of hard prints are similar to market prices, despite excellent service. There is congruence in seven (i.e., "top of the range," "service," "reliability," "attractiveness," "country of origin," "branding," and "selectivity") out of eight cases (87.5%) (see Appendix VI), clearly demonstrating that Spendstre Photo Store is well-positioned in the Ghanaian marketplace.

Shoprite

Content analysis of results from the three populations shows congruence and dominance of five strategies ("service," "value for money," "reliability," "attractiveness," and "branding"). No variations exist in managers' intentions, customers' perceived practice, or researchers' observations. This is attributable to the fact that Shoprite is a global company with many years of marketing experience and thus has perfected its ability to clearly communicate and place its desired positioning strategies in the minds of its target customers (Ries & Trout, 2001; Trout, 2012). To that end, congruence occurs in eight out of eight (100%) cases (see Appendix VII).

Barcelos Restaurant

Content analysis of results from the three populations uncovers consistency in the pursuit of four strategies ("service," "reliability," "attractiveness," and "branding"), with variations in researchers' observations (Appendix VIII). Further analysis shows fit in seven out of eight (87.5%) cases. Ries and Trout (2001) suggest that the key to success is leading in any category in the mind of prospective customers. Care must be taken about the "value for money" strategy espoused by managers and customers but not practiced as observed by the researchers; however, "value for money" is necessary and essential for a restaurant attempting to position itself in a very competitive Ghanaian marketplace. Management is proactive in avoiding the "country of origin" positioning strategy due to the confusion it creates. While the brand name and flagship menu are of Portuguese origin, the franchise originated in South Africa.

Conclusion and implications

The current BoP African business environment, especially Ghana, is very different from that of over 20 years ago (Mmieh & Owusu-Frimpong, 2004; World Bank, 2018). Therefore, determining how retailers pursue positioning strategies constitutes an important and opportune research task. The findings reveal embedded subterranean marketing practices akin to the application of the concept of positioning (de Chernatony & Cottam, 2009; Blankson et al., 2018). This research comes at a time in which the African marketplace is undergoing an influx of foreign retailers and foreign goods as well as an increase in the size of the middle class. Ghana is at the forefront of these changes and thus represents an opportune research setting in which to investigate positioning activities.

The main purpose of this exploratory study in this chapter was to examine the employment of positioning strategies in specific indigenous and foreign retailer contexts and then to determine congruence in the employment of positioning strategies among management (intended/presumed practice), customers (perceived practice), and researcher observations (actual practice) (see also Blankson et al., 2018). The purpose and findings discussed earlier have strong resonance with Schuiling and Kapferer's (2004) research that sought to better understand the real differences between local and international brands. Specifically, the results support the purpose of the study and go further by showing that Western-derived typologies of positioning strategies are applicable in emerging BoP African economies and Ghana in particular (Dadzie, Akaa, & Riordan, 1988; Coffie, 2014). Specifically, indigenous and foreign retailers employ varying positioning strategies in the marketplace, further complementing the utility of Western-developed typologies of positioning strategies in the Ghanaian marketplace. Globalization has paved the way for similar practices of business and marketing. As such, this study adds to the generalizability of the concept of positioning in emerging sub-Saharan African economies, since Ghana is representative of such economies (see Debrah, 2002; Mmieh & Owusu-Frimpong, 2009; Coffie, 2018) and is ripe for business growth.

The study concludes that the key positioning strategies consistently employed by retailers in the Ghanaian marketplace are "service," "reliability," and "attractiveness." In the case of domestic retailers, Life Healthcare Clinic and Accra Mall Pharmacy have convergence in their use of positioning strategies (i.e., "service," "value for money," "reliability," "attractiveness," and "brand name"). Galaxy Perfumery Store, on the other hand, employs "top of the range," "service," "reliability," "attractiveness," "brand name," and "selectivity." This reveals clear disparity in the positioning strategies employed by the Galaxy Perfumery Shop as compared to the pharmacy and clinic. Moreover, there is coherence in customer perceptions for positioning strategies employed by Life Health Care Clinic and the pharmacy, which is not the case for the perfumery. To a degree, these findings show a lack of cohesion in positioning activities within the indigenous retail category.

Concerning foreign retailers, the lack of emphasis on the Spendstre Photo Store's brand name in the mind of customers may have implications for brand recognition for the other branches across the city, as expressed by management. Likewise, the confusion of "country of origin" emanating from the "branding" strategy (as seen in brand name and menu) for Barcelos as well as confusion among customers as to whether Barcelos is a fast food chain or fine dining restaurant due to an overlap in the menu and the average time of order fulfillment have implications for positioning.

Overall, foreign retailers, relative to indigenous retailers, achieve high congruence in positioning activities (87.5%, 87.5%, and 100% compared to 13%, 75%, and 87.5%, respectively). This finding is consistent with Appiah-Adu's (1999) study, which found that although domestic firms achieved high business performance, they were relatively less competitive than foreign firms. Appiah-Adu suggested that domestic firms needed to consider positioning themselves with the long term in mind in order to survive in Ghana's increasingly competitive marketplace, especially with the increase in the presence of international retailers.

The interviews and observations confirm that only Shoprite employs advertising in print and digital media, and as such, the firm achieves 100% congruence in positioning. A challenging market environment calls for managers to proactively emphasize positioning strategies that they intend to follow in marketing communications while ensuring that efforts are consistent with perceptions of target markets (Oyedele, Minor, & Ghanem, 2009). In support, Burton and Easingwood (2006) claim that a firm's communication of its positioning strategy projects an image, communicated category, or emotional selling proposition. Spendstre Photo Store likewise relies on its sponsorship activities of secondary and tertiary institutions' entertainment programs to provide communications about the firm. The positioning strategies identified in this study are the most favored in the study setting (Table 4.1), and to that end, the recommendation is for managers to hone in on these strategies.

Managerial implications

Managers may deliberately and proactively pursue the following two sets of tactics on the basis of the findings: (1) Attitude change, in which managers may direct efforts aimed at altering or re-positioning consumer beliefs about or perceptions of retailer offerings by using the strategies put forward in this research in day-to-day and long-term marketing practices (Oyedele et al., 2009); and/or (2) brand change, in which managers may symbolically or actually modify the offerings' attributes to reflect the positioning strategies identified in this study.

Managers may employ these tactics in marketing communications (e.g., advertising) that reflect in one way or another the contemporary local cultural values, the location, situation, casting, lighting, style, photographs, endorsers, and tone used in each commercial or other type of promotion (Oyedele et al., 2009). This study has, to a degree, responded to Coffie and Owusu-Frimpong's (2014) and Coffie's (2018) call for future research directed at increasing positioning research and generalizability through continued testing and validation using different sample groups, contexts, and, more specifically, emerging African economies. The study offers the opportunity to generalize the adopted typology to developing countries and also provides normative guidelines for managers in these economies.

For foreign retail firms seeking to do business in Africa and Ghana in particular, this study offers a snapshot of the current environment of retailer positioning in the country. While the examined retailers represent only a small fraction of indigenous and foreign retailing activity in Ghana, the findings demonstrate that retailers do engage in positioning activities and that foreign retailers appear to be stronger at positioning than their indigenous counterparts. This finding is attributed to foreign retailers' comparative consistency and congruence in their positioning activities and resource advantage over indigenous firms. As such, foreign retailers seeking to do business in Ghana must enter with a consistent positioning strategy that achieves congruence in order to positively affect customer perceptions thereby attracting and retaining Ghanaian customers. Indigenous firms must capitalize on consistent employment and congruence in positioning strategies while at the same time investing in resources including store expansion, advertising and promotion inducing efforts to positively affect customer perceptions and increase market share, ultimately leading to competitive advantage (de Chernatony & Segal-Horne, 2001).

Note

For the purposes of this chapter, permission was sought and was granted by Wiley Publishers on May 22, 2019, for the extensive use of and consultation of Blankson, Nkrumah, Opare, and Ketron's (2018) article published in Thunderbird International Business Review, *60*(4), 535–548.

References

Aaker, D. A., & Shansby, J. (1982). Positioning your product. *Business Horizons, 25*(3), 56–62.

Alexander, N., & Doherty, A. M. (2010). International retail research: Focus, methodology and conceptual development. *International Journal of Retail & Distribution Management, 38*(11/12), 928–942.

Appiah-Adu, K. (1999). The impact of economic reform on business performance: A study of foreign and domestic firms in Ghana. *International Business Review, 8,* 463–486.

Arnott, D. C. (1992). *Bases of financial services positioning in the personal pension, life assurance and personal equity plan sectors.* Unpublished PhD dissertation, Manchester Business School, University of Manchester, UK.

Ayitey, G. (2001). Ghana is open for business: The economic development agenda. *Ghana Review International Magazine, 78*(1), 15–17.

Babarinde, O. A. (2009, July/August). Africa is open for business: A continent on the move. *Thunderbird International Business Review, 51*(4). https://doi.org/10.1002/tie

Blankson, C. (2004). Positioning strategies and incidence of congruence of two UK store card brands. *Journal of Product & Brand Management, 13*(5), 315–328.

Blankson, C., & Crawford, J. C. (2012). Impact of positioning strategies on service firm performance. *Journal of Business Research, 65*(3), 311–316.

Blankson, C., & Kalafatis, S. P. (2004). The development and validation of a scale measuring consumer/customer-derived generic typology of positioning strategies. *Journal of Marketing Management, 20*(1–2), 5–43.

Blankson, C., & Kalafatis, S. P. (2007). Congruence between positioning and brand advertising. *Journal of Advertising Research, 47*(1), 79–94.

Blankson, C., Kalafatis, S. P., Cheng, J. M. S., & Hadjicharalambous, C. (2008). Impact of positioning strategies on corporate performance. *Journal of Advertising Research, 48*(1), 106–122.

Blankson, C., Nkrumah, M. F., Opare, G., & Ketron, S. (2018). Positioning strategies and congruence in the positioning of high-end indigenous and foreign retailers in sub-Saharan Africa: An illustration from Ghana. *Thunderbird International Business Review, 60*(4), 535–548.

Bruner, E. M. (1996). Tourism in Ghana: The representation of slavery and the return of the black diaspora. *American Anthropologist, 98,* 290–304.

Burt, S. L., & Carralero-Encinas, J. (2000). The role of store image in retail internationalization. *International Marketing Review, 17*(4), 433–453.

Burt, S. L., Dawson, J., & Sparks, L. (2003). Failure in international retailing: Research propositions. *International Review of Retail, Distribution and Consumer Research, 13*(4), 355–373.

Burt, S. L., Mellahi, K., Jackson, T. P., & Sparks, L. (2002). Retail internationalization and retail failure: Issues from the case of Marks & Spencer. *The International Review of Retail, Distribution and Consumer Research, 12*(2), 191–219.

Burton, J., & Easingwood, C. J. (2006). A positioning typology of consumers' perceptions of the benefits offered by successful service brands. *Journal of Retailing and Consumer Services, 13*(5), 301–316.

Cairns, P., Doherty, A. M., Alexander, N., & Quinn, B. (2008). Understanding the international retail divestment process. *Journal of Strategic Marketing, 16*(2), 111–128.

Coe, N., & Bok, R. (2014). Retail transitions in Southeast Asia. *International Review of Retail, Distribution and Consumer Research, 24*(5), 479–499.

Coffie, S. (2014). Congruence of service positioning: Empirical evidence from Ghana. *International Journal of Business and Management Studies, 3*(1), 577–588.

Coffie, S. (2018). Positioning strategies for branding services in an emerging economy. *Journal of Strategic Marketing.* https://doi.org/10.1080/0965254x.2018.1500626

Coffie, S., & Owusu-Frimpong, N. (2014). Alternative positioning strategies for services in Ghana. *Thunderbird International Business Review, 56*(6), 531–546.

Crawford, C. M. (1985). A new positioning typology. *Journal of Product Innovation Management, 2*(4), 243–253.

Dadzie, K., Akaah, I., & Riordan, E. (1988). Incidence of market typologies and pattern of marketing activity performance in selected African countries. *Journal of Global Marketing, 1*(3), 87–107.

D'Andrea, G., Silvestri, L., Costa, L., Fernandes, F., & Fossen, F. (2010). Spinning the wheel of retailing in Latin America: Innovation platforms for emerging consumers. *International Studies of Management & Organization, 40*(2), 52–73.

Debrah, Y. A. (2002). Doing business in Ghana. *Thunderbird International Business Review, 44*(4), 495–514.

Debrah, Y. A., & Toroitich, O. K. (2005). The making of an African success story: The privatization of Kenya Airways. *Thunderbird International Business Review, 47*(2), 205–230.

de Bruyn, P., & Freathy, P. (2011). Retailing in post-apartheid South Africa: The strategic positioning of boardmans. *International Journal of Retail & Distribution Management, 39*(7), 538–554.

de Chernatony, L., & Cottam, S. (nee Drury) (2009). Interacting contributions of different departments to brand success. *Journal of Business Research, 62*(3), 297–304.

de Chernatony, L., & McDonald, M. H. B. (1994). *Creating powerful brands.* Oxford: Butterworth Heinemann.

de Chernatony, L., & Segal-Horn, S. (2001). Building on services' characteristics to develop successful services brands. *Journal of Marketing Management, 17*(7–8), 645–669.

Doherty, A. M. (1999). Explaining international retailers' market entry mode strategy: Internationalization theory, agency theory and the importance of information asymmetry. *International Review of Retail, Distribution and Consumer Research, 9*(4), 379–402.

Doherty, A. M. (2000). Factors influencing international retailers' market entry mode strategy: Qualitative evidence from the UK fashion sector. *Journal of Marketing Management, 16*, 223–245.

Doherty, A. M. (2009). Market and partner selection processes in international retail franchising. *Journal of Business Research, 62*, 528–534.

Donaldson, T. (2015, September 9). A. T. Kearney ranks Africa's 15 most promising retail markets. *R. T. Kearney.*

Dubois, A., & Gadde, L. E. (2002). Systematic combining: An abduction approach to case research. *Journal of Business Research, 55*(7), 553–560.

Eckstein, H. (1998). *Congruence theory explained.* Lanham, MD: Rowman and Littlefield Publishers, Inc.

Eckstein, H., Fleron Jr., F. J., Hoffmann, E. P., & Reisinger, W. M. (1998). *Democracy take root in post-Soviet Russia? Explorations in state-society relations.* Oxford: Rowman and Littlefield Publishers, Inc.

The Economist Magazine. (1997). America loses its Afrophobia, April 26, 20 & 61–62.

The Economist Magazine. (2007). Ghana: Advertisement supplement, December 15–21, 59–62.

Eisenhardt, K. (1989). Building theories from case study research. *Academy of Management Review, 14*(4), 532–550.

Evans, J., & Mavondo, F. T. (2002). Psychic distance and organizational performance: An empirical examination of international retailing operations. *Journal of International Business Studies, 33*(3), 515–532.

Fuchs, C., & Diamantopoulos, A. (2010). Evaluating the effectiveness of brand-position-ing strategies from a consumer perspective. *European Journal of Marketing, 44*(11–12), 1763–1786.

Galperin, B. L., & Lituchy, T. R. (1999). The implementation of total quality management in Canada and Mexico: A case study. *International Business Review, 8,* 323–349.

Gielens, K., & DeKimpe, M. G. (2001). Do international entry decisions of retail chains matter in the long run? *International Journal of Research in Marketing, 18,* 235–259.

Gripsrud, G., & Benito, G. P. G. (2005). Internationalization in retailing: Modeling the pattern of foreign market entry. *Journal of Business Research, 58,* 1672–1680.

Hawkins, T. (1989, July 11). Star pupil comes of age. *Financial Times Survey, Financial Times,* 35–40.

Hollander, S. (2000). Distinguished retrospective viewpoint: Study retailing and see the world? *International Marketing Review, 17*(4/5), 327–333.

Holman, M. (1999, November 4). Leadership to change, reform to continue. *Financial Times Survey, Financial Times,* I–IX.

Hooley, G. J., & Greenley, G. (2005). The resource underpinnings of competitive positions. *Journal of Strategic Marketing, V13*(2), 93–116.

Hooley, G. J., Piercy, N. F., & Nicoulaud, B. (2012). *Marketing strategy and competitive positioning* (5th ed.). London: FT Prentice Hall.

Hutchinson, K., Alexander, N., Quinn, B., & Doherty, A. M. (2007). Internationalization motives and facilitating factors: Qualitative evidence from smaller specialist retailers. *Journal of International Marketing, 15*(3), 96–122.

International Monetary Fund (IMF). (2008). *Direction of trade statistics yearbook.* Washington, DC: International Monetary Fund.

Jarratt, D., & Fayed, R. (2001). The impact of market and organizational challenges on mar-keting strategy decision-making: A qualitative investigation of the business-to-business sector. *Journal of Business Research, 51*(1), 61–72.

Kalafatis, S. P., Tsogas, M., & Blankson, C. (2000). Positioning strategies in business markets. *Journal of Business and Industrial Marketing, 15*(6), 416–437.

Kara, A., Kaynak, E., & Kucukemiroglu, O. (1996). Positioning of fast-food outlets in two regions of North America: A comparative study using correspondence analysis. *Journal of Professional Services Marketing, 14*(2), 99–119.

Kuada, J. (2002). Collaboration between developed and developing country-based firms: Danish-Ghanaian experience. *Journal of Business and Industrial Marketing, 17*(6), 538–557.

Kuada, J., & Buatsi, S. N. (2005). Market orientation and management practices in Ghana-ian firms: Revisiting the Jaworski and Kohli framework. *Journal of International Marketing, 13*(1), 58–88.

Liu, C. L., & Zhang, Y. (2014). Learning process and capability formation in cross-border buyer-supplier relationships: A qualitative case study of Taiwanese technological firms. *International Business Review, 23,* 718–730.

Manwa, H., & Manwa, F. (2007). Applicability of the Western concept of mentoring to African organizations: A case study of Zimbabwean organizations. *Journal of African Business, 8*(1), 31–43.

McGoldrick, P. J., & Blair, D. (1995). International market appraisal and positioning. In P. J. McGoldrick & G. Davies (Eds.), *International retailing: Trends and strategies* (pp. 168–190). London: Pitman Publishing.

McGoldrick, P. J., & Ho, S. S. L. (1992). International positioning: Japanese department stores in Hong Kong. *European Journal of Marketing, 26*(8/9), 61–73.

Miles, S. J., & Mangold, W. G. (2005). Positioning southwest airlines through employee Branding. *Business Horizons, 48*(6), 535–545.

Milliman, J., von Glinow, M. A., & Nathan, M. (1991). Organizational life cycles and strategic international human resource management in multinational companies: Implications for congruence theory. *Academy of Management Review, 16*(2), 316–399.

Mmieh, F., & Owusu-Frimpong, N. (2004). State policies and the challenges in attracting foreign direct investment: A review of the Ghana experience. *Thunderbird International Business Review, 46*(5), 575–599.

Mmieh, F., & Owusu-Frimpong, N. (2009, July/August). The making of a sub-Saharan African success story: The case of cross-border listing of Trust Bank Limited of the Gambia on the Ghana stock exchange. *Thunderbird International Business Review, 51*(4). https://doi.org/10.1002/tie

Nadler, D. A., & Tushman, M. L. (1980). A congruence model for organizational assessment. In E. E. Lawler, D. A. Nadler, & C. C. Cammann (Eds.), *Organizational assessment.* New York, NY: Wiley.

Nwankwo, S. (2000). Assessing the marketing environment in sub-Saharan Africa: Opportunities and threat analysis. *Marketing Intelligence & Planning, 18*(3), 144–153.

Owhoso, V., Gleason, K. C., Mathur, I., & Malgwi, C. (2002). Entering the last frontier: Expansion by US multinationals to Africa. *International Business Review, 11*, 407–430.

Oyedele, A., Minor, M. S., & Ghanem, S. (2009). Signals of global advertising appeals in emerging markets. *International Marketing Review, 26*(4/5), 521–541.

Peterson, R. A., & Merunka, D. R. (2014). Convenience samples of college students and research reproducibility. *Journal of Business Research, 67*, 1035–1041.

Piercy, N. (2005). *Market-led strategic change: A guide to transforming the process of going to Market* (3rd ed.). Oxford: Elsevier Butterworth-Heinemann.

Pieters, R., Wedel, M., & Batra, R. (2010). The stopping power of advertising: Measures and effects of visual complexity. *Journal of Marketing, 74*(5), 48–60.

Poulis, K., Poulis, E., & Plakoyiannaki, E. (2013). The role of context in case study selection: An international business perspective. *International Business Review, 22*, 304–314.

Reardon, T., Timmer, C. P., Barrett, C. B., & Berdegue, J. (2003). The rise of supermarkets in Africa, Asia, and Latin America. *American Journal of Agricultural Economics, 85*(5), 1140–1146.

Republic of Ghana. (2014). *National Economic Forum: Changing the narrative, building national consensus for economic and social transformation.* Retrieved from www.presidency.gov.gh/senchireport.pdf

Ries, A., & Trout, J. (2001). *Positioning: How to be seen and heard in the overcrowded marketplace.* New York, NY: McGraw-Hill.

Schuiling, I., & Kapferer, J. N. (2004). Real differences between local and international brands: Strategic implications for international marketers. *Journal of International Marketing, 12*(4), 97–112.

Si, S. X., & Bruton, G. D. (2005). Knowledge acquisition, cost savings, and strategic positioning: Effects on Sino-American IJV performance. *Journal of Business Research, 58*(11), 1465–1473.

Stewart, D. W. (2009). The role of method: Some parting thoughts from a departing editor. *Journal of the Academy of Marketing Science, 37*(4), 381–383.

Sweeney, J. C., & Chew, M. (2002). Understanding consumer-service brand relationships: A case study approach. *Australian Marketing Journal, 10*(2), 26–43.

Swoboda, B., Berg, B., & Dan–Cristian, D. (2014). International transfer and perception of retail formats: A comparison study in Germany and Romania. *International Marketing Review, 31*(2), 155–180.

Swoboda, B., & Elsner, S. (2013). Transferring the retail format successfully into foreign countries. *Journal of International Marketing, 21*(1), 81–109.

Trout, J. (2012, March). Positioning myopia. *Marketing News Magazine, 15*, 34.

Vida, I., & Fairhurst, A. (1998). International expansion of retail firms: A theoretical approach for future investigations. *Journal of Retailing and Consumer Services, 5*(3), 143–151.

Webster Dictionary. (2004). *The Merriam Webster Dictionary* (New ed.). Springfield, MA: Merriam–Webster, Inc.

Wiig, A., & Kolstad, I. (2010). Multinational corporations and host country institutions: A case study of CSR activities in Angola. *International Business Review, 19*, 178–190.

Wind, Y. (1982). *Product policy, concepts, methods and strategy.* Reading, MA: Addison–Wesley Publishing.

Wolak, R., Kalafatis, S., & Harris, P. (1998). An investigation into four characteristics of services. *Journal of Empirical Generalizations in Marketing Science, 3*, 22–43.

Wrong, M., & Holman, M. (1996, July 9 Tuesday). African trailblazer begins to falter. *Ghana: Financial Times Survey, Financial Times*, I–VI.

Yang, Z., Wang, X., & Su, C. (2006). A review of research methodologies in international business. *International Business Review, 15*(6), 601–617.

Yin, R. K. (2009). *Case study research: Design and methods* (4th ed.). Los Angeles, CA: Sage.

Young, G. J., Meterko, M. M., Mohr, D., Shwartz, M., & Lin, H. (2009). Congruence in the assessment of service quality between employees and customers: A study of a public health care delivery system. *Journal of Business Research, 62*(11), 1127–1135.

Zachary, G. P. (2001, March 14). Tangled roots: For African-Americans in Ghana, the grass isn't always greener. *Wall Street Journal*, A1 & A10.

Web–based references

A. T. Kearney Report. (2015). Retrieved October 27, 2015 from www.atkearney.com/consumer-products-retail/african-retail-development-index/2015/full-report

Doing Business (A World Bank Group). (2014). Retrieved December 21 and 22, 2014 from www.doingbusiness.org/data/exploreeconomies/ghana/

World Bank. (2018). *Country profile.* Retrieved December 30, 2018 from https://databank.worldbank.org/data/views/reports/reportwidget.aspx?Report_Name=CountryProfile&Id=b450fd57&tbar=y&dd=y&inf=n&zm=n&country=GHA

World Investment Report. (2008). *Major FDI indicators.* Retrieved fromhttp://stats.unctad.org/FDI/TableViewer/tableView.aspx?ReportId=1254

Appendix I

Typology of positioning strategies

Typology of Positioning Strategies			
Strategy 1	Top of the range: Upper class, top of the range, status, prestigious, posh	Strategy 5	Attractiveness: Good aesthetics, attractive, cool, elegant
Strategy 2	Service: Impressive service, personal attention, consider people as important, friendly service	Strategy 6	Country of origin: Patriotism, country of origin, youth market
Strategy 3	Value for money: Reasonable price, value for money, affordability	Strategy 7	Branding: The brand name, leaders in the market, extra features, choice, wide range, expensive
Strategy 4	Reliability: Durability, warranty, safety, reliability	Strategy 8	Selectivity: Discriminatory in selection of customers, selective in choice of customers, high principles

Source: Blankson and Kalafatis (2004).

Appendix II

Reliability and validity of case study approach

Test	Case-study tactic	How the tactic was fulfilled
Construct Validity	Use extant typology of positioning strategy	Combined understanding of literature on the concept of positioning and positioning strategies with validation tests in Ghana.
	Systematic combining	Continuously assessed the relationship between the concept of positioning and empirical findings emanating from interviews and observation. In addition, three academics, the CEO of the three indigenous firms, and three managers of the foreign firms interviewed reviewed drafts of the chapter.
Internal Validity	Pattern matching	Researchers checked to ensure that inferences they made are airtight.
Reliability	Use case-study protocol	Documented procedures on the steps and measures taken throughout the data collection and analysis. In addition, all ideas and thoughts pertinent to the study were noted for review and revision if necessary.

Source: Adapted from Sweeney and Chew (2002, p. 30) and Dubois and Gadde (2002, pp. 555–559).

Appendix III

Congruence in the application of positioning strategies at life and health clinic (indigenous retailer)

Positioning Strategies	Managers	Customers	Observation
Top of the range			
Service	*	*	*
Value for money	*	*	*
Reliability	*	*	*
Attractiveness	*	*	*
Country of origin	*		
Branding	*	*	*
Selectivity			

Note: * denotes the employment of a positioning strategy.

Appendix IV

Congruence in the application of positioning strategies at Accra Mall Pharmacy (indigenous retailer)

Positioning Strategies	Managers	Customers	Observation
Top of the range			*
Service	*	*	*
Value for money	*	*	*
Reliability	*	*	*
Attractiveness	*	*	*
Country of origin			
Branding			*
Selectivity			

Note: * denotes the employment of a positioning strategy.

Appendix V

Congruence in the application of positioning strategies at Galaxy Perfumery (indigenous retailer)

Positioning strategies	Managers	Customers	Observation
Top of the range		*	*
Service	*		*
Value for money	*		
Reliability	*	*	
Attractiveness	*	*	*
Country of origin	*		*
Branding	*		
Selectivity		*	

Note: * denotes the employment of a positioning strategy.

Appendix VI

Congruence in the application of positioning strategies at Spendstre Photo Store (foreign retailer)

Positioning strategies	Managers	Customers	Observation
Top of the range			
Service	*	*	*
Value for money	*	*	
Reliability	*	*	*
Attractiveness	*	*	*
Country of origin			
Branding			
Selectivity			

Note: * denotes the employment of a positioning strategy.

Appendix VII

Congruence in the application of
positioning strategies at Shoprite
(foreign retailer)

Positioning strategies	Managers	Customers	Observation
Top of the range			
Service	*	*	*
Value for money	*	*	*
Reliability	*	*	*
Attractiveness	*	*	*
Country of origin			
Branding	*	*	*
Selectivity			

Note: * denotes the employment of a positioning strategy.

Appendix VIII

Congruence in the application of positioning strategies at Barcelos Restaurant (foreign retailer)

Positioning strategies	Managers	Customers	Observation
Top of the range			
Service	*	*	*
Value for money	*	*	
Reliability	*	*	*
Attractiveness	*	*	*
Country of origin			
Branding	*	*	*
Selectivity			

Note: * denotes the employment of a positioning strategy.

5 Social networks, relationships, and positioning of micro and small businesses in Africa

Introduction

The influence of social networks on micro and small business activities, entrepreneurship, and growth is well documented in marketing literature (Obeng & Blundel, 2015; Stokes & Blackburn, 1999; Spring & Rutashobya, 2009). Relying on social identity theory and social capital theory as backdrops to explain the context, this chapter attempts to unravel the virtue of social network relationships, which are pivotal foundations of micro and small business growth in Africa. Social networking can be defined as the process of enabling, creating, and nurturing business and/or social contacts through an interconnected alliance. Social networking is inspired by social identity theory, which accounts for the many roles that an individual plays and for the ways in which group membership dictates the activation and performance of those roles in a given situation. The more the relationships are valued, the more important the role identity is, and thus the more likely it is that the individual (i.e., the customer) will be inclined to maintain that identity (Ashforth, Harrison, & Corley, 2008). Embedded in social identity theory is the existence of a psychological group, defined by Turner (1984) as a collection of people who share the same social identification or define themselves in terms of the same social category membership. A member of a psychological group does not need to interact with or even like other members or be liked and accepted by them. Rather, their perception of being, for example, a member of a tribe, becomes the basis for incorporation of that status into their social identity.

In a rural African context, social networking concerns one's peers who consume privileged information while in social settings and centers on relationships amongst family members, friends, and/or acquaintances who share common interests. The aim of this chapter is to highlight the virtue of social networks and relationships for positioning micro and small businesses within the African cultural context.

Because the employment of positioning and marketing strategies unfolds in social contexts that encode values, beliefs, and acceptable patterns of behavior (Cayla & Arnould, 2008; Anambane, 2017), one infers that culture determines business models and approaches in international markets (Cayla & Arnould,

2008; Gao, 2013). Anambane (2017) examines the relationship between culture and indigenous entrepreneurship in Ghana and concludes that culture acts as a motivational factor for women's entrepreneurship and also limits the growth and expansion of women-owned enterprises. Thus, marketing and positioning activities never occur in a cultural vacuum, and the ability to appreciate the cultural nuances of executing positioning practices in the context of micro and small businesses' activities in Africa, particularly given the contrast between African and Western cultures, is worthy of exploration (see Coffie, 2018; Blankson, Iyer, Owusu-Frimpong, Nwankwo, & Hinson, 2019).

Literature background

An essential component of social networks is a culture that binds interpersonal relationships together. Although Africans share a remarkable cultural unity, they also have significant ethnic, linguistic, religious, and other differences. Notwithstanding these differences, shared characteristics, experiences, and worldviews give Africans a common identity that transcends differences arising from the diversity of languages, ethnic identities, and religions that exist in the country (Oppong, 2003).

In Kluckhohn and Strodtbeck's (1961) *Variations in Value Orientation*, the authors argue that "man-nature orientation" is an important aspect of African culture. They write that those who engage in man-nature orientation "have a needed duty to control or master [nature] (i.e., domination), to submit to nature (i.e., subjugation), or to work together with nature to maintain harmony and balance (i.e., harmony)" (Thomas, 2002, p. 48). Thus, while high-mastery cultures "actively seek to master and change the world, to assert control and exploit it in order to further personal or group interests," high-harmony cultures "accept the world as it is, trying to preserve rather than to change or exploit it" (Munene, Schwartz, & Smith, 2000, p. 341). African culture places man in harmony with the universe. This is evident in Mbiti's (1990 p. 39) writing, where he argues that man is not the master of the universe; he is only the center, the friend, the beneficiary, or the user. For that reason, he has to live in harmony with the universe, obeying the laws of the natural, moral, and mystical orders. Mbiti writes that if these are unduly disturbed, it is man who suffers most. Over the years, African peoples have come to these conclusions through long experience, observation, and reflection.

To the African, "human beings are regarded as an integral part of nature and the idea of dominating or using nature does not exist" (Djangrang, 1998, pp. 6–9). Thus, man must live in the universe, obeying the natural, moral, and mystical orders (Opoku, 1982). It is important to appreciate that the African is nestled in a "religious universe" that permeates every aspect of the African's life. It accompanies a person from conception to long after his or her physical death. There is no separation between religion and philosophy, religion and society, or religion and art. It is within this religious framework that African culture resides (Mbiti, 1990; Darley & Blankson, 2008). In African culture, individuals think of not only themselves and their immediate family but also their extended family members. Ghanaians, for example, depend on and provide support to one another, routinely offering guidance and behavioral modeling for younger members (Zoogah, 2013). At the center of African culture is the virtue of social networks and relationships.

In most African countries, whether an entrepreneur is a small retailer, a small business owner, a street vendor, or someone engaged in a family-owned or non-family-owned formal or informal enterprise, the influence of social networks prevails. In fact, in West Africa, marketplaces are not only avenues for selling products, but they are also places for social gathering, entertainment, dances, and other various social activities. A key component of business social networks in Africa is trust, which manifests in the form of informal credit. For example, Alhaji Mustapha built a successful business using informal credit that contributed to his successful political career in post-independence Sierra Leone (Jalloh, 2003). Similarly, in the early 1950s in Tarkwa and Abontiakoon in the then Gold Coast (now Ghana), Madam Rosemond Blankson (nee Wilson), popularly known as Mama Saalone (because of her Sierra-Leonean origin), built a successful trading company through her informal credit from the local Syrian and Lebanese wholesaler community in African cloths, fabrics, and sewing accoutrements. The practice of using social networks and informal credit to advance one's entrepreneurial career throughout West Africa is well known (see also, Arnould, 1986, 1989, 2001). As a result of social networking relationships, women traders especially excelled in West Africa years before the arrival of European traders (Tardits & Tardits, 1962). According to Tardits and Tardits, Dahomean (now the Republic of Benin) women traders engaged in business relationships with their clients and relied on social networks in order to succeed.

In Kano, Nigeria, the majority of the residents have been primarily engaged in various entrepreneurial activities in the form of micro and small businesses for centuries. Entrepreneurship has been and continues to be a major feature of Kano life (Yusuf, 1975). Despite the impact of Western commercial techniques, traditional savings strategies, and credit relations, socioeconomic networks continue to play major roles in the day-to-day activities of Kano traders; their behaviors are still influenced by sociocultural relationships and social networks which inspire them to seek economic prosperity and accumulate wealth (Yusuf, 1975). In Ghana and Nigeria, for example, young men offer their services to well-off traders ("businessmen") in return for advances of working capital, or cash gifts that enable them to start their own micro enterprises (Yusuf, 1975; Blankson, Cowan, & Darley, 2018). It is important to mention that not all savings go into commercial activity – a considerable fraction is used to strengthen one's social networks. In Nigeria, Ghana, and most of West Africa, money raised from kinsmen is rarely requested back so long as the individual assisted continues to be a worthy and generous member of the family; if successful, he or she will be expected to finance other members of his or her kin group (Yusuf, 1975; Blankson et al., 2018). In Ghana, many Kwahu and Asante micro entrepreneurs have become successful by becoming clients of wealthy businesspeople. Depending upon his or her conduct and the generosity of his or her patron, the client may end up with a reasonable seed fund to establish him or herself independently in whichever business domain he or she chooses. A micro entrepreneur who has been aided in this manner is expected to help fund his or her kinsmen's educations and other basic expenses.

Notwithstanding the generosity, poor credit networks, inadequate book-keeping, price fluctuations, scant market information, poor sales of goods, and lack of marketing skills have been catalysts for the failure of many a Hausa, Kwahu, and Asante trader. One of the key factors leading to bankruptcy within Kano commercial circles is attributed to conspicuous spending – similar to the Asantes in Ghana (Bonsu, 2008). Moreover, as noted earlier, a considerable part of this income from commercial undertakings goes to strengthen kinship and other social networks. While the pursuit of gain and the desire to accumulate wealth for reinvestment are paramount for every African micro or small business owner, so is the urge to maintain one's honor and social prestige; these can be achieved through consistent generosity and public exhibition of wealth (see Bonsu, 2008). Similar to the Asantes in Ghana (Bonsu, 2008), Hausas publicly praise the generous.

The interface of social identity theory and social capital theory

A review of social identity theory literature suggests several factors relevant to rural micro and small businesses that likely increases the tendency to identify with groups (e.g., tribes): Distinctiveness (which serves to separate and differentiate the enterprise from others and provides a unique identity) and prestige of the enterprise or group (based on the argument that through intergroup comparison, social identification affects the self-esteem of the owner–manager and his customers). Mael (1988) found that perceived enterprise prestige was related to the enterprise's identification among a group of university students and religious college alumni. Becoming aware of out-groups (i.e., groups outside the confines of the existing group) reinforces awareness of one's in-group (i.e., the group within which one relates, e.g., alumni, supporters of a football team, a cultural tribe). Identification with a group culture (e.g., Hausa, Igbo, Yoruba in Nigeria; Akyem, Asante, Kwahu, Fante in Ghana) thus directs individuals to engage in and derive satisfaction from activities that are in sync with their identity, to view themselves as an exemplar of the group, and to reinforce social capital: A factor conventionally associated with group formation (Ashforth & Mael, 1989).

Social capital refers to the resources (e.g., trust, norms, and networks) inherent in social relations that facilitate a common purpose, and is defined as the links, bonds, shared values, and culture that enable individuals and groups in a given society to trust and relate to each other. A key component of social capital is a culture of reciprocity, compromise, and pluralistic relationships. Social capital theory thus offers an important backdrop for discussing networks and relationships between micro and small business owner-managers and their customers. Indeed, as noted by Viswanathan, Sridharan, Ritchie, Venugopal, and Jung (2012), social capital theory considers social networks of people as capital and attempts to facilitate information flow and act as a storehouse of value for reciprocation of social obligations in the future. In the context of African marketplaces, the influence of social networks in relationships is pivotal, and the outcomes of social networks in day-to-day interactions have been documented (see Woolcock & Narayan, 2000; Viswanathan, Rosa, & Ruth, 2010).

After extensive ethnographic research covering many developing countries, the World Bank concluded that social networks help us cope with and solve problems related to cultural voicelessness and powerlessness through the enhancement of social identity. Researchers have acknowledged social networks as one of several important categories of "assets" owned by the poor when it comes to "asset vulnerability" and "sustainable livelihood" (Scoones, 1998) frameworks. African culture explains why owner-managers of micro and small businesses celebrate with employees during good times and help them during difficult times. For example, strong ties to one's village of origin and kinship underpin entrepreneurial activities in Western Africa. Businesses feel a responsibility toward their networks in religiosity-infused cultures, which drives businesses to perform better, contrary to Western ideas of business goals (Blankson, Cowan, & Darley, 2018). Especially in rural Ghanaian communities, individuals seek understanding and hope through their faith; individuals thus place a high value on religion and overwhelmingly live by the Golden Rule.

A recent study by Blankson, Cowan, & Darley (2018) revealed how the lives of residents in rural communities in Ghana revolve around religious and moral etiquette that stresses giving back and engaging in relationships with each other. The authors find that owner-managers who are able to find success use it to afford educational opportunities for their children and staff. The authors also find that their interviewees developed ties with local rural bank officers and sought advice from them. Although many of the interviewees rely on customer feedback as a form of information gathering, other owner-managers actually access information about their customers through their own social networks. This is an important facet of these micro and small businesses because both mechanisms help owner-managers improve the way they serve their customers. Blankson, Cowan, & Darley (2018) find that several owner-managers have set up social funds in the form of *susu*: a rotating, member-generated money contribution for funerals, child outdooring and naming ceremonies, school fees, hospitalization, and other emergencies. Ghanaian employees are fond of social funds because being responsible for one another is a virtue in Ghanaian culture. The latter obviously reinforces the notion of "brotherhood" and devotion to expanded networks.

Rural Ghanaian small business owner-managers' relationships with employees are much different from those in other contexts. The employees are individuals to whom owner-managers have a moral obligation to provide. Owner-managers establish social bonds with their employees using non-traditional tactics, such as educational support and gifts. Owner–managers' relationships with staff extend beyond business profit and marketing strategy. Financial assistance allows small businesses to deepen relationships with staff. For instance, owner–managers already provide gifts, help send their employees to additional schooling, and provide financial support when needed. Within the Ghanaian rural community context, the sociocultural characteristics of the marketplace play major roles in the owner–managers' business practices (Blankson, Cowan, & Darley, 2018).

Relationships with staff

Micro and small business owner–managers in rural subsistence Ghana maintain traditional manager–employee relationships. Quite the contrary to formal owner–manager relationships, employee, management, and information dispersion occurs informally. Despite this laxity, most owner–managers speak of "sit[ting] down and talk[ing] about how things are faring" with their employees. This works well. From the arguments, it appears that many issues owner–managers face are less business-focused and more grounded in staff differences. When issues arise, stronger management-implemented solutions overcome difficulties and provide better working environments. In Blankson, Cowan, & Darley (2018), an entrepreneur elaborates, "My staff sometimes had some grudges among themselves. This started by some of the apprentices teasing their colleagues, but it was tribal-based I think. It was based on the dresses some of them wore. I never tolerated tribal teasing between my staff. From that time, I decided that all apprentices should wear uniforms. This stopped the teasing problem." The story illustrates the fact that micro and small business owners sometimes implement moral solutions that do not serve the individual employees but rather the greater good. The latter finding appears to be supported by social identity theory, which stipulates that individuals occupy multiple roles and that the social embeddedness of those roles increases the likelihood of their being activated and performed well in a given situation (Tajfel, 1978).

In rural Ghana, owner–managers treat their employees like family; they would do anything for their welfare. Instead of motivating employees through higher wages, employees stay loyal to the owner–manager because of their treatment. Owners do this not for the sake of the business, but out of religiosity. Sometimes the owner–managers provide bonuses, social gifts, or rewards for hard work, but what matters most are the "family-like" operations of the business. As put by Viswanathan, Sridharan, and Ritchie (2010), social networks play a major role in restoring social identity and eventually prevent psychological imbalances (i.e., powerlessness).

Relationships with customers

Ghanaian rural micro and small business owners treat customers as friends, a behavior consistent with social identity theory. Instead of managing customers by profitability, the owner–manager makes every single customer a priority, almost out of a moral obligation. Their keen attention to customer care is expected because of close-knit communal bonds. An appreciation of social identity theory is evident in customer service, a finding that is in consonance with researches in India (see among others, Viswanathan, Sridharan, and Ritchie, 2010). Owner-managers acknowledge the importance of customer service in business environments and feel the need to "be there for each other." This is evident in Viswanathan, Sridharan, and Ritchie's (2010) study in India, which concludes that business success in subsistence marketplaces requires a different kind of trust revolving around one-to-one social networks, unlike conventional business practices.

The majority of micro and small business owner-managers believe that good customer service promotes positive customer perceptions through word of mouth and sociocultural bonds. By operating their businesses with high morals and treating each customer specially, the owner-managers secure a rich customer network. Blankson, Cowan, & Darley (2018) find that owner-managers who blend marketing tactics with basic social support in an interweaving fashion are unique to rural subsistence cultures. This contextual definition of customer care exceeds those in Western market–orientation strategy. The social support of customers underlies the interdependence of businesses and their customers. Owner-managers place themselves in status positions: They are trustees and the customers are beneficiaries. The owner-managers' social support systems ensure the well-being of each customer, from smaller demonstrations of morality (e.g., the provision of porches [i.e., verandas] in front of stores) to higher levels of financial support (e.g., paying for funerals). Customers also provide marketing intelligence to the business, including advice on sizes of clothing, types of products, and competitive information. Indeed, relationships built early on with customers determine the success or failure of the business. Our assertion is in line with Viswanathan, Rosa, and Ruth's (2010) conclusion that commitment and relationships at the individual level are factors in successful buyer and seller role-based activities in subsistence marketplaces.

Conclusion

In rural Africa, marketing and positioning activities of micro and small businesses result from a shared sense of religiosity within a community and a culture of social networks and relationships. Moreover, relationships with consumers determine competitive positioning and intelligence. Competition exists, but deep consumer relationships appear to mitigate that competition (Blankson, Cowan, & Darley, 2018). Established networks (conversations with consumers, other firms in the villages, or educational institutions) help in gathering marketing intelligence. Networks are vital for micro and small businesses (Viswanathan, Seth, Gau, & Chaturvedi, 2009; Viswanathan, Rosa, and Ruth, 2010). This chapter provides value in its discussion of social identity and social capital theories that are relevant as backdrops for explaining the positioning activities of micro and small business owner-managers in rural subsistence Africa (Arnould, 2001). Overall, the chapter argues that micro and small business owner-managers appreciate certain factors that support positioning and marketing practices: specifically, the virtue of networks and relationships with customers (see also Viswanathan, Rosa, and Ruth, 2010), adherence to religious communality (Bonsu & Belk, 2010), pragmatic social support, and interdependence (Abdelnour & Branzei, 2010; Ingenbleek, Tessema, & van Trijp, 2013). Indeed, owner–managers understand that customer care determines loyalty. They often express the view that if they do not provide a customer-focused business, their competitors will. Hence, this forces them to adapt their positioning and marketing practices (e.g., keeping the workplace clean, creating a welcoming storefront for children to play and elders to relax, ensuring the neat appearance of workers, maintaining cordial relationships between workers and owner–managers, offering quality products geared toward customers' specifications and perceptions) to maintain competitive positioning of their offerings and businesses.

The chapter further concludes that religiosity drives social networks in terms of customer relationships and staff relationships and not only profitability goals. In other words, in rural subsistence Africa, micro and small business owner–managers do not define success solely as profitability, but instead as the ability to provide for family members, staff, and customer friends (see also Yusuf, 1975; Blankson, Cowan, & Darley, 2018). The chapter also reveals that rural micro and small business owner–managers' positioning and marketing practices stem from interdependence and relationships between owner–managers, staff, customers, and rural residents. This agrees with Viswanathan, Rosa, and Ruth's (2010) study in Chennai, India, where subsistence consumer-merchants sustain relationships in three interdependent relationship domains: Vendor, customer, and family. This unique interdependence is borne of a culture that emphasizes "brotherhood" and pragmatic social support. Thus, marketing practices reflect religiosity and adherence to communal and collectivistic cultural systems and informality. It appears that rural African micro and small business positioning and marketing activities reflect simplicity beneath a surface of complexity and sophistication despite apparent naïveté. These bonds run much deeper than those that exist with business practices in the West. The bonds created by social networks and relationships underpin virtue in marketing when it comes to micro and small businesses' operations.

References

Abdelnour, S., & Branzei, O. (2010). Fuel-efficient stoves for Darfur: The social construction of subsistence marketplaces in post-conflict settings. *Journal of Business Research, 63*(6), 617–629.

Anambane, G. (2017). *Culture and women entrepreneurship: A case study of Nabdam District.* Unpublished MPhil Thesis, University of Ghana, Ghana.

Arnould, E. J. (1986). Merchant capital, simple reproduction, and underdevelopment: Peasant traders in Zinder, Niger Republic. *Canadian Journal of African Studies, 20*(3), 323–356.

Arnould, E. J. (1989). Toward a broadened theory of preference formation and the diffusion of innovations: Cases from Zinder Province, Niger Republic. *Journal of Consumer Research, 16*, 239–267.

Arnould, E. J. (2001). Ethnography, export marketing policy, and economic development in Niger. *Journal of Public Policy & Marketing, 20*(2), 151–169.

Ashforth, B. E., Harrison, S. H., & Corley, K. G. (2008, June). Identification in organizations: An examination of four fundamental questions. *Journal of Management, 34*(3), 325–374.

Ashforth, B. E., & Mael, F. (1989). Social identity theory and the organization. *Academy of Management Review, 14*(1), 20–39.

Babarinde, O. A. (2009). Africa is open for business: A continent on the move. *Thunderbird International Business Review, 51*(4), 329–339.

Blankson, C., Cowan, K., & Darley, W. K. (2018). Marketing practices of rural micro and small businesses in Ghana: The role of public policy. *Journal of Macromarketing, 38*(1), 29–56.

Blankson, C., Iyer, P., Owusu-Frimpong, N., Nwankwo, S., & Hinson, R. (2019). Positioning strategies of foreign and indigenous firms in an African culture Milieu. *Journal of Business Research*. https://doi.org/10.1016/j.jbusres.2019.03.001

Bonsu, S. K. (2008). Ghanaian attitudes towards money in consumer culture. *International Journal of Consumer Studies* (ISSN: 1470–6423), *32,* 171–178.

Bonsu, S. K., & Belk, R. W. (2010). Marketing a new African god: Pentecostalism and material salvation in Ghana. *International Journal of Nonprofit and Voluntary Sector Marketing, 15*(4), 305–323.

Cayla, J., & Arnould, E. J. (2008). A cultural approach to branding in the global marketplace. *Journal of International Marketing, 16*(4), 86–112.

Coffie, S. (2018). Positioning strategies for branding services in an emerging economy. *Journal of Strategic Marketing*. https://doi.org/10.1080/0965254x.2018.1500026.

Darley, W. K., & Blankson, C. (2008). African culture and business markets: Implications for marketing practices. *Journal of Business & Industrial Marketing, 23*(6), 374–383.

Djangrang, N. B. (1998, March). Africa: The breath of life. *UNESCO Courier, 51,* 6–9.

Gao, M. H. (2013). Culture determines business models: Analyzing Home Depot's failure case in China for international retailers from a communication perspective. *Thunderbird International Business Review, 55*(2), 173–191.

Ingenbleek, P. T. M., Tessema, W. K., & van Trijp, H. C. M. (2013). Conducting field research in subsistence markets, with an application to the market orientation in the context of Ethiopian pastoralists. *International Journal of Research in Marketing, 30*(1), 83–97.

Jalloh, A. (2003). Informal credit and politics in Sierra Leone. *African Economic History, 31,* 91–110.

Kluckhohn, F. R., & Strodtbeck, F. L. (1961). *Variations in value orientation.* Westport, CT: Greenwood Press.

Mael, F. (1988). *Organizational identification: Construct re-definition and a field application with organizational alumni.* Doctoral dissertation, Wayne State University, Detroit.

Mbiti, J. S. (1990). *African religions and philosophy.* Oxford: Heinemann International.

Munene, J. C., Schwartz, S. H., & Smith, P. B. (2000). Development in sub-Saharan Africa: Cultural influences and managers' decision behavior. *Public Administration and Development, 20*(4), 339–351.

Obeng, B. A., & Blundel, R. K. (2015). Evaluating enterprise policy interventions in Africa: A critical review of Ghanaian small business support services. *Journal of Small Business Management, 53*(2), 416–435.

Opoku, K. A. (1982). The world view of the Akan. *Tarikh (26 Akan History and Culture), 7*(2), 61–73.

Oppong, J. R. (2003). Culture, conflict, and change in sub-Saharan Africa. In S. Aryeetey-Attoh (Ed.), *Geography of sub-Saharan Africa* (2nd ed.). New York, NY: Prentice-Hall.

Scoones, I. (1998). *Sustainable rural livelihood: A framework for analysis.* IDS Discussion Paper No. 72, University of Sussex, Brighton, UK.

Spring, A., & Rutashobya, L. K. (2009). Gender-related themes in African entrepreneurship: Introduction to the articles. *Journal of African Business*, *10*(1), 1–10.

Stokes, D., & Blackburn, R. (1999). *Entrepreneurship: Building for the future*. Working Paper Series, Small Business Research Centre, Kingston University, UK.

Tajfel, H. (1978). Social categorization, social identity and social comparison. In H. Tajfel (Ed.), *Differentiation between social groups: Studies in the social psychology of intergroup relations* (pp. 61–76). London: Academic Press.

Tardits, C., & Tardits, C. (1962). Traditional market economy in South Dahomey. In P. Bohannan & G. Dalton (Eds.), *Markets in Africa* (Chapter 3, pp. 897–24102). Chicago, IL: Northwestern University Press.

Thomas, D. C. (2002). *Essentials of international management: A cross-cultural perspective*. Thousand Oaks, CA: Sage.

Turner, J. C. (1984). Social identification and psychological group formation. In H. Tajfel (Ed.), *The social dimension: European developments in social psychology* (2nd ed., pp. 518–538). Cambridge: Cambridge University Press.

Viswanathan, M., Rosa, J. A., & Ruth, J. A. (2010). Exchanges in marketing systems: The case of subsistence consumer-merchants in Chennai, India. *Journal of Marketing*, *74*(3), 1–17.

Viswanathan, M., Seth, A., Gau, R., & Chaturvedi, A. (2009). Ingraining product-relevant social good into business processes in subsistence marketplaces: The sustainable market orientation. *Journal of Macromarketing*, *29*(4), 406–425.

Viswanathan, M., Sridharan, S., & Ritchie, R. (2010). Understanding consumption and entrepreneurship in subsistence marketplaces. *Journal of Business Research*, *63*(6), 570–581.

Viswanathan, M., Sridharan, S., Ritchie, R., Venugopal, S., & Jung, K. (2012). Marketing interactions in subsistence marketplaces: A bottom-up approach to designing public policy. *Journal of Public Policy & Marketing*, *31*(2), 159–177.

Woolcock, M., & Narayan, D. (2000). Social capital: Implications for development theory, research, and policy. *World Bank Research Observer*, *15*(2), 225–249.

Yusuf, A. B. (1975). Capital formation and management among the Muslim Hausa traders of Kano, Nigeria. *Africa*, *45*, 167–182.

Zoogah, D. B. (2013). Career motivation, mentoring readiness, and participation in workplace mentoring programs: A cross-cultural study. *Journal of African Business*, *14*(1), 19–32.

6   Branding nation–states
South Africa and Ghana

Introduction

Brands abound in our daily activities, from the choice of products we are offered, to services and to an individual's sense of worth of his or her own "brand" value. In the corporate world, established brands serve as identifiers but also play emotional roles as reminders of what an organization stands for. Brands are also a source of profit which emanates from the worth consumers attach to them (Cravens & Piercy, 2013; Riley, 2016). Therefore, strong brands yield benefits to both the consumer and the organization.

This recognition of the valuable role brands and branding can play in the life of the organization has spilled over into country branding, and is partly responsible for the developing interest of nation–states in brands. The potential contribution toward the development of tourism and the strategic role it can play in marketing nation–states' economic development are among the driving forces of brand interest. The strategic roles that branding can play include attracting foreign direct investments to the relevant sectors of the economy on the path of development. Youde (2009) notes that country branding should also be viewed as an integral part of foreign policy as a vehicle for achieving specific objectives.

Papadopoulos, Hamzaoui-Essoussi, and Rojas-Mendez (2016, p. 459) explain that notionally, country branding may not be "new," as different terminologies appear to have been used interchangeably in the past (although in some cases differently) to refer to country branding. Such terminologies have included references to places, countries, nations, cities, regions, and neighborhoods. What is probably inherent in these descriptions is that there is a sense of purpose and process for such "places" as part of the larger goals affecting the nation-state. What may be "new" is the strategic orientation that nation branding has assumed. This strategic orientation now appears to be applicable to other areas, such as tourism, goods, and services originating in the countries under consideration. The logic is that one affects the other; as these are interlinked in purpose; and this is more strategic than has been in the past. The quest for development, globalization, and the attendant competitive spirit associated with the process have also contributed to the strategic nature of country orientation. The most potent explanation for the surge in interest in country branding has been the growth in interest in branding as a concept and practice. Emerging in the 1960s, the concept and practice have grown over the past decades, reaching the high points around the 2000s, and in the process spilling over to the branding of almost "everything" (Papadopoulos et al., 2016).

In addition, the development of models for the purpose of explaining and supporting how countries should brand or have branded is a relatively recent evolution. Anholt (2003, 2006) attempted to develop a model aimed at reflecting the global public perception of countries in terms of their governance, culture and heritage, attitudes, tourism, investment, immigration, reputation, export performance, and city/place characteristics. These pioneering classifications appear to have gained currency and remain the best known and consequently most applied to determine the "brand status" of countries. In bottom of the pyramid markets (BoPM), branding becomes even more critical as a means of restoring the negative image associated with products and services from such countries. In this regard, there appears to be a linkage between products and services and the countries of origin. Papadopoulos et al. (2016) note that developing countries tend to have mostly such negative associations, and it is imperative that marketing efforts are made to change the status quo alongside the offerings from such countries.

This chapter builds on the work of Coffie and Darmoe (2016), and discusses branding issues from BoPM countries in Africa and uses South Africa and Ghana as proto-type countries from the continent. The purpose is to outline the challenges faced by BoPM African countries in their branding efforts, to evaluate those efforts by South Africa and Ghana in spite of their challenges, and to suggest ways forward.

Branding in BoPMs: issues and challenges

Branding at the base of the pyramid – including sub-Saharan African countries – has been beset by a number of challenges. Generalization and stereotyping have made it difficult to achieve a positive image. These stereotypes include corruption, poverty, poor governance, limited economic resources, a wide range of cultures, and others (Anholt, 2003, 2005; Chikweche & Fletcher, 2011; Versi, 2009b). Versi (2009b, p. 2) captures these issues in this way:

> [B]randing of Africa as backward, primitive, childlike and violent goes back centuries to when Europe made contact with the continent. It worsened during the slave trade, during which Africa's supposed backwardness provided the excuse for dealing in this horrific enterprise and the projection of Africa as "uncivilised" provided the excuse for its colonial exploitation.

In sum, these historical prejudices that cast Africa in a bad light still abound and serve as challenges in positively branding countries and organizations on the continent. In addition, the charity-centered approach to solving problems only serves to perpetuate Africa's negative image. Charity campaigns such as Food Aid for Ethiopia in 1985 and Make Poverty History in 2005 serve as constant reminders of a continent always carrying a begging bowl (Versi, 2009b).

Adegoju (2017, p. 161) argues that the negative portrayal of Africa tends to emanate predominantly from the Western media and is often based on a snapshot of a situation. For example, in December 2006, during an American Broadcasting Company (ABC) News *20/20* piece, Lagos (Nigeria's commercial nerve center) was described as "a sprawling, crime-ridden, corrupt, disgrace of a city, home to more than 20 million people where the average income is a dollar a week." In another part of the broadcast, Nigeria is also characterized as "a desperately poor country." Here the image created of Lagos is one of a dangerous and unsafe city in a country where people live in squalor and degradation. In a 2007 CNN documentary on the Niger Delta situation entitled *Rebels Revealed*, reporter Jeff Koinange focused on the despicable activities of the Niger Delta militants who were then still holding 24 Filipinos hostage (Adegoju, 2017, p. 161). The CNN report again suggests that much of Nigeria is bedeviled by such activities, attitudes, and behaviors. Such reportage will surely create a sense of fear and add to the aforementioned negative portrayal and might deter or obstruct a foreigner who may be considering investing in Nigeria. Anholt (2005) describes this as a negative brand effect that overshadows what is good in the continent of Africa.

On economic challenges, Chikweche and Fletcher (2011) identify issues including low GDP, low income, instability of currencies, high inflation, and poor capital inflows. Infrastructural challenges such as poor electricity supply and poor transport networks that affect distribution constitute part of the economic difficulties that BoPMs face. These, together with levels of corruption and poor governance, work against confidence in investment and productivity and perpetuate a low quality of life among the majority. The cumulative effect of the negative portrayal is the negative perception of countries in sub-Saharan Africa, and in consequence, low perception of products and services from such places. Such countries are often treated as one homogeneous market (Anholt, 2003; Chikweche & Fletcher, 2011; Chikweche, 2013). With such a myriad of negatives, it is not surprising to see the emergence of Brand Africa (www. brandafrica.org) as a "pan-African intergenerational movement to inspire a great Africa through creating a positive image of Africa, celebrating its diversity and inspiring its competitiveness."

Branding South Africa

South Africa is better off economically and is perceived as the "gateway to the rest of the continent, consisting infrastructural and industrial advance relative to its neighbors and the resultant investment opportunities and access to the African market that it offered" (Cornelissen, 2017 p. 536). In spite of this, South Africa suffers from the negative continent effect from a poor image abroad in its attempt at branding the country. Given the country's checkered political history of apartheid and subsequent liberation through key personalities such as Nelson Mandela, this section discusses how South Africa's branding/rebranding of the country rests on four key elements: Leverage on its political history, exploitation of key personalities from the liberation process, successful organization of international events (FIFA 2010), and emphasis of its internationally acclaimed products such as South African wines (Youde, 2009).

South Africa suffered a prolonged, painful, and unforgettable history of apartheid until the country's final liberation in 1994. Notwithstanding the treatment and horrors visited on the "natives," South Africans of color remain at peace with their white counterparts today (Bannister, 2010). This provides an opportunity for South Africa to tout itself as a peacemaker nation at the international level based on its history and experience. This also allows South Africa to promote itself as a young and new country with a diverse population that is tolerant in its approach to dealing with issues of race and tribal affiliation (Youde, 2009). In essence, South Africa's efforts in this direction reflect attempts at rebranding that the country has used to its advantage in international relations. As noted by Goff and Dunn (2004), image and international relations are critically important aspects of what a country stands for in the eyes of the world, and therefore affects how other countries view and treat issues affecting the country in question. It is argued here that South Africa should do more to capitalize on this "peacemaker" perception to further develop the country's brand and its international relations. Papadopoulos et al. (2016, p. 461) observe that such an approach to branding a nation is "systematic and strategic in orientation." Youde (2009, p. 135) reports that "South Africa has used this new brand image in numerous places around the world. It has offered its services as an international mediator in places such as Israel, Northern Ireland, the Great Lakes region of Central Africa, East Timor, Zimbabwe, Sudan, Nigeria, and Côte d'Ivoire, among other places."

South Africa's international role is a key subject in the work of Cornelissen (2017, p. 532), who observes that "Given the context for South Africa's reintegration into the international arena and the new political elite's appraisal of the domestic imperatives they faced, it is noteworthy that they constructed an internationalist and activist foreign policy that was legitimated in terms of South Africa's socioeconomic and developmental priorities." The author here argues that given the country's history of apartheid, it is imperative for its leaders to seek a measure of reintegration of the people and the country in general into the world order. Doing so on its own is important, but it is also strongly linked to the developmental purpose of the nation-state. In this regard, this chapter buttresses the point that South Africa's attempt to carve a role for itself as an international mediator creates a positive international presence and this process is often associated with economic benefits that are likely to emerge strategically from the process.

Closely associated with South Africa's peacemaker image is the drive to leverage the personality of the leading figure of the country's struggle against the apartheid system: Nelson Mandela. Mandela himself around the world is well respected and is perceived as a peace lover who suffered for decades in search of unity for the nation and equality and dignity for the black race. This notion of branding as reflected in persons and their personality finds support in the work of Papadopoulos et al. (2016) – namely, that humans necessarily express emotions towards objects, products, services, and of course countries. In this regard, the positive image of Mandela and his personality recalls the peacemaker that he was, and he is therefore symbolically drawn upon as a measure of what South Africa represents. This idea also finds much support in the influential work of Aaker (1997) in discussing the development and construct of brand personalities as they affect entities. In application, South Africa has drawn on what Mandela personifies for the purpose of tourism. This peacemaker brand may be enviable, but the country must actually carry out the ideals of its brand in order for this notion to be continuously leveraged in order to achieve the maximum impact for marketing purposes.

One element in South Africa's attempt to rebrand itself across the globe is to capitalize on global events as occasions for selling itself to the world. In the last decade, perhaps the most evident was the country's successful hosting of the FIFA World Cup in 2010. Since it was the first time the event was held in Africa, it served as a strong avenue for advertising the country's ability to effectively organize and implement international activities. In that event, South Africa represented itself as well as the continent of Africa as a whole, and demonstrated what they were capable of at the world stage during one of the largest and most prestigious sports events in the world. Bannister (2010, p. 37) asks this:

> Having risen to the challenge in the eyes of the world, the critical issue of the 2010 FIFA World Cup, is now: can we maintain standards at that level and can we create the ultimate legacy and use the event as a springboard to establish a new value proposition and positioning for Brand South Africa?

The answer has to be "yes" to illustrate the continuity of using international events as pivots and springboards for branding and marketing positive news about the country. Cornelissen (2017, p. 539) reports that language used in description of the 2010 FIFA World Cup such as "the African World Cup," "to strengthen the African and South African image," and "promote new partnerships with the world" are just a few examples of the positive and enduring effect of South Africa's hosting. It clearly signaled to the leaders that South Africa is a key gateway to reawaken all that is good in Africa. In this regard, South Africa is cast in the role of a continent leader, which clearly plays to the image of the country.

South Africa can also harness its strengths by emphasizing a product it is well known for as a vehicle for country branding: Its wines. Although the focus of this chapter is on country branding, country branding tends to lean on some entities or variables the country can add to the positive elements it already possesses for branding purpose. Herstein, Berger, and Jaffe (2014) argue that in brand development for products (services) and places, there can be an element of a "vice versa" relationship. This means that countries can draw on the positives associated with their products to advance their country's image. South Africa's wines appear to have a good reputation in most parts of the world. In this sense, it is a feasible proposition to associate the positives of the wine with its place of origin. So communications can be built on slogans such as this: "South Africa, where the best wines are made." Such a statement would be in consonance with countries such as Japan and Germany that are inextricably associated with the reliability and durability of the vehicles that are manufactured in their countries.

Developing brand Ghana

In attempting to change the negative narrative, African countries such as Ghana have shown some evidence of branding and positioning. Focusing on tourism positioning, Blankson, Owusu-Frempong, and Mbah (2004) examine the Ghanaian government's efforts to encourage tourism in the country. This recognizes the expectation that, within two decades, tourism is set to become an internationally recognized economic and social sector in Africa (Asiedu, 2008; UNWTO, 2007). Ghana has enjoyed a relatively stable democracy and a growing tourism sector amid economic recovery programs by successive governments since 1983 (Ghana Budget, 2002). The purpose of a study by Blankson et al. (2004) was to investigate the development of tourism in Ghana and to establish the perceived brand positioning of Ghana on tourism from the perspective of experts and government ministries responsible for tourism (the Ministry of Tourism, the Ghana Tourism Board, and the Ministry of Trade). The study (Blankson et al., 2004) uncovered that, overall, Ghana aims to be a middle-class, niche tourist destination by targeting tourists from North America and Europe, Africans in diaspora, and Ghanaians living abroad. The Ministry of Tourism therefore focused its research on the target audience in order to position Ghana as a tourist destination to suit the needs of the target market. A lack of funds hindered efforts to create any meaningful brand and positioning through communication and other activities. Word of mouth communication was used to reach out to the target audience. In general, low-level promotional activities were mainly employed. The functional objective emerged most strongly from the ministries and experts interviewed for the ongoing promotional efforts, whereas symbolic and experiential goals were reserved for the long term. The key branding and positioning focuses were service, value for money, culture, selectivity, attractiveness, reliability of manpower development, quality controls, and ecology. The Blankson et al. (2004) study suggests a lack of clarity and focus in what Ghana wants to achieve with respect to tourism branding and positioning. It appears that Ghana's effort to brand and position the tourism industry is at an early stage and no dominant perspective exists.

There were further efforts by the late President John Evans Atta Mills in the first year of his presidency in 2009 to brand Ghana through packaging the country's values, socio-economic and political environment, and heritage in order to present a collective image of the country to the outside world. The Brand Ghana Office was established in 2009 as a first step to achieving this objective. The country's citizens were to represent brand Ghana, and in a sense, "their education, abilities and aspirations that ultimately deliver what our country is and create the potential for tourism, business, and cultural, social and political exchange. Without some sense of the people and their particular nature and ability, the country Ghana is an empty landscape" (brandghana.gov.gh). Although the original website still contains some information about the purpose and direction for brand Ghana, the pursuit of the agenda has not followed the cohesive trajectory intended since the passing of the late president in 2012. It appears that subsequent governments have not pursued the brand Ghana initiative with the same enthusiasm as was intended by the late president. The brand Ghana office has been replaced with committees and bodies under the Ghana Tourism Authority that work with Ghana Investment Promotion Centre (GIPC), Ghana Exports Promotion Authority (GEPA), and the Free Zones Board to promote Ghana (myjoyonline.com).

Evidence suggests that Ghana's identity appears to be based on a number of other associations that Angus (2010) identifies over a period of time. In the early days after independence, Ghana was regarded as the "star" of Africa, as its president at the time, Dr. Kwame Nkrumah, spearheaded the search for independence among other African countries with the mantra, "the black man is capable of managing his own affairs." The perception of Ghana as an independent and democratic country was short-lived, as the country soon suffered a number of military coups along the lines of many other African countries. The "democratic" credentials appear to have been revived since the 1990s, and the country has held a number of successful democratic elections. However, a recent event at the Ghanaian supreme court in which the leading opposition party challenged the results following the 2012 elections produced evidence to suggest all is not well with the "star" of sub-Saharan Africa. Recently, Ghana was touted as one of the fastest-growing economies in the world following the 2011 discovery of oil (Epic Global Media, 2012). However, during the last quarter of 2014, the country was in discussion with the IMF for a bailout to help support the economy, which was hugely indebted (Daily Guide, 2014).

One target group for tourism that potentially defies the "negative" associations of hunger, poverty, deprivation, disease, and squalor on the continent may be that of Visiting Friends and Relatives (VFR) in Ghana. This is because most of this target group are Ghanaians who reside in other countries, including Europe and North America. This category often regards visits to relatives in Ghana as a necessity, and therefore is not easily dissuaded; thus reducing "the potential social apprehensions and tensions' associated with the continent" (Asiedu, 2008, p. 619). Therefore it is tentatively arguable that while there are varied attempts either to create a brand or to associate certain positive values with the country, none appears to have been a sustained basis for brand Ghana. This position is corroborated by the work of Opoku and Hinson (2005) involving an online study of the brand personality of ten African countries. Opoku and Hinson (2005) concluded that none of the ten African countries – including Ghana – appeared to have a distinct brand personality.

According to Versi (2009a, 2009b), in many countries, the national brand has an umbrella effect on its companies and institutions. In the case of Ghana, there appears to be an inverse approach in the sense that efforts to brand state institutions are seen as part of the state/national branding strategy. One tertiary educational institution that has recently been successfully rebranded is the Kwame Nkrumah University of Science and Technology (KNUST) in Ghana. Williams, Osei, and Omar (2012, p. 72) observe that "higher education is repeatedly positioned by the international community as a central site for facilitating the skills, knowledge, and expertise that are essential to economic and social development in low-income countries." Williams et al. (2012), examine the renaming of KNUST and its strategic implications on branding Ghana. In South Africa, for example, the Nelson Mandela Business School was named after Mandela in order to "associate the institution with hard work, integrity, and sincerity of the country's first black president" (Williams et al., 2012, p. 75). In Ghana, by changing the name from the University of Science and Technology (UST) to Kwame Nkrumah University of Science and Technology (KNUST), the institution was imitating the example of Mandela Business School in South Africa. In fact, the renaming of UST as KNUST marked a return to the original name of the institution before it was changed to UST in 1966 following a political upheaval and a change of government in Ghana. The return to the original name was intended to reinforce the founding objectives of the institution and to associate it with the positive image of Ghana's first president. As observed by Edu-Buandoh (2011) and Williams et al. (2012), the institution was seeking to exploit the positive image of Ghana's first president, and this, by association, is strongly linked to Ghana's search for identity through institutional naming and actions.

The emerging picture of branding in Ghana is a varied one, marked by inconsistency and a lack of concrete and sustainable bases for country branding. There is also "mixed" evidence in the literature of consumer expectations and bases for brand selection, as well as the ways in which organizations seek to brand. With a country, the negative effect of homogeneous branding of the continent and its effect on organizations suggest that any redress should take a dual approach to improve the country image as well as the organizations within the country. Such an approach can have a positive, synergistic effect on a country and its organizations. The key question is this: How should countries and their organizations focus their branding efforts in order to move forward?

One way of successfully branding Ghana as a country will be to harness and focus on its strengths in areas that could provide competitive advantages. On competitive advantage, Mpoyi, Festervand, and Sokoya (2006) argue that sub-Saharan Africa should dwell on its products and its environment as key bases for distinctiveness through low-cost strategy. This observation is further buttressed by Versi (2009a, p. 3), who provides more specific details on the point of environment: "Africa with its wonderful scenery, its mountains, rivers, lakes, jungles, wildlife and the extraordinary diversity and vitality of peoples and cultures, not to mention its tremendous economic potential, should be a continent made in heaven for imaginative branding." The point is that the natural environment should be exploited for branding. While this is acknowledged to be a strong possibility for sub-Saharan Africa, including Ghana, it must be admitted that the physical environment cannot be treated as a "standalone" factor in branding; it has to be viewed alongside other factors that have contributed to the creation of negative brand perception.

This notion of branding from "within" is a key subject of discussion in the work of Bonsu and Godefroit-Winkel (2016). The authors explore contemporary notions of branding that involve an element of co-creation. The consumer is not just a docile recipient of what is produced or is available, and therefore the active involvement of the consumer in developing the "preferred" brand is more likely to produce better outcomes that reflect consumer preferences. Drawing on the consumer then should culminate in the development and expression of a mutual relationship that defines the quality sought from the product or service. In this regard, the capitalist notion – the profit-seeking motive of the organization – is developed as a shared responsibility with the consumer in order to put out what may be most relevant and applicable to their needs and situation. In BoPMs, these ideas should culminate in the search for and discovery of what is unique and local. In 2014, Guinness launched an African version of the advertisement "made of more; made of black" in Ghana, which was intended to metaphorically draw on the inner strengths of the African to emphasize what is good, creative, and authentic about the color black, as it recalls the color of the Guinness beer. Here, "made of black" assumes a positive connotation, contrary to the sometimes derogatory use of "black" in relation to the history of colonization and racism. We see here that what is most relevant to the search for a successful country brand is for African countries to apply what their strengths are from within their environment and to embellish and present that as a basis for branding to the outside world.

Therefore, within the environment and culture of sub-Saharan African countries are areas of focus for branding efforts; this falls in line with the conceptualizations of Abimbola (2006). While these cultures and traditions may seem "normal" to the inhabitants of sub-Saharan Africa, they may not seem so to people on other continents. It is therefore possible to look for positive aspects of country-of-origin elements and associate them with products intended for export. The historical relics of sub-Saharan Africa will serve a very useful purpose here. In the case of Ghana, the "nostalgia" (Abimbola, 2006) associated with the slave dungeons, for example, can be better utilized for a tourist attraction. In addition, Ghana's history as the first independent country in Africa, as well as its relative political stability and "good" governance can be associated with products for export and for attracting tourists to the country (Kuada, 2013a; Kuada, 2013b).

Adding value to primary products and adopting low-cost strategies can create competitive advantage (Mpoyi et al., 2006) in order to enhance the allocation of such advantages to the country through image transfer (Gotsi, Lopez, & Andriopoulos, 2011). For example, BMW's recognition as the "ultimate driving machine" plays a part in the regard for Germany's engineering excellence. Thus, there is a synergistic effect between Germany and BMW; both country and company benefit from each other. In Ghana, natural fruit drinks can be promoted well in

export markets by emphasizing their "organic" and "ecological" nature (Abimbola, 2006; Kuada, 2013a). These expectations account for why Kastner (2005)
bemoans Ghana's failure to build and develop competitive advantage through the
exploitation of its natural produce in the world market. Kastner's study (2005)
identified a clear lack of competitive positioning strategy by Ghanaian horticultural firms attempting to export their products. Focusing on the competitiveness
of Ghana's horticultural export sector, Kastner argues that it is a natural space for
Ghana to gain a competitive advantage in the world market. The two dominant
products – pineapple and yam – together constituted about 25% of the total horticultural exports in Ghana in 2005; there exist growth capabilities to contribute
even more to Ghana's economy (Kastner, 2005). Limited barriers to entry exist in
the horticultural sector, and it is necessary to encourage and promote the sector
through a policy of openness. The industry, however, is fragmented and comprised
of a large number of small producers. This situation is attributable to factors such
as the low-level capital requirement for entry, minimal differentiation, a low level
of trust among competitors, and a tendency toward an increase in transaction costs
emanating from the aforementioned fragmented nature of the industry. Overall,
such negative factors work against competitiveness in the world market. The key
point here is that Ghana should exploit its environment, ecology, and "originality"
to sell and brand the country. Such products can serve as the driving forces for
branding the country and will include the forests, wildlife, sea coast, mountains,
and the history of its the slave dungeons. It is critical to emphasize the originality
of these products for exports to thrive in the developed world.

Conclusion

Country branding has been gaining importance as a means of marketing tourism and as part of general efforts at country development. For BoPM countries
in Africa, branding efforts include the aforementioned factors, but for such
economies branding also serves the purpose of correcting negatives image often
associated with them (Papadopoulos et al., 2016; Youde, 2009).

This chapter has presented the challenges – in terms of image, economy, and
more – encountered in branding efforts of African countries. For South Africa,
the options available for branding include leveraging its checkered political history, taking advantage of key personalities from the struggle to end apartheid, and
drawing on successful organization of globally significant events. Coming out of
a prolonged period of apartheid, it is feasible for the country to turn its historical agonies into international relations advantages. This will mean presenting the
"new" country as a peacemaker in international arbitrations. For the country to
do this successfully, it will have to be seen as exhibiting internal peace beyond the
apartheid years in order to have the credibility to arbitrate in the international
sphere on matters of race and racial discrimination. Internal peace is a precursor
for international involvement and cannot be taken for granted. This is because
countries tend to have their own challenges, both internal and international. For
example, the political acrimony in 2018 surrounding the departure of the former

president Jacob Zumah had the potential to cause the alienation of some world leaders. The key here is that South Africa was able to handle this well, even as it led to a change of leadership. In this way, the country and its leaders can project themselves as peacemakers. A dimension of this brand relates to the domineering image of Nelson Mandela as an international statesman and peaceful fighter. This has been drawn on by his family members for attracting tourists to Mandela's hometown, for example. South Africa can extend and project this well beyond Mandela's immediate family background for a greater national advantage.

The successful organization of the 2010 FIFA World Cup in South Africa surely drew the world's attention as well. Being the first African country to host this event, and doing so successfully (Bannister, 2010), the country can highlight its strengths for future benefit. In addition, South Africa is renowned for quality wines, and as noted by Herstein et al. (2014), place and product images can be interlinked. In this sense, South Africa can take advantage of its wine image around the world for positioning and branding purposes as well.

In the case of Ghana, the pioneering role in obtaining independence in Africa, and its level of relative stability and good governance, are among its positive achievements. However, the umbrella painting of sub-Saharan Africa as corrupt, dominated by poor governance, and plagued by severe economic challenges has had a negative effect on many sub-Saharan African countries, including Ghana. A number of bases for improving country branding are discussed, bearing in mind that country branding can improve the fortunes of organizations; branding success by organizations can also affect country image (Gotsi et al., 2011; Versi, 2009a, 2009b). Key among these is the need to exploit the positive elements of the environment, culture, history, and other factors in order to create nostalgia for originality. Regarding ecology as part of the heritage for branding (Abimbola, 2006) is critical as well. For example, these may manifest in artefacts as a way of boosting performance in tourism.

Different African countries may be faced with different challenges in the efforts at branding. What appears to be a predominant commonality for the majority is a negative image: Underdevelopment, hunger, corruption, poor leadership, and more. Each country will have to work to resolve these challenges, and above all, BoPM countries in Africa should individually seek to brand depending on their strengths, be they political, historical, or ecological, or even their product and service capabilities.

References

Aaker, J. L. (1997). Dimensions of brand personality. *Journal of Marketing Research, 34*(3), 347–356.

Abimbola, T. (2006). Market access for developing economies: Branding in Africa. *Place Branding, 2*(2), 108–117.

Adegoju, A. (2017). We have to tell our own story: Semiotics of resisting negative stereotypes of Nigeria in the heart of Africa nation branding campaign. *Social Semiotics, 27*(2), 158–177. http://doi.org/10.1080/10350330.2016.1172827

Angus, M. (2010, October). Marketing focus – Ghana. *Brands and Branding Intelligence*, 52–53.

Anholt, S. (2003). *Brand new justice: The upside of global branding*. Oxford: Butterworth-Heinemann.

Anholt, S. (2005). *Brand new justice: How branding places and products can help the developing world* (Revised ed.). Oxford: Butterworth-Heinemann.

Anholt, S. (2006). The Anholt: GMI city brands index: How the world sees the world's cities. *Place Branding and Public Diplomacy*, 2(1), 18–31.

Asiedu, A. B. (2008). Participants characteristics and economic benefits of visiting friends and relatives tourism: An international survey of the literature with implications for Ghana. *International Journal of Tourism Research*, 10, 609–621.

Bannister, P. (2010). South Africa: Key lessons in nation branding. *Brands and Branding Intelligence*, 37–39.

Blankson, C., Owusu-Frempong, Y., & Mbah, C. H. N. (2004). An investigation of Ghana's tourism positioning. *Journal of African Business*, 5(2), 113–136.

Bonsu, S. K., & Godefroit, D. (2016). Guinness in Africa: Contemporary branding at the base of the pyramid. In F. D. Riley, J. Singh, & C. Blankson (Eds.), *The Routledge companion to contemporary brand management* (pp. 391–403). Abingdon: Routledge.

Chikweche, T. (2013). Marketing at the bottom of pyramid: Market attractiveness and strategic requirements. *Marketing Intelligence and Planning*, 31(7), 764–787.

Chikweche, T., & Fletcher, R. (2011). Branding at the base of the pyramid: A Zimbabwean perspective. *Marketing Intelligence and Planning*, 29(3), 247–263.

Coffie, S., & Darmoe, J. (2016). Branding in the base of the pyramid: Bases for country and organisations in Ghana. In F. D. Riley, J. Singh, & C. Blankson (Eds.), *The Routledge companion to contemporary brand management* (pp. 378–390). Abingdon, UK: Routledge.

Cornelissen, S. (2017). National meaning-making in complex societies: Political legitimation and branding dynamics in post-apartheid South Africa. *Geopolitics*, 22(3), 525–548. https://doi.org/10.1080/14650045.2017.1278695

Cravens, D. W., & Piercy, N. F. (2013). *Strategic marketing*. New York, NY: McGraw-Hill.

Daily Guide. (2014). *IMF, Ghana begin formal talks today*. Retrieved from www.ghanaweb.com/GhanaHomePage/NewsArchive/artikel.php?ID=330340#

Edu-Buandoh, D. F. (2011). Discourse in institutional administration of public universities in Ghana: A shift towards a market paradigm? *African Nebula*, 3, 86–98.

Epic Global Media. (2012). *A documentary and branding commercial on Ghana*. Retrieved from www.epicglobalmedia.com

Ghana Budget. (2002). *Government of Ghana budget statement presented by the minister of finance to parliament*. Retrieved from www.ghanaweb.com

Goff, P., & Dunn, K. (2004). Introduction: In defence of identity. In P. Goff & K. Dunn (Eds.), *Identity and global politics*. Basingstoke: Palgrave Macmillan.

Gotsi, M., Lopez, C., & Andriopoulos, C. (2011). Building country image through corporate image: Exploring the factors that influence the image transfer. *Journal of Strategic Marketing*, 19(3), 255–272.

Herstein, R., Berger, R., & Jaffe, E. D. (2014). How companies from developing and emerging countries can leverage their brand equity in terms of place branding. *Competitiveness Review*, 24(4), 293–305.

Kastner, A. N. A. (2005). Competitiveness of Ghana's horticultural export sector. In J. Kuada (Ed.), *Internationalisation and enterprise development in Ghana* (pp. 25–53). London: Adonis and Abbey.

Kuada, J. (2013a). Danso fruit drinks Ghana limited. In G. Tesar & J. Kuada (Eds.), *Marketing management and strategy: An African casebook* (pp. 164–175). London: Routledge.

Kuada, J. (2013b). Ghana craft company. In G. Tesar & J. Kuada (Eds.), *Marketing management and strategy: An African casebook* (pp. 235–243). London: Routledge.

Mpoyi, R. T., Festervand, T. A., & Sokoya, S. K. (2006). Creating a global competitive advantage for sub-Saharan African companies. *Journal of African Business*, 7, 119–137.

Myjoyonline.com. (2019). Retrieved from www.myjoyonline.com/business/2018/june-25th/brand-ghana-office-doesnt-exist-tourism-authority-boss.php

Opoku, R., & Hinson, R. (2005). Online brand personalities: An exploratory analysis of selected African countries. *Place Branding*, 2(2), 118–129.

Papadopoulos, N., Hamzaoui-Essoussi, L., & Rojas-Mendez, J. I. (2016). From nation to neighbourhood: Branding and marketing places. In F. D. Riley, J. Singh, & C. Blankson (Eds.), *The Routledge companion to contemporary brand management* (pp. 458–472). Abingdon: Routledge.

Riley, F. D. (2016). Brand definitions and conceptualisations: The debate. In F. D. Riley, J. Singh, & C. Blankson (Eds.), *The Routledge companion to contemporary brand management* (pp. 3–12). Abingdon: Routledge.

Versi, A. (2009a). Branding Africa's products. *African Business*, 358.

Versi, A. (2009b). The power of branding. *African Business*, 358.

Williams Jr., R., Osei, C., & Omar, M. (2012). Higher education institution branding as a component of country branding in Ghana: Renaming Kwame Nkrumah University of Science and Technology. *Journal of Marketing For Higher Education*, 22(1), 71–81.

World Tourism Organization. (2007). Looking forward to fourth year of sustained growth. *UNWTO News*, 1.

Youde, J. (2009). Selling the state: State branding as a political resource in South Africa. *Place Branding and Public Diplomacy*, 5(2), 126–140.

7 Corporate reputation, brand crisis, and customer loyalty in BoPMs and developed economies

"Successful global marketing is about collaboration, strong organizational structures and a clear brand vision," says Lego's chief marketing officer, Julia Goldin.

(Bewick, 2017, p. 33)

Introduction

The contemporary global business environment is both challenging and very different from the global business landscape of 20 years ago. Many international firms are combining multi-domestic marketing approaches to global marketing approaches, impacting their brand purpose and branding strategies (Schuiling & Kapferer, 2004; Adekambi, Ingenbleek, & van Trijp, 2015; Aaker, 2017). Simultaneously, the globalization of markets has placed brands, both global and local, at the center of competition (Ozsomer & Altaras, 2008; Bewick, 2017) which makes them prone to trust-damaging crises (Aaker, 2017). As stated by Jonathan Gabay, brand psychologist, and author: "there have been so many crises that we're in serious danger of getting to a point where brands are simply perceived to be protecting their own interests" (Catalyst, 2016, p. 20).

In the 1970s, for example, Pinto fuel system design decisions resulted in Ford introducing and selling a vehicle that presented a serious fire hazard in rear-end collisions (Teagarden, 2017, p. 139). In 2010, Toyota was embroiled in a scandal relating to faulty accelerator pedals that caused vehicles to suddenly accelerate. Toyota's delay in responding to the problem resulted in the deaths of 89 people and the subsequent recall of 8.8 million vehicles at a cost of US$3.1 billion (Teagarden, 2017). Then, in September 2015, Volkswagen made headlines when they were forced to recall nearly 500,000 diesel cars in the United States. Within a few days, Volkswagen saw a massive sell-off of its stock, wiping out US$16.9 billion of the firm's market value (Jung & Park, 2017, p. 127). Major damage to the company's brand image was incurred when Volkswagen's CEO apologized for "cheating on emissions tests" (Bomey, 2015, p. 1A) and went on to admit that its 11 million diesel vehicles worldwide were equipped with a defect device that disguised emission levels in laboratory diesel-exhaust emissions tests. In spite of the much-publicized Volkswagen and Toyota brand crises in recent years, unfortunately, little is documented about the reaction of individuals who are already loyal to a firm following a crisis (Jung & Park, 2017; Catalyst, 2016). This gap in the extant literature has given the impetus for this chapter.

In the midst of challenges posed by varying cultural dimensions in the global marketplace (Cayla & Arnould, 2008; Guzman & Paswan, 2009) exists the pressing question of how loyal customers' trust in brands works (see Dimofte, Johansson, & Ronkainen, 2008), especially during times of brand crises (Jung & Park, 2017; Aaker, 2017). At the same time, continuous research on corporate reputation for firms that seek to successfully accumulate competitive advantages and subsequently position themselves in the market has been called for by marketing scholars and practitioners (Klein & Dawar, 2004; Abd-El-Salam, Shawky, & El-Nahas, 2013). Corporate reputation is a critical factor in the overall evaluation of firms' competitive advantage (Sarstedt, Wilczynski, & Melewar, 2012) because of the strength that lies in customers' perceptions of a firm (Mahon, 2002). The importance of understanding the links between corporate reputation, brand crisis, and customer loyalty is called for by both marketing scholars and practitioners (e.g., Aaker, 2017; Cretu & Brodie, 2007; Bewick, 2017) and underscores the potential contribution of this chapter.

Although research has shown that a relationship exists between corporate reputation and customer loyalty (Merchant, Rose, Moody, & Mathews, 2015; Nguyen & Leblanc, 2001), there remains a need for an ongoing understanding of how the customer loyalty construct is influenced either directly or indirectly by corporate reputation (Abd-El-Salam et al., 2013; Cretu & Brodie, 2009) and in different environments: both base of the pyramid markets (BoPMs) and developed markets.

In spite of the interest shown in corporate reputation literature, there have been contradictory findings about the role corporate reputation plays when a brand crisis occurs. While studies show corporate reputation can act as an "insurance policy" or buffer if developed prior to the occurrence of a brand crisis (Decker, 2012; Roberts & Dowling, 2002), others purport that a strong corporate reputation can be detrimental to a firm in the event of a crisis (Keh & Xie, 2009; Rhee & Haunschild, 2006). Furthermore, studies have shown that brand crisis can alter customers' knowledge of a brand as well as their favorability of associations, affecting their perceptions of brands (e.g., Dawar & Pillutla, 2000). Unfortunately, despite the frequency and severe consequences of brand crisis, little research about its impact on key marketing constructs – such as brand evaluations, loyalty, or purchase likelihood (Dawar & Lei, 2009) – exists (see Appendix 1). These are important issues, worthy of empirical research; hence, the need for this study.

Responding to calls from Nguyen and Leblanc (2001), Zins (2001), and Dawar and Lei (2009) in order to close the gaps in the literature, the purpose of the research discussed in this chapter is to examine the relationships among corporate reputation, brand crisis, and customer loyalty. Pursuant to the purpose of this study, the main objective of this research is to examine how corporate reputation influences customer loyalty and how brand crisis, in turn, influences corporate reputation and customer loyalty (Aaker, 2017). More specifically, the study seeks to do the following:

1   Explore the established relationship between corporate reputation and customer loyalty.
2   Investigate the influence of brand crisis on corporate reputation.
3   Investigate the influence of brand crisis on customer loyalty.
4   Investigate if and whether attributions moderate the relationship between brand crisis and corporate reputation.

Apart from serving as the prelude to a stream of research in this domain, this study has been necessitated by calls for more attention to and the stronger integration of the loyalty concept into nomological relationships with other constructs of marketing theory (Opare, Blankson, and Nkrumah, 2017). It also seeks to expand the limited research on the impact of a brand crisis on customers who are already loyal to the firm that is in difficulty (Dawar & Lei, 2009). Further, to the best of our knowledge, most of the studies related to the research topic have not only been conducted in advanced developed economies (see Merchant et al., 2015; Decker, 2012; Yannopoulou, Koronis, & Elliott, 2011) to the exclusion of fast-expanding markets in BoPMs in Africa (Kuada & Buatsi, 2005), but studies comparing two culturally and economically different economies at varying levels of economic development (e.g., Ghana and the United States) have been overlooked by marketing scholars (see Appendix I).

Ghana and the United States serve as illustrations for this research. In international marketing, context matters in explaining the relationship between corporate reputation, brand crisis, and customer loyalty. Although our selection of these two countries was convenience based, we were interested in a variation on perceptions of the constructs (corporate reputation, brand crisis, and customer loyalty). Further, because most cross-national studies have overlooked the fast-expanding economies of Africa, choosing two samples that vary culturally and economically will present a more robust framework for the constructs under study.

Two key contributions intended to fill substantive, theoretical, managerial, and contextual gaps in the literature emerge from this research. First, this chapter identifies sources of sustainable competitive advantages that enhance the deployment of distinctive, inimitable, and protected marketing strategies (Mahon, 2002). Thus, by extending corporate-reputation and consumer-behavior literatures, this study provides organizations with knowledge and understanding of how corporate reputation influences customer loyalty. Second, in the absence of research activity comparing data from BoPMs and developed economies, this study comes at an opportune time in a changing, complex, and often dysfunctional business environment (Diwan, 2016) while serving as an overture to new research in branding in the international marketplace (Cayla & Arnould, 2008; Ozsomer & Altaras, 2008; Kuada & Buatsi, 2005; Orth et al., 2012).

The subsequent sections of the chapter are organized as follows. First, the literature review and conceptual framework underpinning the study and related hypotheses are presented. This is followed by the methodology, the results of the analyses in study one and study two, the discussion, and conclusion. Theoretical and managerial implications are then discussed, followed by limitations of the study and avenues for further research.

Literature and conceptual framework

In order to highlight the gaps in the literature – and upon suggestions from three academic experts – a thorough search of published articles relating to corporate reputation, brand crisis, and customer loyalty was conducted. The content of these articles (see Appendix I) was thoroughly analyzed, and it reveals two main gaps that further underscore the impetus for this research: Namely, the lack of comprehensive studies and frameworks exploring the links between corporate reputation, brand crisis, and customer loyalty, and the missing discourse on the latter in comparative studies involving fast-expanding African economies such as Ghana and advanced developed economies such as the United States. For both scholars and practitioners, these two culturally and economically different countries are compared to enhance understanding and appreciation of approaches to branding in a changing global marketplace (see also Cayla & Arnould, 2008; Guzman & Paswan, 2009; Kuada & Buatsi, 2005; Adekambi et al., 2015).

Corporate reputation

Fombrun and Shanley (1990) define corporate reputation as a perceptual representation of a company's past actions and future prospects that describe the firm's overall appeal to all its key constituents when compared to other leading rivals. According to Whetten and Mackey (2002), corporate reputation is "a particular type of feedback received by a firm from its stakeholders (customers, investors, employees, etc.), concerning the credibility of the organization's identity claims." In more practical terms and consistent with Coombs (2007), a firm's reputation is characterized as the result of the impressions of all stakeholders, both internal and external (Chun, 2005). Thus, in general, the perceptual nature of corporate reputation cannot be overemphasized since researchers consider corporate reputation to be an organizational attribute associated with stakeholders' perceptions of the firm.

How, then, is corporate reputation formed? Mahon (2002) argues that corporate reputation is built over time as a result of complex interrelationships and exchanges between a firm and its stakeholders. Furthermore, the beliefs that a customer holds about a firm based upon their experiences with the firm, their relationship to it, as well as their knowledge gained through word of mouth or mass media all shape a firm's corporate reputation in the mind of the consumer (Barnett, Jermier, & Lafferty, 2006; York, Gumbus, & Lilley, 2008).

Corporate reputation is considered to be a critical factor in the overall evaluation of any firm because of the strength that lies in customers' perceptions of a firm. Research has shown that corporate reputation is a valuable resource for the firm (Sarstedt et al., 2012) because it creates and enhances sustainable competitive advantage (Mahon, 2002) by attracting more and possibly higher-caliber employees, investors, and customers (Walker, 2010; Gardberg & Fombrun, 2002). More so, Fombrun and Shanley (1990) argue that firms are in competition for reputation just as they are for customers, and since firms operate in markets characterized by imperfect information, a favorable corporate reputation will enhance a competitive and differential advantage (Dawar & Pillutla, 2000).

Brand crisis

The concept of brand crisis has gained a wider understanding in recent years by both academics and practitioners. Brand crises have been widely defined by researchers as "the unexpected events that threaten a brand's perceived ability to deliver expected benefits" (Ahluwalia, Burnkrant, & Rao, 2000; Dawar & Lei, 2009; Pullig, Netemeyer, & Biswas, 2006). However, for the purpose of this chapter, the most preferred definition is that of Dutta and Pullig (2011), who assert that brand crises are adverse events that threaten brand reputations.

Crises involving brands such as Coca Cola in Europe, Firestone in the United States, Snow Milk in Japan, and more recently, Volkswagen in the United States and in Europe (Bomey, 2015; Ewing, 2016) have created customer and media awareness and sensitivity around the world. A rather untoward example of brand crises is that of Sanlu, an infant formula manufacturing company based in China: In September 2008, 6,244 babies were diagnosed with numerous ailments after ingesting poisonous infant formula (People Daily, 2008). Having used all of its cash reserves for product recall and medical payments, Sanlu was declared bankrupt in 2009, and the company folded. This example clearly corroborates the devastating effects of brand crises on firms.

Brand crises are conceptualized in two broad types: Performance-related and values-related (Pullig et al., 2006). Performance-related crises usually involve defective products, and primarily reduce a brand's perceived ability to deliver functional benefits (Dawar & Pillutla, 2000). On the other hand, values-related crises, which are the main focus of this study since they are the most observed form of brand crisis in the global marketplace (Kim & Atkinson, 2014), do not directly involve the product or attributes that deliver functional benefits, but instead involve social or ethical issues that implicate the values espoused by the brand (Aaker, 2017). These crises call into question the brand's ability to deliver symbolic and psychological benefits (Pullig et al., 2006). Thus, performance-related crises largely affect confidence related to functional benefits and values-related crises affect confidence related to symbolic benefits, though both affect common outcomes such as overall brand attitude or brand choice (Pullig et al., 2006; Kim & Atkinson, 2014; Aaker, 2017).

Attribution theory

Attributions are defined as the causal explanations that individuals use to interpret events viewed as important, novel, unexpected, and negative (Martinko, Harvey, & Dasborough, 2011). Weiner (1980) identifies two traits of attributions –

unexpected and negative – as key drivers of a person's need to search for the causes of an event. Weiner's (1980) attribution model conceptualizes three causal dimensions of attribution that lead to an overall judgment of responsibility or blame: First, the locus of the behavior (the event that triggers the crisis), which can be internal or external to the actor (in this case, the firm); second, the stability of the behavior, which can be unchanging or temporary; and finally, the controllability of the behavior, which can be within or outside the control of the actor.

In the event of a negative situation, people seek a causal explanation (Whelan & Dawar, 2016). In a customer context, the latter involves determining whether the brand in question had control over the outcome (i.e., attributions of *controllability*) and assessing the likelihood that the outcome will reoccur (i.e., attributions of *stability*) (Whelan & Dawar, 2016). Attribution theory has been applied in the marketing domain to explain customers' brand evaluations. Klein and Dawar (2004) find corporate social responsibility (CSR) associations may have a significant impact when customers rely on corporate associations to inform their judgments. Furthermore, Lei, Dawar, and Gürhan-Canli (2012) conducted an investigation to determine whether attributions that are influenced by base-rate information affect customers' blame of a brand in the event of a crisis. Their findings suggest that less blame is ascribed to brands with positive prior beliefs if the crisis is similar to others in the industry, and in the absence of similarity information, a low base-rate of crisis leads to less blame toward the brand. Orth et al. (2012) find that brand-related attributions fully mediate the influence of pleasure and satisfaction on brand attachments. Also, the study results of Zhou and Whitla (2013) reveal the crucial role of the evaluation of moral reputation in shaping respondents' reactions to a poorly behaving celebrity and their endorsed brands.

From a marketing perspective and for the purpose of this study, attributions are important because they form the basis of customers' perceptions and opinions about a brand which has weathered a crisis (Aaker, 1996; Kim & Atkinson, 2014). Furthermore, it is important for firms to know how customers make attributions in the event of a crisis, since customers rely on information, including corporate associations, to construct these attributions. Specifically, the impact of a brand crisis on customers' brand perceptions and brand reputations can be devastating. Thus, even if a brand is later exonerated, the damage already caused by customer attributions of blame can be irreversible, leading to customer complaints, negative word of mouth, decreased brand loyalty, and subsequent reduction in purchase intentions (Whelan & Dawar, 2016, pp. 285–286). Along these lines and consistent with the aforementioned studies, this study examines whether attributions moderate the relationship between corporate reputation and brand crisis.

Customer loyalty

A critical issue for the continued success of a firm is its capability to retain its current customers and make them loyal to its brand (Sathish, Kumar, Naveen, & Jeevanantham, 2011). This is because there is a general consensus among marketing scholars that it costs more to gain a new customer than it does to retain an existing one (Dawar & Lei, 2009). Moreover, developing, maintaining, and enhancing customer loyalty toward a firm's products or services is generally considered the central thrust of marketing activities (Dick & Basu, 1994). Andreassen and Lindestad (1998) claim that customer loyalty expresses an intended behavior related to the firm, which includes the willingness to repurchase from the firm in the future and the willingness to provide positive word of mouth about the firm and recommend the patronage of the firm to others. For the purpose of this study, it is assumed that a loyal customer is one who repurchases from the same firm whenever possible and who continues to recommend or maintains a positive attitude towards the firm.

There have been a number of attempts to develop typologies of loyalty. The marketing literature suggests that customer loyalty can be defined in two distinct dimensions: Attitudinal and behavioral (Oliver, 1999; Zeithaml, 2000). The first defines loyalty as an attitude whereby different feelings create an individual's overall attachment to a product, service, or firm (Fornier, 1994). These feelings define the individual's (purely cognitive) degree of loyalty. The second definition of loyalty is behavioral. The loyalty behavior includes continuing to purchase from the same firm, increasing the scale and or scope of a relationship with a firm, or the act of recommending the firm to others (Yi, 1990). This is consistent with prior studies that have used both attitudinal and behavioral measures to define and assess customer loyalty (Jacoby & Kyner, 1973; Dick & Basu, 1994). Similarly, Odin, Odin, and Florence (2001) assert that there are two basic approaches to defining customer loyalty: Stochastic and deterministic loyalty. The stochastic approach assumes that customer loyalty is a behavior while the deterministic approach assumes customer loyalty is an attitude.

Loyalty can be of substantial value to both customers and to the firm. Customers are willing to invest their loyalty in a firm that can deliver superior value relative to the offerings of competitors (Reichheld, 1996). Ahluwalia et al. (2000) have shown that loyal customers are much less susceptible to negative information about a brand than non-loyal customers. Furthermore, loyal customers are inclined to forgive customer-service mishaps, display decreased sensitivity to price, and disseminate positive word of mouth about the firm to others (Heskett, 2002). Moreover, building on the preceding literature review, this study proposes that corporate reputation impacts customer loyalty while brand crisis influences the "reputation-loyalty" relationship. This study further posits that attributions moderate the relationship between brand crisis and corporate reputation. Figure 7.1 depicts the conceptual framework showing the specific relationships among the constructs together with the hypotheses that are discussed in the subsequent section.

The relationship between brand crisis and customer loyalty

Available studies have shown the effects of brand crisis on customer loyalty (e.g., Huber, Vollhardt, Matthes, & Vogel, 2010; Dawar & Lei, 2009; Cleeren, Dekimpe, & Helsen, 2008). Yannopoulou et al. (2011) assert that brand crises

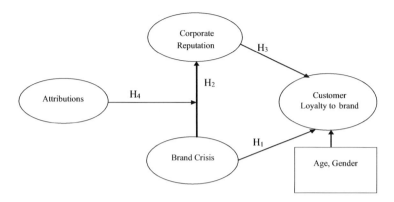

Figure 7.1 Conceptual framework exploring the links between corporate reputation, brand crisis, and customer loyalty

initiate perceptions of risk, and perceptions of risk negatively affect brand trust. According to Coombs (2007) and Aaker (2017), brand crises can cause a firm's stakeholders, including customers, to end their associations with the firm and make negative statements to others concerning the firm. Literature reveals that brand crisis can change customers' purchase behaviors and, in extreme cases, drive away some customers of the brand altogether (Ma, Zhang, Li, & Wang, 2010; Bomey, 2015). Along these lines, the first hypothesis of this study is this:

H1: Brand crises have a negative relationship with customer loyalty.

The relationship between brand crisis and corporate reputation

Extant literature indicates contradictory findings about the role corporate reputation plays in brand crises. Decker (2012) asserts that a good reputation can act as an "insurance policy" or buffer if it has been developed prior to the occurrence of a brand crisis; this is in line with cognitive dissonance theory. According to this theory, people are motivated to resolve inconsistencies in their perceptions, and in doing so exhibit a confirmatory bias toward perceiving later information in a manner that is consistent with earlier information (Grunwald & Hempelmann, 2010). This assertion suggests that even in the event of brand crises, a firm with a favorable corporate reputation will benefit from positive consumer impressions. Thus, the consumer may consider brand crises as exceptions to his or her impression of the firm as a whole (see Opare, Blankson, and Nkrumah, 2017).

Conversely, another school of thought purports that having a strong corporate reputation can be detrimental, particularly when firms are faced with crises (Keh & Xie, 2009). Rhee and Haunschild (2006) illustrate the liability of good reputation through a study of product recalls in the United States automobile industry. Specifically, their findings reveal that firms with good reputations suffer more than those with poor reputations when they make mistakes, which may be due to the contrasting effect of the disconfirmation of high expectation (Herr, 1989).

More generally, the literature reveals that brand crises can alter customers' knowledge of a brand as well as their perception of favorability of associations (Dawar & Pillutla, 2000; Keller, 1993). Klein and Dawar (2004) note that brand crises can imperil long-standing favorable customer impressions about a brand. In the same vein, Coombs (2007) contends that brand crises can threaten a firm's reputation because they give people reasons to think negatively of the firm, and since such crises are usually sudden and unexpected, they threaten to disrupt a firm's operations and pose financial and reputational problems. Clearly, brand crises can seriously harm stakeholders, including customers, physically, emotionally, and/or financially, as well as endanger a brand's performance; in extreme cases, they can even destroy a company, as in the case of Sanlu. These assertions suggest the presence of a close relationship between brand crisis and corporate reputation. Consequently, a second hypothesis is put forward:

H2: Brand crisis has a negative relationship with corporate reputation.

The relationship between corporate reputation and customer loyalty

Existing literature has identified a close relationship between corporate reputation and customer loyalty. Walsh and Beatty (2007) proffer the idea that a firm's reputation is a surrogate indicator of the quality of its offerings, and since customers tend to prefer to deal with firms that have proven reliable in the past, a favorable reputation may stimulate continuous purchase by simplifying decision procedures for customers, consequently making them loyal. Empirical evidence also demonstrates the effect of corporate reputation on customer loyalty (Merchant et al., 2015; Abd-El-Salam et al., 2013; Walsh & Beatty, 2007). Studies conducted on corporate reputation and customer loyalty include that of Nguyen and Leblanc (2001) who empirically test the nature of the relationship between corporate reputation and corporate image and their effects on customers' retention decisions using data from three service industries: The retail, telecommunications, and educational sectors. The results of the study suggest that when the perceptions of both corporate reputation and corporate image are strongly favorable, the degree of customer loyalty has a tendency to be higher.

Cretu and Brodie (2009) provide support for the argument that what most influences the likelihood of a customer engaging with a specific product or service is the association the customer has with about the product or service (Keller, 1993). Keh and Xie (2009) assert that corporate reputation has a positive influence on customer trust and identification and that customer commitment mediates the relationships among customer trust, customer identification, and behavioral intentions. Abd-El-Salam et al. (2013) provided empirical support for the significant relationships among corporate image and reputation, overall service quality, customer satisfaction, and customer loyalty based on a case study in an international environment. In a recent study, Merchant et al. (2015) examine the impact of heritage and reputation of nonprofit universities when it comes to the attitudes of prospective students. The results of this study show that there are significant relationships among university heritage, university reputation, student attitudes, intentions to recommend, and intentions to pay premium. Consistent with the aforementioned views, a firm's reputation is positively associated with customers' loyalty to the firm, which leads to the formulation of the third hypothesis of this study:

H3: Corporate reputation has a positive relationship with customer loyalty.

The moderating role of attributions on the relationship between brand crisis and corporate reputation

Theoretical support for the postulated effects of brand crisis on corporate reputation can be derived from the *Attribution theory* (Weiner, 1980). It is logical to connect brand crises and attribution theory because they both share two key traits; namely, they are unexpected and negative. Indeed, extant research forges a link between brand crises and attribution theory (Jorgensen, 1996; McDonald & Hartel, 2000). Moreover, by extension of attribution theory, it is logical to expect customers to engage in making attributions about a firm's corporate reputation, especially if the firm has suffered a crisis. According to Johar (1996), in the event of brand crisis, customers are likely to start thinking about the crisis event and why it happened if they had not previously perceived a pattern of crisis-prone behavior in the firm's activities. More so, Johar, Birk, and Elnwiller (2010) assert that consumers reading or hearing about brand crises are likely to make attributions about the cause of these crises. They will assess crisis responsibility by asking themselves a predictable set of questions including the following: Is it true? Was the crisis a result of situational factors or something the firm did? Will the brand do this again? What does this event say about the brand? If the firm is deemed responsible, its reputation will suffer. In turn, customers may exit the relationship and/or create negative word of mouth about the brand.

Although customers are unlikely to respond in a homogeneous manner when brand crises occur due to their unique prior expectations about a firm (Dawar & Pillutla, 2000), their level of commitment towards the brand (Ahluwalia et al., 2000), the firm's corporate reputation (Siomkos & Kurzbard, 1994), or the brand's personality (Aaker, Fournier, & Brasel, 2004), they spontaneously construct attributions of blame (Folkes, 1984). Existing studies that have applied Weiner's (1980) model to customers' attributions in the context of brand crisis have provided compelling evidence for the effects of attributions on customers' attitudes and behavior (Folkes, 1984; Jorgensen, 1996). Consequently, this study anticipates that attributions will moderate the relationship between brand crises and firms' corporate reputations. This leads us to the next hypothesis:

H4: Attributions moderate the relationship between brand crisis and corporate reputation such that brand crisis will have a positive effect on corporate reputation for individuals with low attributions about the crisis and have a negative effect on corporate reputation for individuals with high attributions.

Control variables

Demographic characteristics are useful in obtaining information about consumer attitudes and consumer behavior in general. Past literature has cited demographic characteristics – including age, gender, and education – as control variables (see Ndubisi, 2006; Homburg & Giering, 2001). Moreover, previous studies link demographic characteristics to the ways in which people choose to explain and justify their actions and evaluations of organizations' marketing activities (see Galan-Ladero, Casquet, & Singh, 2015). In order to rule out alternative explanations, we considered demographic characteristics – including age and gender – as control variables, which is not without precedent (see for example Ndubisi, 2006).

STUDY ONE

Methodology

Our discussion with academic experts and practitioners in our initial pilot studies in Ghana and the United States suggested the importance of obtaining perceptions from executives prior to surveying the general public. The latter is consistent with Ertekin's (2009) study of foreign-based franchises in the fast food sector. To that end, following Kim and Atkinson (2014), and to shed light on the topic, in study one, a qualitative method involving unstructured face-to-face and telephone interviews was used in our two environments (Ghana and the United States) in order to gauge executives' actual thoughts and views about the relationships among corporate reputation, brand crisis, and customer loyalty and thereby elicit in-depth accounts of their perspectives, thereby enhancing our understanding of the study and our appreciation of the study settings (Davis, Golicic, Boerstler, Choi, & Oh, 2013). The use of multiple research methods in marketing research is important and is called for in the wake of mounting criticisms for overreliance on a small set of quantitative methods which has the potential to delimit the scope of inquiries and its attendant lack of trust in findings (see Davis et al., 2013, pp. 1245–1246, p. 1248).

Sample and data collection

Convenience and snowball techniques were employed in the selection of respondents. The Ghana Club 100 (2010) directory of firms in Ghana and the Yellow pages directory covering firms in a large metropolitan area in the state of Texas,

United States, provided the sample frames for the populations. The formal definition of these populations includes brand managers, marketing managers, heads of marketing, corporate communication specialists, chief executives, and academic experts with an interest in and focus on branding. The decision to seek information from executives and experts is in line with Dalebout and Wierenga's (1997) suggestions about the importance of soliciting executives' and experts' opinions and perceptions about complex marketing knowledge. In addition, using experts in business-related research is accepted by scholars as a valid way of obtaining consensus and developing a holistic appreciation of relevant issues (Winkler, 1981).

A total of 21 respondents from small, medium, and large firms in the Accra-Tema Metropolitan area in the Greater Accra region of Ghana and 18 respondents from similar industry domains in the Dallas Fort-Worth Metroplex in the state of Texas, United States, participated in face-to-face and telephone interviews. The samples were representative across all industries: Industrial, B2B, FMCG, services, and manufacturing sectors. Following email and telephone introductions, an interview guide (see Frey, 1989) was sent via email to some of the respondents who requested them. Appointments for the interviews were arranged through emails and follow-up telephone calls.

Topics explored in the interviews were based on the objectives of this study – the determination of a link between corporate reputation, brand crisis, and customer loyalty. The interview questions were open-ended, thereby encouraging the respondents to express their views (Frey, 1989; Kim & Atkinson, 2014). The interviews lasted between 20 and 60 minutes. During these interviews, the discussion was allowed to develop naturally while the interviewers ensured that key areas were also addressed (McCracken, 1998). Respondents were allowed to expand upon the interview topics, thereby generating richer information (illustrated through quotes) to bring the qualitative data to life (Daymon & Holloway, 2004). Participants were offered anonymity, and notes were taken concurrently with an audio tape recording made during each interview. The interviews were carried out intermittently over a period of two months (February and March) in 2015 in Ghana and two months (April and May) in 2015 in the United States.

Reliability and validity

In view of the subjective nature of qualitative data, we adhered to Sweeney and Chew's (2002) and Dubois and Gadde's (2002) suggestions for validity and reliability in qualitative research by testing "pattern matching." The latter involved researchers checking to ensure that inferences made are airtight. In addition, we sent a summary of the findings, including the emanating themes, to three marketing academics and two brand experts in the United States and two marketing academics and two brand experts in Ghana for their comments and suggestions. The experts and academics agreed with the inferences and the resulting themes. Their suggestions were subsequently incorporated into the final version of this study.

Analysis and results

The responses gathered from our notes and audio recording were thematically analyzed following suggestions of Mishler (1990). Thematic analysis is a search for themes that emerge which are important to the description of a phenomenon. The process involves the identification of themes through "careful reading and re-reading of the data." The analysis was informed by the approach of Miles and Huberman (1994) as well as that of Obeng and Blundel (2015), where responses that demonstrated semantic similarity were attached to one of the defined dimensions derived from questions. To that end, the responses gathered from each respondent were carefully read after the interviews were carried out to gain familiarity with what the respondents articulated and to develop initial ideas about the meaning of their statements and their relationships to other statements noted in the entire interview process and in the literature. Furthermore, the responses gathered from the interviewees were consistently reread by the authors, both separately and in combination, to help identify and select major themes, develop categories, explore similarities and differences that run through the responses, and discover relationships based on inductive reasoning (Sweeney & Chew, 2002; Dubois & Gadde, 2002). The emerging themes from the qualitative studies are placed in Appendix II. Detailed verbatim comments from the qualitative studies are available upon request from the authors.

Conclusion

Study one highlights the close relationships among the research constructs and thus supports the study hypotheses. All interviewees acknowledged the significant impact of brand crisis on corporate reputation. The interviewees acknowledged that brand crisis both directly and indirectly influences customer loyalty. However, the views about the relationship between corporate reputation and consumer loyalty to the brand were not uniform, although they all pointed to the fact that a relationship does exist between the two. The interviewees also confirmed the link between brand crisis and attribution as established in the literature, suggesting the possibility of a moderating effect of attribution on the relationship between brand crisis and corporate reputation.

STUDY TWO

Methodology

Data collection and sample

The data for study two consist of responses from 525 Ghanaian and 321 American consumers. In order to appreciate the study setting and test the questionnaire, prior to the main study, a pilot study involving 50 MBA students at a major university in Accra, Ghana, was undertaken in April and May 2015. A similar pilot study involving 38 MBA students and 10 doctoral students at a large public university in the southwestern United States was undertaken in September and October 2016. Not only did these approaches provide an opportunity to ensure clarity of the questionnaire items, avoid vague concepts, and keep the questions as simple, "respondent-friendly," specific, and concise as possible (Dillman, Smyth, & Christian, 2009), but they also solicited customers' opinions and perceptions about marketing activities (Dalebout & Wierenga, 1997).

The study in Ghana was conducted between April and May 2015 and involved a drop-off-and-collect (Ibeh, Brock, & Zhou, 2004) simple random sampling approach involving self-completion of a four-page survey. Specifically, 35 MBA and MPhil students and 2 faculty members from a leading business school in Accra were hired and worked with one of the authors to personally administer the questionnaires to respondents' homes; 700 questionnaires were administered in a one-wave drop-off and collect survey to a random sample of members of the general public across ten residential areas in Accra (specifically, Adenta, Ashongman Estates, Labone Estates, North Kaneshie, Laterbiokorshie, Osu, Dzorwulu, West Legon, East Legon, and North Legon). There were 525 fully completed questionnaires collected after two rounds of questionnaire pick-up, giving an overall response rate of 75%. As shown in Appendix III, the gender pattern of the respondents clearly shows that there were more women (270, i.e., 51.4%) than men (48.6%). The results show that 305 out of the 525 respondents had completed either a polytechnic or university degree (58.1%), and the remaining had either a secondary school certificate, master's degree, or professional certification.

Similar to the study in Ghana, data collection commenced in November 2016 through March 2017 in the United States. Unlike Ghana, the postal system of the United States is highly developed and hence a slightly different approach was used in this setting. For extra credit in classes taught by one of the authors and two classes taught by two doctoral students, students using the mall intercept approach randomly distributed questionnaires to members of the general public in a major metropolitan area in the southwestern United States via a drop-off and mail-back technique (see Ibeh et al., 2004). The 700 questionnaires distributed yielded 380 responses. After eliminating incomplete responses, 321 questionnaires were kept for analysis (a 45.8% response rate) in a one-wave survey. The results reveal that more men completed the survey than women (55% and 45%, respectively) And 65% of the respondents were in college compared to 13.4% with a college degree and 13.7% with a graduate degree (i.e., Master's) (see Appendix III).

Measures

We adapted tested and proven measures from prior studies to build our questionnaire. The items used in this study were anchored on a seven-point Likert scale, ranging from "1: strongly disagree" to "7: strongly agree." We measured attribution using three items taken from Dawar and Pillutla (2000) and Weiner (1980). The four-item scales for corporate reputation, brand crisis, and customer loyalty were adapted from Cretu and Brodie (2007), Yang and Peterson

(2004), and Zeithaml, Berry, and Parasuraman (1996), respectively. In order to rule out alternative explanations in which people chose to explain and justify their loyalty attitudes, evaluations, and actions, we also included two control variables (gender and educational level) (see also Ndubisi, 2006). Worthy of note is that following suggestions from four senior academic experts in branding and eight doctoral students, at the top of page two of the questionnaire and specifically, prior to the set of statements on brand crisis, we introduced a "scenario qualifier" stating:

> Now, keeping in mind the recent "Volkswagen gas emission control" crisis and the "Toyota Prius brake" crisis as examples (or cases in point), kindly answer the following questions.

This is consistent with Nariswari and Chen's (2016, p. 708) scenario qualifier in their exploration in the negative consequences of engaging customer participation through voting mechanisms.

Data analysis and results

Common method bias

Because the data came from a single survey in each country and was obtained from single respondents, there is the possibility for the presence of common method bias. We tested for common method bias in several ways. First, we used the CFA approach to Harman's one-factor test to ensure that results are not biased because of a single respondent (Podsakoff & Organ, 1986). We conducted a confirmatory factor analysis (CFA) and examined the fit indices (Malhotra, Kim, & Patil, 2006). The fit for the one factor, which is an equivalent of a "Methods factor" that signifies the existence of bias due to the method of data collection, showed very poor fit (χ^2 (52) = 1754.41, p-value = 0.00; RMSEA = 0.198, CFI = 0.595, TLI = 0.485, and SRMR = 0.16). The fit of the one-factor model was significantly worse than that of the measurement model (χ^2 (46) = 120.82, p-value = 0.00; RMSEA = 0.044, CFI = 0.982, TLI = 0.974, and SRMR = 0.032), suggesting that common method bias is not a serious concern. Considering the limitation of Harman's one-factor test, we also used Lindell and Whitney's (2001) marker-variable technique to test for common method bias. This technique requires the selection of a variable that is theoretically unrelated to the nomological network of the variables involved in the study. For the purposes of testing, we used age as a suitable marker variable commonly used research studies (Williams, Hartman, & Cavazotte, 2010; Visinescu, Sidorova, Jones, & Prybutok, 2015). Results showed that the marker variable correlation with other variables in the model is low and not statistically significant. These insignificant correlations indicate that they will not have any real impact on the model, suggesting that common method variance is not a problem.

Measurement evaluation

Initial examination of the descriptive statistics for the 28 items revealed good fit of the data sets and the correlation matrices for Ghana and the United States (see Appendices IVa and IVb) showed a considerable degree of inter-item correlation for the 28 items. Next, we employed covariance-based structural equation modeling using STATASE 14 to analyze the research model. Following Anderson and Gerbing's (1988) two-stage approach, we (1) assessed the measurement model using confirmatory factor analysis (CFA), and (2) evaluated the hypothesized structural model. We used CFA to validate the measures used in this study. The fit indices for the measurement model were (χ^2 (46) = 120.82, p-value = 0.00; RMSEA = 0.044, CFI = 0.982, TLI = 0.974, and SRMR = 0.032), indicating that the model is good. These indices exceed the threshold levels that Hu and Bentler (1999) suggested. In addition to the global fit indices, we display the loadings of the items measurement model for both the combined, Ghana, and the United States samples (Table 7.1). We calculated both the internal consistency reliability and average variance extracted (AVE) values using the CFA results (Anderson & Gerbing, 1988). The composite reliability scores for all constructs are greater than 0.70, supporting our measures of internal consistency. Acceptable convergent validity was supported with (1) all standardized loadings above 0.5, and (2) all four constructs having AVEs exceeding 0.50 (Bagozzi & Yi, 1988) (Table 7.1). All our squared inter-construct correlations (φ^2) in Table 7.2 were below the AVEs for the respective constructs, indicating acceptable discriminant validity (Fornell & Larcker, 1981).

Table 7.1 CFA model fit and item loadings

Latent variable	Item	Combined sample			Ghana sample			United States sample		
		Loadings	CR	AVE	Loadings	CR	AVE	Loadings	CR	AVE
Customer loyalty	CL1	0.81	0.76	0.61	0.81	0.75	0.60	0.80	0.80	0.66
	CL2	0.75			0.74			0.83		
Corporate reputation	CR1	0.81	0.70	0.50	0.85	0.70	0.51	0.80	0.70	0.50
	CR2	0.68			0.66			0.66		
	CR3	0.61			0.60			0.61		
Brand crisis	BC1	0.76	0.82	0.59	0.74	0.80	0.56	0.79	0.84	0.65
	BC2	0.86			0.83			0.92		
	BC3	0.72			0.71			0.73		
	BC4	0.72			0.71			0.75		
Attribution	ATT1	0.78	0.84	0.64	0.75	0.83	0.62	0.85	0.87	0.69
	ATT2	0.85			0.85			0.85		
	ATT3	0.77			0.76			0.79		

Table 7.2 Evidence of discriminant validity in the three samples

Combined	CL	BC	ATT	CR	Ghana	CL	BC	ATT	CR	United States	CL	BC	ATT	CR
CL	**0.61**				CL	**0.6**				CL	**0.66**			
BC	0.02	**0.59**			BC	0.03	**0.56**			BC	0.01	**0.65**		
ATT	0.15	0.031	**0.64**		ATT	0.12	0.08	**0.62**		ATT	0.21	0	**0.69**	
CR	0.35	0.051	0.17	**0.51**	CR	0.38	0.05	0.17	**0.51**	CR	0.31	0.04	0.178	**0.5**

Note: The diagonal elements are AVEs. Entries below the diagonals are squared correlations. CL= customer loyalty, BC=brand crisis, ATT=attribution, and CR=corporate reputation

Table 7.3 Measurement invariance tests

Model	df	CFI	TLI	SRMR	RMSEA	Δ	Δ df	p-value
1 Configural invariance	324.41	96	0.947	0.928	0.045	0.076	—	
2 Full metric invariance	326.78	104	0.949	0.935	0.046	0.072	2.372	8	0.967
3 Scalar invariance	418.57	116	0.93	0.921	0.061	0.079	91.79	12	0.000

** $p<0.01$

Measurement invariance

Since the data used in this research were collected in two countries, we tested for measurement invariance between the two samples (Table 7.3). First, we tested for configural invariance, which requires no differences in the pattern of salient and nonsalient loadings across samples (Steenkamp & Baumgartner, 1998; Srinivasan & Swink, 2015) between the two samples. The results of our analysis support configural invariance across the two countries with a satisfactory model fit (χ^2 (96) = 324.408; CFI = 0.947; TLI = 0.928; SRMR = 0.045; RMSEA = 0.076). Next, we tested for metric invariance by constraining the factor loadings to be the same across the countries. The chi-square difference between model 1 and model 2 did not result in statistically significant differences in measurement loadings between the two samples (Table 7.4). Next, we tested for scalar invariance, which assesses the mean structure across groups is the same, by constraining the intercepts to be equal across the two samples. Although the model fit was satisfactory (χ^2 (116) = 418.57; CFI = 0.949; TLI = 0.935; SRMR = 0.046; RMSEA = 0.072), the chi-square difference test revealed that the two samples did not exhibit scalar invariance (Table 7.3). Researchers recommend partial measurement invariance as a sufficient condition when testing across different samples since the omnibus test will frequently not hold (Steenkamp & Baumgartner, 1998). Thus, our tests indicate that with the exception of scalar invariance, the samples satisfy a rigorous test of measurement invariance; as a result, we can combine the two samples to test our hypotheses.

Table 7.4 Results of SEM analyses

	Combined (n=833)		Ghana (n=525)		United States (n=308)	
	B	SE	B	SE	B	SE
Direct effects						
Brand Crisis → Customer Loyalty	0.01	0.04	0.05	0.06	−0.07	0.06
Brand Crisis → Corporate Reputation	0.23**	0.04	0.22**	0.06	0.21**	0.07
Corporate Reputation → Customer Loyalty	0.62**	0.06	0.65**	0.07	0.56**	0.09
Indirect (Mediated) Effects						
Brand Crisis → Corporate Reputation → Customer Loyalty	0.14**	0.03	0.14**	0.04	0.12**	0.04

**$p < 0.01$

Structural model

Finally, the hypothesized structural model for the combined sample was estimated using SEM. The overall fit of this structural model is acceptable, with χ^2 (22) = 49.51; CFI = 0.99; TLI = 0.98; SRMR = 0.026; RMSEA = 0.039 (Hu & Bentler, 1999). While the direct relation between brand crisis and customer loyalty was not significant (B=0.01; p>0.1), the direct relations between brand crisis and corporate reputation (B=0.26; p<0.01) and corporate reputation and customer loyalty (B=0.62; p<0.01) were positive and statistically significant. In addition, the results from these two countries also confirm support for the relationship between brand crisis and corporate reputation, and between corporate reputation and customer loyalty. We did not find support for the relationship between brand crisis and customer loyalty (Table 7.4). Thus, H1 is not supported, but H2 and H3 are supported. A post hoc analysis confirms the full mediating role of corporate reputation in the relationship between brand crisis and customer loyalty for both the combined sample and the individual countries because the corresponding indirect effects are positive and significant (Table 7.4).

Moderation effects of attribution

We followed a number of steps to examine the moderating role of attribution in the brand crisis/corporate reputation relationship. First, the scale items for each construct were averaged to create a composite score for testing the moderation hypotheses. Second, the variables were standardized to reduce the threat of multicollinearity (Aiken, West, & Reno, 1991). Third, we regressed corporate reputation on attribution, brand crisis, and the interaction term (i.e., brand crisis

Table 7.5 Hierarchical regression results

Variables	Model 1		Model 2		Model 3		Effect size η^2
	Beta	SE	Beta	SE	Beta	SE	
Constant	0.12	0.12	0.13	0.11	0.14	0.11	
Control variables							
Age	−0.08*	0.04	−0.08**	0.04	−0.08**	0.04	0.01
Gender	0.00	0.07	−0.01	0.06	−0.02	0.06	0.00
Main effects							
Brand crisis			0.16***	0.03	0.16***	0.03	0.03
Attribution			0.31***	0.03	0.30***	0.04	0.09
Interaction effects							
Brand crisis X attribution					−0.06*	0.03	0.01
F	1.99		32.48		26.83		
R^2	0.01		0.135		0.139		
Adj. R^2	0.01		0.132		0.135		
R change			0.125		0.004*		

***$p < 0.01$; **$p < 0.05$; *$p < 0.1$

X attribution) using hierarchical linear regression to detect the incremental fits of the model. As shown in Table 7.5, hierarchical linear regression results of the control variable-only (model 1), control variables and main effects (model 2), and all variables (model 3) models show significant improvement of the model fit with model 3 displaying the largest percentage of variance explained (R^2 = 0.139). Our model 3 results also did not show issues of multicollinearity as the variance inflation factors (VIFs) were all below 5 with the largest being 1.04.

In model 1, age was the only significant control variable while gender was not (Table 7.5). The main effects in model 2, brand crisis (β = 0.16; $p < 0.01$) and attribution (β = 0.30; $p < 0.01$), had positive effects on corporate reputation. The results in model 3 (Table 7.5) provide support for the negative interaction effect between brand crisis and attribution (β = −0.06; $p < 0.1$) on corporate reputation in the combined sample, indicating that higher levels of attribution significantly lowers the impact of brand crisis on corporate reputation. Thus, H4 is supported. Since the interaction effect was significantly different in the combined sample, we further tested the effect of this interaction in both the Ghana and United States samples to ascertain which of the samples had a more pronounced interaction/moderating effect. We found the interaction effect of brand crisis and attribution to be negative and statistically significant in the United States sample (β = −0.13; $p < 0.05$) but not significant in the Ghana sample (β = −0.04; $p > 0.05$).

Discussion

Even though knowledge of the relationship between corporate reputation and customer loyalty exists (see Walsh & Beatty, 2007; Cretu & Brodie, 2009; Abd-El-Salam et al., 2013), knowledge of the nature of the relationship is very limited (Nguyen & Leblanc, 2001) and as such this research has not only strengthened and expanded the literature on corporate reputation and customer loyalty but has also provided an extension of the literature by integrating corporate reputation, customer loyalty, and brand crisis into a conceptual framework that is operationalized in two differing economies.

The framework provides evidence of statistically significant relationships among brand crisis, corporate reputation, and customer loyalty. Moreover, there is an indirect relationship between brand crisis and customer loyalty. Although this finding is in line with prior studies (Dawar & Pillutla, 2000), it also contradicts studies that have shown the negative effects of brand crisis on customer loyalty (e.g., Huber et al., 2010; Dawar & Lei, 2009). Nonetheless, the qualitative analysis provides evidence for explaining these contradictory findings, highlighting the importance of mixed-method approaches in marketing research (Davis et al., 2013). As we gathered from the executives and experts, not only does brand crisis influence customer loyalty, but the reverse relationship also exists. Thus, when brand crisis occurs, loyal customers tend to be accommodating, forgiving, and sympathetic with a firm or brand, and sometimes even serve as advocates to the firm or brand. This finding demonstrates that using qualitative and quantitative data sequentially provides a better appreciation of the underlying phenomena (Davis et al., 2013) and further shows that the relationship existing between brand crisis and customer loyalty is indeed an indirect relationship after all.

Accepting hypothesis two – that is, that brand crisis has a statistically significant positive relationship with corporate reputation – in conjunction with the qualitative results helps to overcome the confusion and contradictory findings about the role corporate reputation plays in the occurrence of brand crisis by confirming Decker's (2012) assertion that a good reputation can act as an "insurance policy" or buffer if it has been developed prior to the occurrence of a brand crisis. This finding implies that, all things being equal, when a customer perceives a firm as reputable, the firm will continue to benefit from positive impressions even in the event of brand crisis. Thus, a customer may consider brand crisis as an exception to his or her whole impression of the firm.

Moreover, hypothesis three, which tested the relationship between corporate reputation and customer loyalty, was supported by both qualitative and quantitative analyses, showing that corporate reputation has a statistically positive relationship with customer loyalty. This particular finding suggests that when a customer perceives a firm as highly reputable, the customer tends to be more loyal to the firm or brand. Thus customer loyalty increases through accumulated positive impressions of the firm in the mind of the customer. Based on qualitative and quantitative data, the fourth hypothesis – indicating that attributions significantly moderate the relationship between brand crisis and corporate reputation (Klein & Dawar, 2004) – is supported, meaning that while the occurrence of brand crisis may directly affect how reputable a customer perceives a firm to be, the effect appears to be more pronounced in customers who engage in making attributions about brand crisis. Besides, we found that this effect is more prevalent in the United States (a developed Western market) than in Ghana (a fast-expanding African BoPM). A plausible explanation for this result is that obviously there are not many brand alternatives in the Ghanaian marketplace compared to the United States that will motivate customers to switch brands should a brand face some crisis. Hence, irrespective of the information given on a brand in crisis, Ghanaian customers do not consider diminishing the reputation of a firm's brand and rather are inclined to patronize the "failing brand" mainly because they have no viable brand alternatives. However, the United States sample showed a negative effect of attribution and brand crisis on corporate reputation. Incidentally, the United States customer has various brand alternatives to choose from should his or her preferred brand be in crisis. Thus, when faced with more information on a brand in crisis, American individuals tend to decrease their perceptions of the corporate reputation of the brand and proceed to search for a better and reputable firm that can meet their needs.

Worthy of note is that the discourse in the qualitative study elicited some appreciable findings; specifically, that the causes of brand crisis could be natural or unnatural. Examples of natural causes include floods, fire outbreaks, and earthquakes. Also, a decline in the growth stage of a brand's life cycle, inappropriate use of marketing tools in a brand's life cycle, a shortfall in the value chain of a brand, and negligence on the part of the firm in question are examples of unnatural causes of brand crisis.

Conclusion and implications

To a degree, this research has answered the calls from Nguyen and Leblanc (2001), Zins (2001), and Dawar and Lei (2009) to extend the limited knowledge of the nature of the relationship between corporate reputation and customer loyalty, to pay more attention to the stronger integration of the loyalty concept into nomological relationships with other constructs of the marketing theory, and to expand the limited research on the impact of brand crisis on key marketing constructs, respectively. In this quest, this chapter sought to explore the relationships among corporate reputation, brand crisis, and customer loyalty by assessing how corporate reputation influences customer loyalty and how brand crisis, in turn, influences the corporate reputation and customer loyalty constructs in the context of two differing economies, a fast-expanding African BoPM (i.e., Ghana) and an advanced developed market (i.e., the United States). The study concludes that there is evidence of the moderating effect of attribution on the relationship between brand crisis and corporate reputation. Our findings thus respond to Kim and Atkinson's (2014, p. 662) call for researchers to explore the role of brand experience in a crisis in order to enhance targeted crisis communications and in Davis et al's (2013) suggestion for mixed methods in marketing research.

Theoretical and managerial implications

On the theoretical front, this chapter contributes contextually to the body of knowledge on corporate reputation and customer loyalty by extending the literature to two culturally, socially, and economically different countries. Following Merchant et al. (2015) and Abd-El-Salam et al. (2013), who uncovered the relationship between corporate reputation and customer loyalty, this study fills a theoretical gap by providing a comprehensive approach to the research problem in its employment of a triangulation method of analysis. This research finds that the relationship between brand crisis and customer loyalty is indirect and therefore provides clarification to the contradictory findings on "brand crisis–customer loyalty" discourse (Huber et al., 2010; Ma et al., 2010). The use of the mixed-method analysis sequentially provides a comprehensive and a better understanding of underlying phenomena (Davis et al., 2013).

Concerning managerial implications, this research makes a substantive contribution to international marketing literature, as it provides managers in BoPMs and developed economies as well as those multinational firms interested in doing business in both developed economies and BoPM with insight into how corporate reputation influences customer loyalty and how brand crisis, in turn, influences the corporate reputation and customer loyalty constructs (Adekambi et al., 2015). By uncovering the important role corporate reputation plays in brand management, international marketing managers will take a keen interest in carving out targeted crisis marketing communications to curb the effects of brand crisis (Kim & Atkinson, 2014). To a degree, this research also provides international marketing managers with insight about how to confront challenging questions when developing the ideal international brand portfolio, as they must decide how to build their international and local brands, which brands to eliminate, which brands to promote, and which brands to assimilate into a local culture (e.g., "cultural brands") (see Guzman & Paswan, 2009; Cayla & Arnould, 2008; Schuiling & Kapferer, 2004).

This chapter also provides managers with knowledge about how to enhance customer loyalty through brand crisis management. The study makes it clear from the analysis and model developed that brand crisis influences corporate reputation, especially when customers make attributions about the crisis. This implies that managers must develop pertinent marketing and positioning strategies, including the remedies to brand crisis suggested in this study, to rectify the occurrence of brand crisis in the shortest possible time since attributions about brand crisis are likely to be made when the crisis drags on for too long. The chapter finds that corporate reputation is a very strong predictor of customer loyalty, and as such, managers should endeavor to work at improving their firms' overall appeal to customers using public relations and positioning tactics and strategies. Also, when faced with brand crisis, public relations are essential in the management of crisis situations in order to provide assurance to customers of the brand. Thus, firms can adopt timely, constant, and clear communication, apologies, and sometimes compensation as remedies to the crisis.

Indeed, as Aaker suggests, "crisis communications cannot be the only tactic firms use to smooth over breaches of customer trust. They need to deploy a thoughtful combination of programs and messaging that conveys a higher purpose" (Aaker, 2017, p. 18). We concur with Aaker's (2017) three key courses of actions that brands should take to address or prevent a crisis:

1 The firm must create a higher-purpose mission, value set, or culture that will enable the firm to have meaning apart from generating sales and profits.
2 Managers should develop a higher-purpose program that not only engenders trust but can redirect the discourse during a crisis incident. This action should form part and parcel of the brand and should leverage the firm's staff and resources toward social good.
3 The firm should distribute messages about the brand's higher purpose using stories of real and loyal customers.

References

Aaker, D. (1996). *Building strong brands.* New York, NY: Free Press.
Aaker, D. (2017, April/May). How does a brand regain trust? *Marketing News, 51*(4), 18–19.
Aaker, J., Fournier, S., & Brasel, A. S. (2004). When good brands do bad. *Journal of Consumer Research, 31*(6), 1–18.
Abd-El-Salam, E. M., Shawky, A. Y., & El-Nahas, T. (2013). The impact of corporate image and reputation on service quality, customer satisfaction and customer loyalty: Testing the mediating role. *Business and Retail Management Review, 8*(1), 130–153.
Adekambi, S. A., Ingenbleek, P. T. M., & van Trijp, H. C. M. (2015). Integrating producers at the base of the pyramid with global markets: A market learning approach. *Journal of International Marketing, 23*(4), 44–63.
Ahluwalia, R., Burnkrant, R. E., & Rao, U. H. (2000). Consumer response to negative publicity: The moderating role of commitment. *Journal of Marketing Research, 37*(2), 203–215.
Aiken, L. S., West, S. G., & Reno, R. R. (1991). *Multiple regression: Testing and interpreting interactions.* Thousand Oaks, CA: Sage.
Anderson, J. C., & Gerbing, D. W. (1988). Structural equation modeling in practice: A review and recommended two-step approach. *Psychological Bulletin, 103*(3), 411.
Andreassen, T. W., & Lindestad, B. (1998). The effect of corporate image in the formation of customer loyalty. *Journal of Service Research, 1*(1), 82–92.
Bagozzi, R. P., & Yi, Y. (1988). On the evaluation of structural equation modeling. *Journal of the Academy of Marketing Science, 16*(1), 74–94.
Barnett, M. L., Jermier, J., & Lafferty, B. L. (2006). Corporate reputation: The definitional landscape. *Corporate Reputation Review, 9*, 26–38.
Bewick, M. (2017). Building a global brand. *Catalyst,* The Chartered Institute of Marketing (CIM), 32–35.
Bomey, N. (2015, September 21, Monday). VW halts diesel sales. *USA Today,* 1A.
Catalyst Magazine. (2016, January). Brand in crisis. *Viewpoint, The Chartered Institute of Marketing* (CIM), 18–22.

Cayla, J., & Arnould, E. J. (2008). A cultural approach to branding in the global marketplace. *Journal of International Marketing, 16*(4), 88–114.

Chun, R. (2005). Corporate reputation: Meaning and measurement. *International Journal of Management Review, 7*(2), 91–109.

Cleeren, K., Dekimpe, M. G., & Helsen, K. (2008). Weathering product-harm crises. *Journal of the Academy of Marketing Science, 36*, 262–270.

Coombs, T. W. (2007). Protecting organization reputations during a crisis: The development and application of situational crisis communication theory. *Corporate Reputation Review, 10*(3), 163–176.

Cretu, A. E., & Brodie, R. J. (2007). The influence of brand image and company reputation where manufacturers market to small firms: A customer value perspective. *Industrial Marketing Management, 36*(2), 230–240.

Cretu, A. E., & Brodie, R. J. (2009). Business-to-business brand management: Theory, research and executive case study exercises. *Advances in Business Marketing and Purchasing, 15*, 263–387.

Dalebout, A., & Wierenga, B. (1997). Qualitative modelling of sales promotion decision making based on verbal data. *26th EMAC Conference Proceedings*, 20–23 May, Warwick Business School, Warwick.

Davis, D. F., Golicic, S. L., Boerstler, C. N., Choi, S., & Oh, H. (2013). Does marketing research suffer from methods myopia? *Journal of Business Research, 66*(9), 1245–1250.

Dawar, N., & Lei, J. (2009). Brand crises: The roles of brand familiarity and crisis relevance in determining the impact on brand evaluations. *Journal of Business Research, 62*, 509–516.

Dawar, N., & Pillutla, M. (2000). Impact of product-harm crises on brand equity: The moderating role of consumer expectations. *Journal of Marketing Research, 37*, 215–226.

Daymon, C., & Holloway, I. (2004). *Qualitative research methods in public relations and marketing communications.* London: Routledge.

Decker, W. H. (2012). A firm's image following alleged wrongdoing: Effects of the firm's prior reputation and response to the allegation. *Corporate Reputation Review, 15*(1), 20–34.

Dick, A. S., & Basu, K. (1994). Customer loyalty: Toward an integrated conceptual framework. *Journal of the Academy of Marketing Science, 22*(2), 99–113.

Dillman, D. A., Smyth, J. D., & Christian, L. M. (2009). *Internet, mail, and mixed-mode surveys: The tailored design method.* Hoboken, NJ: Wiley.

Dimofte, C. V., Johansson, J. K., & Ronkainen, I. A. (2008). Cognitive and affective reactions of American consumers to global brands. *Journal of International Marketing*, Article Postprint, *16*, 1–43.

Diwan, S. P. (2016). Investigating the relationship among desired, actual, and perceptual positioning strategies of Indian car brands. *Journal of Global Marketing, 29*(5), 315–323.

Dubois, A., & Gadde, L. (2002). Systematic combining: An abduction approach to case research. *Journal of Business Research, 55*(7), 553–560.

Dutta, S., & Pullig, C. (2011). Effectiveness of corporate responses to brand crises: The role of crisis type and response strategies. *Journal of Business Research, 64*, 1281–1287.

Ertekin, S. (2009). *An Assessment of consumers' willingness to patronize foreign-based business format franchises: An investigation in the fast-food sector.* Unpublished PhD dissertation, University of North Texas, Denton, TX.

Ewing, J. (2016, April 22, Friday). VW agrees to a settlement, with many blanks to be filled in. *Business Day – The New York Times*, B1.

Folkes, V. S. (1984). Consumer reactions to product failure: An attributional approach. *Journal of Consumer Research, 10*(4), 398–409.

Fombrun, C. J., & Shanley, M. (1990). What's in a name: Reputation building and corporate strategy. *Academy of Management Journal, 33*(2), 233–258.

Fornell, C., & Larcker, D. F. (1981). Structural equation models with unobservable variables and measurement error: Algebra and statistics. *Journal of Marketing Research,* 382–388.

Fornier, S. (1994). *A consumer-based relationship framework for strategic brand management.* PhD dissertation, University of Florida.

Frey, J. H. (1989). *Survey research by telephone.* Newbury Park, CA: Sage.

Galan-Ladero, M. M., Casquet, C. G., & Singh, J. (2015). Understanding factors influencing consumer attitudes toward cause-related marketing. *International Journal of Nonprofit and Voluntary Sector Marketing, 20,* 52–70.

Gardberg, N. A., & Fombrun, C. J. (2002). The global reputation quotient project: First steps towards a cross-nationally valid measure of corporate reputation. *Corporate Reputation Review, 4*(4), 303–307.

Ghana Club 100 Magazine. (2010, September). Enhancing partnership between domestic & foreign investors for sustained economic development. *Ghana Investment Promotion Center, 10.*

Grunwald, G., & Hempelmann, B. (2010). Impacts of reputation for quality on perceptions of company responsibility and product-related dangers in times of product-recall and public complaints crises: Results from an empirical investigation. *Corporate Reputation Review, 13,* 264–283.

Guzman, F., & Paswan, A. K. (2009). Cultural brands from emerging markets: Brand image across host and home countries. *Journal of International Marketing, 17*(3), 71–86.

Herr, P. M. (1989). Priming price: Prior knowledge and context effects. *Journal of Consumer Research, 16*(1), 67–75.

Heskett, J. L. (2002). Beyond customer loyalty. *Managing Service Quality: An International Journal, 12*(6), 355–357.

Homburg, C., & Giering, A. (2001). Personal characteristics as moderators of the relationship between customer satisfaction and loyalty: An empirical analysis. *Psychology and Marketing, 18*(1), 43–66.

Hu, L., & Bentler, P. M. (1999). Cutoff criteria for fit indexes in covariance structure analysis: Conventional criteria versus new alternatives. *Structural Equation Modeling: A Multidisciplinary Journal, 6*(1), 1–55.

Huber, F., Vollhardt, K., Matthes, I., & Vogel, J. (2010). Brand misconduct: Consequences on consumer-brand relationships. *Journal of Business Research, 63,* 1113–1120.

Ibeh, K., Brock, J. K., & Zhou, Y. J. (2004). The drop and collect survey among industrial populations: Theory and empirical evidence. *Industrial Marketing Management, 33*(2), 155–165.

Jacoby, J., & Kyner, D. B. (1973). Brand loyalty vs. repeat purchasing behavior. *Journal of Marketing Research, 2,* 1–9.

Johar, G. V. (1996). Intended and unintended effects of corrective advertising on beliefs and evaluations: An exploratory analysis. *Journal of Consumer Psychology, 5*(3), 209–230.

Johar, G. V., Birk, M. M., & Elnwiller, S. A. (2010). How to save your brand in the face of crisis. *MIT Sloan Management Review,* 57–64.

Jorgensen, B. K. (1996). Components of consumer reaction to company-related mishaps: A structural equation model approach. *Advances in Consumer Research, 23,* 346–351.

Jung, J. C., & Park, S. B. (2017). Case study: Volkswagen's diesel emissions scandal. *Thunderbird International Business Review, 59*(1), 127–137.

Keh, H. T., & Xie, Y. (2009). Corporate reputation and customer behavioral intentions: The roles of trust, identification and commitment. *Industrial Marketing Management, 38,* 732–742.

Keller, K. L. (1993). Conceptualizing, measuring, and managing customer-based brand equity. *Journal of Marketing, 57*, 1–22.

Kim, S., & Atkinson, L. J. (2014). Responses toward corporate crisis and corporate advertising. *Journal of Promotion Management, 20*(5), 647–665.

Klein, J., & Dawar, N. (2004). Corporate social responsibility and consumers' attributions and brand evaluations in a product-harm crisis. *International Journal of Research in Marketing, 21*, 203–217.

Kuada, J., & Buatsi, S. N. (2005). Market orientation and management practices in Ghanaian firms: Revisiting the Jaworski and Kohli framework. *Journal of International Marketing, 13*(1), 58–88.

Lei, J., Dawar, N., & Gürhan-Canli, Z. (2012). Base-rate information in consumer attributions of product-harm crises. *Journal of Marketing Research, 49*(6), 336–348.

Lindell, M. K., & Whitney, D. J. (2001). Accounting for common method variance in cross-sectional research designs. *Journal of Applied Psychology, 86*(1), 114.

Ma, B., Zhang, L., Li, F., & Wang, G. (2010). The effects of product-harm crisis on brand performance. *International Journal of Market Research, 52*(4), 443–458.

Mahon, J. F. (2002). Corporate reputation: A research agenda using strategy and stakeholder literature. *Business and Society, 41*(4), 415.

Malhotra, N. K., Kim, S. S., & Patil, A. (2006). Common method variance in IS research: A comparison of alternative approaches and a reanalysis of past research. *Management Science, 52*(12), 1865–1883.

Martinko, M. J., Harvey, P., & Dasborough, M. T. (2011). Attribution theory in the organizational sciences: A case of unrealized potential. *Journal of Organizational Behavior, 32*, 144–149.

McCracken, G. (1998). *The long interview.* Sage University Paper. Newbury Park, CA: Sage.

McDonald, L., & Hartel, C. E. J. (2000). Applying the involvement construct to organizational crises. Proceedings of *the Australian and New Zealand Marketing Academy Conference, Visionary Marketing for the 21st Century: Facing the Challenge,* Griffith University, Department of Marketing, Gold Coast, 799–803.

Merchant, A., Rose, G. M., Moody, G., & Mathews, L. (2015). Effect of university heritage and reputation on attitudes of prospective students. *International Journal of Nonprofit and Voluntary Sector Marketing, 20*, 25–37.

Miles, M. B., & Huberman, M. A. (1994). *Qualitative data analysis: An expanded sourcebook.* Los Angeles: Sage.

Mishler, E. G. (1990). Validation in inquiry-guided research: The role of exemplars in narrative studies. *Harvard Educational Review, 60*(4), 415–442.

Nariswari, A. G. A., & Chen, Q. (2016). Siding with the underdog: Is your customer voting effort a sweet deal for your competitors? *Marketing Letters, 27*, 701–713. https://doi.org/10.1007/s11002-015-9372-z

Ndubisi, N. O. (2006). Effect of gender on customer loyalty: A relationship marketing approach. *Marketing Intelligence & Planning, 24*(1), 48–61.

Nguyen, N., & Leblanc, G. (2001). Corporate image and corporate reputation in customers' retention decisions in services. *Journal of Retailing and Consumer Services, 8*, 227–236.

Obeng, B. A., & Blundel, R. K. (2015). Evaluating enterprise policy interventions in Africa: A critical review of Ghanaian small business support services. *Journal of Small Business Management, 53*(2), 416–435.

Odin, Y., Odin, N., & Florence, P. V. (2001). Conceptual and operational aspects of brand loyalty an empirical investigation. *Journal of Business Research, 53*, 75–84.

Oliver, R. L. (1999). Whence customer loyalty? *Journal of Marketing, 63*, 33–44.

Opare, G., Blankson, C. and Nkrumah, M. (2017). When a Brand Faces Crisis, who you gonna call? Corporate Reputation, Brand Crisis, and Customer Loyalty. *7th Conference on Marketing in Emerging Economies*, IIMA, Ahmedabad, India, January 11–13, pp. 324–328.

Orth, U. R., Stöckl, A., Veale, R., Brouard, J., Cavicchi, A., Faraoni, M.,. . . Wilson, D. (2012). Using attribution theory to explain tourists' attachments to place-based brands. *Journal of Business Research*, 65, 1321–1327.

Ozsomer, A., & Altaras, S. (2008). Global brand purchase likelihood: A critical synthesis and an integrated conceptual framework. *Journal of International Marketing*, Article Postprint, *16*.

People Daily. (2008, September 17). The number of baby sufferers of milk powder incident reached 6244, among which 158 suffered from acute renal failure. Retrieved from http://society.people.com.cn/ GB/86800/8060739

Podsakoff, P. M., & Organ, D. W. (1986). Self-reports in organizational research: Problems and prospects. *Journal of Management*, 12(4), 531–544.

Pullig, C., Netemeyer, R. G., & Biswas, A. (2006). Attitude basis, certainty, and challenge alignment: A case of negative brand publicity. *Journal of the Academy of Marketing Science*, 34(4), 528–543.

Reichheld, F. F. (1996). Learning from customer defections. *Harvard Business Review*, 74, 56–67.

Rhee, M., & Haunschild, P. R. (2006). The liability of a good reputation: A study of product recalls in the U.S. automobile industry. *Organization Science*, 17, 101–117.

Roberts, P. W., & Dowling, G. R. (2002). Corporate reputation and sustained superior financial performance. *Strategic Management Journal*, 23(12), 1077–1093.

Roehm, M. L., & Brady, M. K. (2007). Consumer responses to performance failures by high-equity brands. *Journal of Consumer Research*, 34(4), 537–545.

Sarstedt, M., Wilczynski, P., & Melewar, T. C. (2013). Measuring reputation in global markets – A comparison of reputation measures' convergent and criterion validities. *Journal of World Business*, 48(3), 329–339.

Sathish, M., Kumar, K. S., Naveen, K. J., & Jeevanantham, V. (2011). A study on consumer switching behavior in cellular service provider: A study with reference to Chennai, far East. *Journal of Psychology and Business*, 2(2), 71–81.

Schuiling, I., & Kapferer, J. (2004). Real differences between local and international brands: Strategic implications for international marketers. *Journal of International Marketing*, 12(4), 97–112.

Siomkos, G. J., & Kurzbard, G. (1994). The hidden crisis in product-harm crisis management. *European Journal of Marketing*, 28(2), 30–41.

Srinivasan, R., & Swink, M. (2015). Leveraging supply chain integration through planning comprehensiveness: An organizational information processing theory perspective. *Decision Sciences*, 46(5), 823–861.

Steenkamp, J. B. E., & Baumgartner, H. (1998). Assessing measurement invariance in cross-national consumer research. *Journal of Consumer Research*, 25(1), 78–90.

Sweeney, J. C., & Chew, M. (2002). Understanding consumer-service brand relationships: A case study approach. *Australian Marketing Journal*, 10(2), 26–43.

Teagarden, M. B. (2017). The multidimensional drivers of corporate scandal. *Thunderbird International Business Review*, 59(1), 139–140.

Visinescu, L. L., Sidorova, A., Jones, M. C., & Prybutok, V. R. (2015). The influence of website dimensionality on customer experiences, perceptions and behavioral intentions: An exploration of 2D vs. 3D web design. *Information & Management*, 52(1), 1–17.

Walker, K. (2010). A systematic review of the corporate reputation literature: Definition, measurement, and theory. *Corporate Reputation Review*, 12(4), 357–387.

Walsh, G., & Beatty, S. E. (2007). Measuring customer-based corporate reputation: Scale development, validation, and application. *Journal of the Academy of Marketing Science, 35*(1), 127–143.

Weiner, B. (1980). *Human motivation*. New York, NY: Holt, Rinehart and Winston.

Whelan, J., & Dawar, N. (2016). Attribution of blame following a product-harm crisis depend on consumers' attachment styles. *Marketing Letters, 27*, 285–294. https://doi.org/10.1007/s11002-014-9340-z

Whetten, D. A., & Mackey, A. (2002). A social actor conception of organizational identity and its implications for the study of organizational reputation. *Business Review, 41*(4), 393.

Williams, L. J., Hartman, N., & Cavazotte, F. (2010). Method variance and marker variables: A review and comprehensive CFA marker technique. *Organizational Research Methods, 13*(3), 477–514.

Winkler, R. L. (1981). Combining probability distributions from dependent information sources. *Management Science, 27*(4), 479–488.

Yang, Z., & Peterson, R. T. (2004). Customer perceived value, satisfaction, and loyalty: The role of switching costs. *Psychology & Marketing, 21*(10), 799–822.

Yannopoulou, N., Koronis, E., & Elliott, R. (2011). Media amplification of a brand crisis and its effect on brand trust. *Journal of Marketing Management, 27*(5–6), 530–546.

Yi, Y. (1990). A critical review of consumer satisfaction. In V. Zeithaml (Ed.), *Review of marketing* (pp. 68–123). Chicago, IL: American Marketing Association (AMA).

York, C. C., Gumbus, A., & Lilley, S. (2008). Reading the tea leaves: Did Citigroup risk their reputation during 2004–2005? *Business and Society Review, 113*, 199–225.

Zeithaml, V. A. (2000). Service quality, profitability, and the economic worth of customers: What we know and what we need to learn. *Journal of the Academy of Marketing Science, 28*, 67.

Zeithaml, V. A., Berry, L. L., & Parasuraman, A. (1996). *Delivery quality service: Balancing customer perception and expectation*. New York: The Free Press.

Zhou, L., & Whitla, P. (2013). How negative celebrity publicity influences consumer attitudes: The mediating role of moral reputation. *Journal of Business Research, 66*, 1013–1020.

Zins, A. H. (2001). Relative attitudes and commitment in customer loyalty models: Some experiences in the commercial airline industry. *International Journal of Service Industry Management, 12*(3–4), 269–294.

Appendix I

A sample of studies dealing with corporate reputation, brand crisis, and customer loyalty

Author	Objective / Research Question	Sample	Variables	Method & Tool of Analysis	Findings
Merchant et al. (2015)	Examine the impact of heritage and reputation of nonprofit universities on attitudes of prospective students	208 community college students in the United States	Dependent: Student attitudes, intentions to recommend and intentions to pay premium Independent: University heritage and university reputation	Survey; Structural equation modeling	• There are significant relationships among university heritage, university reputation, student attitudes, intentions to recommend and intentions to pay premium • Students' nationality moderates the relationships between university heritage, reputation, and attitudes

(Continued)

Author	Objective / Research Question	Sample	Variables	Method & Tool of Analysis	Findings
Abd-El-Salam et al. (2013)	Explore the impact of corporate image and reputation on service quality, customer satisfaction and customer loyalty in an international service company	650 respondents	Dependent: Service quality, customer satisfaction and customer loyalty Independent: Corporate image and reputation	Case study; Questionnaires; SPSS; Regression analysis	• There are significant relationships among corporate image and reputation, service quality, customer satisfaction and customer loyalty
Decker (2012)	Explore the impact of trust-related components of corporate reputation on observers' impressions of corporate wrongdoing and investigate the potential moderating variables that impact corporate reputation	395 undergraduate students at a mid-Atlantic university	Dependent: Trustworthiness, expertise, magnitude of harm Independent: Firm reputation, response to allegation of wrongdoing, type of industry	Survey; Factor analysis, ANOVA	• Firm's reputation has a strong impact across a range of harm magnitudes • Firm's response to an allegation has a significant impact on in impressions of both firm's trustworthiness and expertise • Admitting wrongdoing is generally more effective than either denial or declining comment
Yanno-poulou et al. (2011)	Explore consumers' perceptions of risk and its effect on brand trust in the case of a crisis	22 respondents, 143 articles	Dependent: Brand trust, perception of risk Independent: Brand crisis	Case study; depth interviews Content analysis	• Brand crisis initiates perception of risk • The perception of risk negatively affects brand trust

(Continued)

Author	Objective / Research Question	Sample	Variables	Method & Tool of Analysis	Findings
Ma et al. (2010)	Understand how a product-harm crisis influences brands (including both crisis brand and non-crisis brands) and market structure	Secondary data	Product-harm crisis, market share, penetration, purchase frequency, SCR	NBD-Dirichlet model	• Product-harm crisis can greatly damage the crisis brand's market share and penetration • Product crisis can change customers' purchase behaviors by driving away some customers of the crisis brand • Purchase frequency and SCR (Share of category requirements) were not damaged at similar levels as market share and penetration
Keh and Xie (2009)	Explore the underlying mechanism by which corporate reputation influences customer behavioral intentions	351 customers of three Chinese B2B service firms	Dependent: Customer trust, customer identification, customer commitment, purchase intention, price premium Independent: Corporate reputation	Survey; Structural equation modeling with the maximum likelihood estimation method	• Corporate reputation has positive influence on customer trust and identification • Customer commitment mediates the relationships between customer trust and customer identification, and behavioral intentions • Customer identification and customer commitment relate closely, but are distinct constructs in the B2B setting

Author	Objective / Research Question	Sample	Variables	Method & Tool of Analysis	Findings
Dawar and Lei (2009)	Investigate the effects of brand crises on consumers' brand evaluations	Two brands selected from 24 subjects with subjects drawn from pairs of brands within a product category with well-defined but distinct brand associations	Dependent: Perceptions of seriousness of the crisis, brand attitude, brand trust Independent: Crisis relevance, brand familiarity	Two experiments with subjects drawn from pairs of brands within a product category with well-defined but distinct brand associations; ANOVA; Full factorial between subject designs	• Crisis relevance interacts familiarity in its effects on brand evaluations • The effect of crisis is mediated by perceived crisis seriousness and moderated by prior brand familiarity • Crisis can have a differential effect on the brand evaluations of two differently positioned brands
Cretu and Brodie (2007)	Examine the influences of brand image and company reputation on customers' perceptions of product and service quality; customer value, and customer loyalty	377 salons	Dependent: Product and service quality, customer value, and customer loyalty Independent: Company reputation, brand image	Mixed method; telephone interviews and questionnaires; Confirmatory factor analysis; structural equation modeling (LISREL)	• Brand image has a more specific influence on the customers' perceptions of the quality loyalty • Company's reputation has a broader influence on perceptions of customer value and customer loyalty

(Continued)

(Continued)

Author	Objective / Research Question	Sample	Variables	Method & Tool of Analysis	Findings
Coombs (2007)	Explore the relationship between crisis, anger, and behavioral intention	167 undergraduate students	Dependent: Negative word of mouth, purchase intention Independent: Crisis responsibility, anger	Experimental design; regression analysis	• Crisis responsibility has an impact on negative word of mouth and purchase intention • Anger has a stronger impact on negative word of mouth and purchase intention
Roehm and Brady (2007)	Explore conditions that mitigate negative customer reactions to high-equity brand failures	116 graduate business students, 59 participants for experiments 1 and 2 respectively	Brand equity, failure severity, evaluation timing, distraction	Experimental design; ANOVA	• High-equity brands fare best when responses are timed immediately after the failure • In the absence of failure severity, evaluation timing, and distraction, high-equity brand evaluations appear to be adversely affected by a performance lapse

Author	Objective / Research Question	Sample	Variables	Method & Tool of Analysis	Findings
Klein and Dawar (2004)	Examine whether attributions that are influenced by CSR mediate the impact of brand crisis on consumers' brand evaluations	150 respondents for both studies	Dependent: Brand evaluation, buying intentions, judgments of blame, attributions Independent: Corporate social responsibility (CSR), brand crisis	Two studies involving three between-subjects conditions (positive CSR, negative CSR, and a control condition in which no information about CSR was provided), and accordingly, three versions of Questionnaires, Mall intercept; ANOVA, Structural equation modeling (LISREL)	• CSR associations have a strong and direct impact on consumers' attributions and brand evaluations • The impact of CSR associations on consumers' attributions translates into blame and consequently brand evaluations and purchase intentions
Roberts and Dowling (2002)	Examine the impact of corporate reputation on financial performance	3,141 firms	Dependent: Profitability Independent: Corporate reputation	Autoregressive profit models; proportional hazards regression	• Corporate reputation is an important strategic asset that contributes to firm-level persistent profitability

Appendix II

Themes emanating from two extensive qualitative studies: study one

Theme	Definition	Description of Statements Identified from Respondents
Causes of brand crisis	There are two causes of brand crisis. Natural and unnatural causes	"Brand crisis is caused by natural and unnatural factors."; "Brand crisis could be as a result of natural or unnatural occurrence."; "Brand crisis may occur through natural or unnatural means."
Remedies of brand crisis	How a firm or brand can avoid the devastating effects of brand crisis	"Brand crisis can be remedied by constant and clear communication, apologies and sometimes compensation."; "Timely and constant communication, apologies and sometimes compensations can be good remedies to brand crises."; "Usually, PR is essential in the management of crises situations in order to provide assurance to customers the brand."; "Communication on the part of the brand in crisis and the information given out by the brand at the time of the crisis are very important since customers are likely to understand the situation."
Types of corporate reputation	There are two types of corporate reputation	"Corporate reputation could be positive or negative."; "Corporate reputation can be positive or negative and enables customers to identify a company with a set of common descriptors."; "A positive corporate reputation is an asset to a company, especially in the services domain due to its intangible nature."; "More often than not firms assume they have a positive reputation but this is only true when the customers perceive it as reputable."
Influence of corporate reputation on brand crisis	In addition to the conventional knowledge about the influence of brand crisis on corporate reputation, the reverse relationship exists	"When a company has a solid corporate reputation, especially in the delivery of superior services, then customers are more forgiving when brand crisis occurs."; "Customers are ready to forgive a brand mishap based on the reputation they have about the brand and how loyal they are to the company."

Theme	Definition	Description of Statements Identified from Respondents
Influence of consumer loyalty to brand on brand crisis	In addition to the conventional knowledge about the influence of brand crisis on customer loyalty, the reverse relationship exists	"A highly loyal customer will sympathize and stay with a firm in crisis. He or she is likely to ask questions as to why the crisis occurred and if possible offer support to the firm."; "Where customers are loyal they tend to accommodate failure or crisis." "Loyal customers tend to sympathize with an organization in the event of a crisis and may serve as advocates for the organization."
Determining factors of the relationship between brand crisis and consumer loyalty to brand	The nature, degree, and frequency of the crisis; the reputation of the brand; the degree of loyalty to a brand; crisis communication; and crisis management are determining factors of the relationship between brand crisis and customer loyalty	"The effect of brand crisis on customer loyalty depends on the degree of loyalty on the part of customers and at the same time the degree of the brand crisis."; "Customer loyalty is affected by brand crisis if it persists for more than the tolerable limits of the customers."; "The impact of brand crisis on customer loyalty is dependent on the nature of the crises and how professionally and promptly it is managed."; "If not managed or handled professionally, brand crisis can affect customer loyalty to a very large extent. The relationship is also dependent on the nature of the crisis and the reputation the customers have about the brand."; "Communication on the part of the brand in crisis and the information given out by the brand at the time of the crisis are very important since customers are likely to understand the situation and make informed judgments about their loyalty to the brand."

Appendix III

Demographic characteristics of respondents
in Ghana and the United States (study two)

Demographic Variable	Ghana (N=525)		United States (N=321)	
	Number of Respondents	Percentage of Respondents (%)	Number of Respondents	Percentage of Respondents (%)
Gender				
Male	255	48.6	170	55
Female	270	51.4	139	45
Age				
18–30 years	343	65.3	251	79.7
31–40 years	129	24.6	37	11.7
41–50 years	33	6.3	11	3.5
51–60 years	14	2.7	2	0.6
61–70 years	6	.2	8	2.5
71 and over	n/a	n/a	6	1.9
Education				
High school graduate or equivalent	85	16.2	22	7.0
Some college education	21	4.0	204	65.0
Commercial or Vocational School	14	2.7	n/a	n/a
Polytechnic/University Degree	305	58.1	59	18.3
Master's Degree/ Post-graduate diploma	55	10.5	26	8.3
Professional or Doctoral Degree	38	7.2	3	1.0
Other qualification	7	1.3	1	.3
Total	525	100.0*	321	100.0*

Note: *percentages are rounded off

Appendix IVa

Correlation and descriptive statistics of items for Ghana sample (N=525)

	1	2	3	4	5	6	7	8	9	10	11	12	13	14	15	16	17	18	19	20	21	22	23	24	25	26	27	28
1	1																											
2	.64**	1																										
3	.48**	.48**	1																									
4	.41**	.34**	.60**	1																								
5	.38**	.41**	.57**	.56**	1																							
6	.35**	.46**	.51**	.51**	.66**	1																						
7	.29**	.26**	.34**	.27**	.31**	.31**	1																					
8	.26**	.24**	.37**	.38**	.40**	.36**	.56**	1																				
9	.23**	.27**	.26**	.26**	.34**	.29**	.40**	.56**	1																			
10	.31**	.25**	.42**	.41**	.39**	.35**	.47**	.65**	.52**	1																		
11	.23**	.27**	.35**	.27**	.33**	.33**	.42**	.56**	.55**	.56**	1																	
12	.18**	.27**	.26**	.22**	.22**	.24**	.31**	.46**	.47**	.50**	.62**	1																
13	.23**	.20**	.19**	.18**	.20**	.19**	.32**	.45**	.34**	.40**	.45**	.53**	1															
14	.20**	.20**	.12**	.11*	.12**	.18**	.35**	.34**	.35**	.37**	.40**	.48**	.54**	1														
15	.25**	.21**	.28**	.17**	.22**	.23**	.30**	.37**	.44**	.41**	.46**	.47**	.47**	.53**	1													
16	.11*	.07	.09*	.11*	.15**	.07	.17**	.27**	.21**	.20**	.26**	.25**	.26**	.30**	.23**	1												
17	.14**	.21**	.21**	.16**	.17**	.24**	.27**	.31**	.31**	.28**	.23**	.28**	.24**	.28**	.23**	.22**	1											
18	.18**	.21**	.27**	.19**	.20**	.25**	.14**	.23**	.22**	.26**	.16**	.22**	.23**	.21**	.19**	.08	.57**	1										

(Continued)

(Continued)

	1	2	3	4	5	6	7	8	9	10	11	12	13	14	15	16	17	18	19	20	21	22	23	24	25	26	27	28
19	.17**	.13**	.14**	.13**	.14**	.14**	.22**	.20**	.19**	.17**	.26**	.19**	.28**	.26**	.24**	.11*	.28**	.21**	1									
20	.10*	.12**	.12**	.15**	.03	.05	.15**	.16**	.17**	.09*	.16**	.17**	.23**	.24**	.23**	.09*	.25**	.11*	.61**	1								
21	.12**	.15**	.07	.08	.03	.06	.14**	.08	.16**	.08	.18**	.13**	.17**	.20**	.23**	.15**	.19**	.06	.50**	.61**	1							
22	.08	.11*	.01	.03	-.03	.01	.16**	.08	.19**	.02	.20**	.18**	.19**	.25**	.27**	.10*	.18**	.09*	.55**	.58**	.69**	1						
23	.16**	.18**	.22**	.16**	.14**	.18**	.23**	.25**	.26**	.21**	.24**	.22**	.32**	.29**	.27**	.14**	.28**	.20**	.46**	.44**	.43**	.51**	1					
24	.16**	.17**	.24**	.19**	.23**	.19**	.13**	.25**	.19**	.31**	.23**	.28**	.31**	.28**	.27**	.15**	.28**	.36**	.24**	.23**	.22**	.18**	.38**	1				
25	.12**	.16**	.21**	.19**	.18**	.13**	.20**	.24**	.19**	.24**	.22**	.18**	.31**	.23**	.21**	.12**	.17**	.29**	.23**	.20**	.14**	.14**	.33**	.59**	1			
26	.17**	.13**	.22**	.16**	.14**	.15**	.22**	.29**	.20**	.27**	.16**	.25**	.25**	.19**	.28**	.06	.33**	.35**	.16**	.15**	.08	.10**	.25**	.39**	.37**	1		
27	.14**	.17**	.22**	.16**	.18**	.18**	.22**	.26**	.24**	.26**	.19**	.27**	.26**	.20**	.25**	.13**	.39**	.35**	.19**	.23**	.08	.13**	.30**	.32**	.35**	.65**	1	
28	.15**	.23**	.27**	.26**	.26**	.25**	.25**	.30**	.18**	.29**	.21**	.27**	.26**	.18**	.22**	.15**	.44**	.39**	.25**	.20**	.17**	.14**	.27**	.38**	.35**	.55**	.64**	1
M.	5.0	5.0	5.8	5.7	5.7	5.6	5.1	5.3	5.1	5.6	5.3	5.0	4.9	5.0	5.0	5.5	4.8	4.9	4.6	4.6	4.6	4.3	4.9	5.2	5.4	5.0	5.0	5.2
Std.	1.9	1.7	1.6	1.6	1.4	1.4	1.7	1.6	1.6	1.4	1.5	1.6	1.6	1.6	1.5	2.1	1.5	1.5	1.5	1.6	1.7	1.8	1.6	1.6	1.5	1.6	1.4	1.5

Appendix IVb

Correlation and descriptive statistics of items for the United States sample (N=301)

	1	2	3	4	5	6	7	8	9	10	11	12	13	14	15	16	17	18	19	20	21	22	23	24	25	26	27	28
1	1																											
2	.74**	1																										
3	.56**	.52**	1																									
4	.39**	.36**	.67**	1																								
5	.23**	.23**	.25**	.22**	1																							
6	.19**	.22**	.22**	.20**	.93**	1																						
7	.33**	.27**	.42**	.35**	.23**	.18***	1																					
8	.31**	.26**	.47**	.43**	.20**	.18**	.55**	1																				
9	.13*	.14*	.22**	.21**	.07	.09	.42**	.46**	1																			
10	.24**	.19**	.32**	.42**	.12*	.12*	.40**	.52**	.45**	1																		
11	.14*	.10	.29**	.30**	.04	.03	.41**	.50**	.60**	.54**	1																	
12	.19**	.16**	.30**	.34**	.09	.08	.41**	.50**	.43**	.48**	.64**	1																
13	.27**	.24**	.32**	.28**	.24**	.21**	.39**	.60**	.34**	.43**	.44**	.37**	1															
14	.37**	.34**	.41**	.39**	.25**	.21**	.40**	.62**	.35**	.46**	.45**	.41**	.81**	1														
15	.21**	.19**	.35**	.31**	.03	.02	.38**	.50**	.55**	.49**	.59**	.58**	.39**	.44**	1													
16	.21*	.17**	.25*	.31**	.17**	.14*	.38**	.60**	.43**	.50**	.46**	.43**	.55**	.57**	.44**	1												
17	.36**	.43**	.42**	.34**	.25**	.21**	.44**	.42**	.24**	.28**	.30**	.34**	.45**	.44**	.28**	.33**	1											
18	.27**	.24**	.28**	.24**	.15**	.17**	.26**	.39**	.27**	.28**	.30**	.30**	.39**	.36**	.29**	.37	.54**	1										
19	.05	.10	.06	.10	.02	.03	.19**	.13*	.12*	.16**	.13*	.10	.14*	.16**	.12*	.13*	.16**	.08	1									

(Continued)

(Continued)

	1	2	3	4	5	6	7	8	9	10	11	12	13	14	15	16	17	18	19	20	21	22	23	24	25	26	27	28
20	.09	.15**	.06	.07	.05	.06	.20**	.09	.14*	.15**	.10	.12*	.15**	.12*	.16**	.10	.11*	-.01	.74**	1								
21	.09	.15**	.06	.06	.11	.11	.22**	.08	.16**	.23**	.09	.15**	.14*	.10	.15**	.11	.16**	-.02	.59**	.66**	1							
22	.11	.21*	.10	.08	.10	.09	.16**	.06	.14*	.17**	.05	.10	.13*	.15*	.16**	.08	.13*	-.06*	.58**	.70**	.76**	1						
23	.09	.14*	.15**	.14**	.11	.10	.18**	.16**	.13*	.23**	.08	.14*	.19**	.19**	.13*	.21**	.23**	.10	.54**	.51**	.50**	.61**	1					
24	.14*	.17**	.22**	.22**	.05	.06	.19**	.22**	.15**	.17**	.19**	.18**	.24**	.28**	.18**	.29**	.25**	.34**	.10	.05	-.01	.02	.24**	1				
25	.20**	.17**	.27**	.20**	.10	.11	.26**	.33**	.17**	.18**	.18**	.16**	.21**	.26**	.21**	.25**	.37**	.39**	.12*	.03	-.00	.02	.26**	.73**	1			
26	.30**	.21**	.34**	.27**	.18**	.17**	.34**	.37**	.25**	.26**	.22**	.18**	.26**	.32**	.22**	.28**	.48**	.47**	.06	.00	-.01	-.07	.15*	.35**	.40**	1		
27	.29**	.23**	.30**	.28**	.21**	.17**	.26**	.36**	.27**	.28**	.21**	.16**	.29**	.34**	.25**	.34**	.44**	.42**	.04	.01	-.01	-.05	.17**	.39**	.44**	.75**	1	
28	.31**	.22**	.37**	.35**	.22**	.22**	.34**	.38**	.28**	.34**	.27**	.31**	.29**	.39**	.31**	.32**	.41**	.35**	.09	.03	.01	-.02	.18**	.42**	.51**	.68**	.66**	1
M.	4.8	4.8	5.8	6.0	4.6	4.6	4.9	5.5	4.9	5.4	5.3	5.3	5.1	5.0	5.2	5.7	4.8	5.4	4.5	4.3	4.1	3.7	4.6	5.4	5.6	5.2	5.3	5.5
Std.	1.5	1.4	1.3	1.2	1.8	1.9	1.4	1.4	1.5	1.3	1.4	1.4	1.5	1.4	1.4	1.3	1.5	1.4	1.3	1.3	1.4	1.5	1.4	1.5	1.4	1.2	1.3	1.4

Notes: ** Correlation is significant at the 0.01 level (two-tailed); * Correlation significant at the 0.05 level (two-tailed); M = Mean; Std. = Standard Deviation.

8   Conclusion

This text has focused on BoPM in Africa in exploring the concepts and practices of branding and positioning. Even in BoPM, branded products serve as avenues and pivots of attraction to the values that are seen embedded in given products and services. In this perspective, the text has presented how the concepts and practice of branding and positioning apply in the context BoPM in Africa. This application of course takes place against the backdrop of many issues – economic, socio-cultural and other environmental factors that impinge on the milieu and lifestyles in BoPM in Africa. Consequently, the key learning points that emerge from the studies and within the text are keenly notable in this concluding chapter.

Positioning strategies, particularly when based on consumer preferences, are found to be appropriate for branding as they reflect the service and product preferences of customers in the market (Chapter 2). This suggests that organizations need to test service attributes in each target market to arrive at the best branding decisions. Not all positioning strategies are appropriate for branding in all markets; appropriateness and relevance to the ideology and consumer expectations are important, and this is not different in base of the pyramid markets (BoPM) in Africa.

Organizations operating in Africa therefore stand to make the "best" branding decisions that will inure to the benefit of the consumer and the organization when the necessary background work has been carried out to enhance the consumer contribution and centeredness of branding decisions. One acknowledges that well-branded services offer benefits to both the consumer and the service provider. To the consumer, such benefits may include an assurance of the quality and dependability of the service, while to the organization, successful branding results in customer loyalty and higher profitability. In BoPM in Africa, and as denoted in the illustrative cases (Chapter 3), there are a range of economic, sociocultural, technological, and infrastructural challenges that could potentially obstruct the successful development, introduction, and growth of brands. In order to develop successful service brands, organizations need to be more imaginative in addressing the environmental challenges posed in the context of BoP consumers in Africa. Products and services that meet the needs of the majority may have a good chance of success, as in the case of M-Pesa in the telecommunications market in Kenya. The ease of money transfer via mobile technology allows well-off persons to perform their social and financial responsibilities, often towards their rural relatives. In this regard, targeting, positioning, and the development of an imaginative marketing mix become very important. Corporate Social Responsibility (CSR) as a strategy and working with non-governmental organizations (NGOs) will augment the efforts of the organization in identifying core social and service needs to help organizations both local and foreign meet the needs of the majority. Pricing to meet the target audience – urban or rural – is important. In general, low-margin, high-volume pricing for the majority will improve the chances of successful branding and marketing. Distribution through multi-level channels, with proximity and small volumes as key principles for most services used by the majority, may provide the answers to success. Promotion – predominantly via below-the-line methods – emphasizing word of mouth through community groups and associations might be the key for reaching out to the majority in BoP service markets in Africa.

For foreign retail firms seeking to do business in Africa, and Ghana in particular (Chapter 4), this study offers a snapshot of the current environment of retailer positioning in the country. While the examined retailers represent only a small fraction of indigenous and foreign retailing activity in Ghana, the findings demonstrate that retailers do engage in positioning activities and that foreign retailers appear to be stronger at positioning than their indigenous counterparts. This finding is attributed to foreign retailers' comparative consistency and congruence in their positioning activities and resource advantage over indigenous firms. As such, foreign retailers seeking to do business in Africa must enter with a consistent positioning strategy that achieves congruence with consumer expectations in order to positively affect customer perceptions, thereby attracting and retaining customers. Indigenous firms must capitalize on consistent employment and congruence in positioning strategies while at the same time investing in resources including store expansion, advertising, and promotion-inducing efforts to positively affect customer perceptions and increase market share, ultimately leading to competitive advantage.

The role of social networks, culture, and religion for developing and building competitive advantage are pronounced (Chapter 5). Religion drives social networks in terms of customer relationships and staff relationships as vehicles for achieving profitability goals. In other words, in rural subsistence Africa, micro and small business owner-managers do not define success solely on profitability, but additionally on the ability to provide for family members, staff, and customer friends. Rural micro and small business owner-managers' positioning and marketing practices stem from interdependence and relationships between owner-managers, staff, customers, and rural residents. There is a suggestion that, in rural Africa, this unique interdependence is borne out of a culture that emphasizes "brotherhood" and pragmatic social support. Thus, marketing practices reflect religiosity and adherence to communal and collectivistic cultural systems and informality. It appears that rural African micro and small business positioning and marketing activities reflect simplicity beneath a surface of complexity and sophistication despite apparent naïveté. These bonds run much deeper than those that exist with business practices in the West. The bonds created by social networks and relationships underpin virtue in marketing when it comes to micro and small businesses' operations.

Country branding has been gaining importance as a means of marketing tourism and as part of general efforts at country development (Chapter 6). For BoP countries in Africa, branding efforts include the mentioned factors, and for such economies branding also serves the purpose of correcting the negative image they are often associated with. Different African countries may be faced with different challenges in the efforts at branding. What appears to be a predominant commonality for the majority is the negative image: Underdevelopment, hunger, corruption, poor leadership, and more. Each country will have to work to resolve these challenges, and above all, BoP countries in Africa should individually seek to brand depending on their strengths, be they political, historical, ecological, or product and service capabilities.

The research presented in the penultimate chapter (Chapter 7) makes a substantive contribution to international marketing literature. It provides managers in BoP markets and developed economies and those multinational firms interested in doing business in both developed and BoPM with insight into how corporate reputation influences customer loyalty and how brand crisis in turn influences the corporate reputation and customer loyalty constructs. By uncovering the important role corporate reputation plays in brand management, international marketing managers will take a keen interest in carving out targeted crisis marketing communications to curb the effects of brand crisis. Brand crisis influences corporate reputation especially when customers make attributions about the crisis. This suggests that managers must develop pertinent marketing and positioning strategies to help remedy brand crisis in the shortest possible time since attributions about brand crisis are likely to be made when the crisis drags on for too long. Corporate reputation is a very strong predictor of customer loyalty, and, as such, managers should endeavor to work at improving their firms' overall appeal to customers using public relations and positioning tactics and strategies, as well as to provide assurance to customers of the brand. Managers should develop a higher-purpose program that not only engenders trust but can redirect the discourse during a crisis incident. This action should form part and parcel of the brand and should leverage the firm's staff and resources toward social good. These measures are necessary for firms operating in BoPM as well as other settings.

In a nutshell, organizations operating in BoPM in Africa need to be socially conscious, and develop products and services bearing in mind environmental relevance as reflected in cultural understanding and economic well-being of the targeted group – rural or urban. Ultimately, the success of branding and positioning of products and services will be via understanding such social milieu factors in addition to others for competitive success in BoPM in Africa.

Index

Note: Numbers in **bold** indicate a table. Numbers in *italics* indicate a figure.

Aaker, D. 93, **20**, 109, 124
Abd-El-Salam, E. 110, 123, **131**
Abontiakoon (Gold Coast/Ghana) 81
Accra 55, 56, 114, 115
Accra Mall 48, 50–53, 59; food court 60
Accra Mall Pharmacy 49, 51–53;
    application of positioning strategies 56,
    61, 62, 64, **74**
Accra-Tema Metropolitan area 113
Adegoju, A. 91
Africa 1–4; businesses 30; central 28; culture
    30, 80, 81; economic challenges 91;
    economies 64, 65, 105; global trade 46;
    negative portrayal of 90–91; pan- 91;
    positioning strategies for branding in 7;
    prejudices against 90; "religious universe"
    81; rural 25–26, 85; social networks 81,
    83; society 31; sociocultural values 31,
    32, 35, 84, 85, 143; socioeconomics 4,
    81, 92, 94; socio-political challenges 47,
    94; strengths 144; as study setting 46–48;
    see also base of pyramid markets (BoPM);
    Ghana; Nigeria; South Africa
Agyemang, O. 10
Ahluwalia, R. 108
Akyem (Ghana) 82
Alexander, N. **42**, 44, 49, 50
American Broadcasting Company (ABC)
    News 91
Andreassen, T. W. 108
Ansong, A. 10
apartheid 26–27, 91, 92, 98
Appiah-Adu, K. 36, 64
Arnott, D. C. **20**, 35
Aryee, G. 3
Asante (Ghana) 81, 82
Asia Pacific region 37

Assimeng, M. 11, 15
Atkinson, L. 112, 122
attractiveness 10, **20**, **42**, 49, 51
attractiveness positioning strategy 59, 60, **61**,
    62, 63, 64; case studies **71–78**, 94
attribution(s) *109*, **117–118**; and brand
    crisis 114, **120**, 123, 145; customer 122,
    123, 145; measuring 115; moderating
    effects of 104, 108, 112, 114, 119–120;
    negative effects of 122; positioning
    strategies case studies **71**, **73–78**
attribution theory 106–107, 111
Australasia 37
Austria 37
availability of service **12**, 14, 32

Bannister, P. 93
Barcelos Restaurant 49, 51, 53–54, 63, 64;
    application of positioning strategies
    59–61, **61**, **78**
base of the pyramid markets (BoPM) in
    Africa 1–4, 7, 16, 22–24, 32, 144–145;
    challenges 22, 24, 27, 33, 35, 90, 143; and
    developed economies 102–105, 122–124;
    dynamics of branding 25–30; marketing
    mix strategies for service brands in
    30–32; positioning research in 36; *see also*
    brand crisis; branding; customer loyalty;
    positioning
batteries 25
Beatty, G. 110
Belk, R. 3
Benin, Republic of 81
Benito, G. P. G. **41**
Berger, R. 93
Berry, L. **20**, 116
Bharadwaj, A. 3

Birk, M. 111
black: (color) 97; man 95; president 96; race 92; urban areas 26, 33
Blankson, Charles 3, 6, 7, 9, 36, 45, 46, 50; on brand identity 35; inductive reasoning 54; on owner-managers 83, 85; on positioning views of executives 13; on *susu* 83; on tourism positioning 94
Blankson, Rosemond 81
Blundel, R. 114
BMW 16, 97
Bonsu, S. 2, 3, 97
Botswana 54
Brady, M. K. **134**
brand: associations 11, 13; change 65; company **20**; established 22; evaluations **135**; failure **134**; identity 35, **41**; international 64; management 7; marketing 23; name **21**, 54, 56, 60, **61**, 64; performance 8; positioning 56, 59; preference 10, 97; quality 10; strength 10, 13; store 51; successful 22; uncertainty 8; well-known 53
Brand Africa 91
"Brand" and "brand" 8
brand crisis 102–106; and corporate reputation 105–106, 109–110, 111–112, **117–119**, 145; and customer loyalty 108–109, *109*, 121–124, **130–137**
Brand Ghana Office 94
"brand status" 90
branding 62, 63, 64; in base of the pyramid markets (BoPMs) 1–4, 9, 90–91; as a concept 90; "standalone" 97; from "within" 97
branding and positioning 7–10, 13–16, 44, 45–46, 94, 144; BoPM illustration 9–13, **12**; case studies **71**, **73**, **74**, **75**, **76**, **77**, **78**
branding nation-states 89–90, 98–99; Ghana 94–98; issues and challenges 90–91; South Africa 91–94
branding services 23–24, 31, 32, 33; in base of pyramid markets (BoPMs) 24–30; *see also* service brands
"branding strategy" 11–13, **12**, 16, 96, 102
Brock, J. 10
Broderick, A. **20**
Brodie, R. J. 103, 110, 115, 121, **133**
"brotherhood" 83, 86, 144
Brown, H. E. **20**
Burt, S. L. 35, 37, **39–41**, 44
Burton, J. 65
Buskirk, R.K. **20**

Cairns, P. **40**, 44
Canada 54
Caribbean 37
Carnevale, M. 8
Carralero-Encinas, J. 35, 37, **39**
Cateora, P. 16
Celuch, K. 15
Chakraborty, G. 8
Chen, Q. 116
Chennai, India 86
Chernatony, L. de 7, 23, 45, 48, 49, 50, 61
Chew, M. 55, 113
Chikweche, T. 91
China 47, 55, 106
Chu, R. 10
Cleff, T. 12
Coca-Cola 16, 106
Coffie, Stanley 7, 9, 10, **21**, 31, 51, 65
coherence/fit 45, 48, 62, 64
comfort **12**, 14
common method bias 116
congruence 35, 36, 37, 44, 62; with consumer expectations 144; among managers' intentions 48; in positioning deliberations 60–61; in positioning strategies 65, 66, **73–78**; in retailer positioning 45–46, 50
consumer-based positioning typology 9, 13
controllability 107
control variables 112, 116, **120**
convenience 9, **12**, 14, 53, 58, 104, 112
Coombs, T. 105, 109, 110, **134**
Cornelissen, S. 92, 93
corporate reputation 103, 105–106, *109*, 115, **117–119**, **130–136**; *see also* brand crisis; customer loyalty
corporate social responsibility (CSR) 10–11, 15, 31, 33, 107, **135**, 144
Côte d'Ivoire 92
Cottam, S. 48, 49, 50, 61
country branding 89, 93, 96, 97, 98, 99, 145
country of origin: positioning strategies case studies **71**, **73–78**
Cowan, K. 83, 85
Crawford, C. M. **20**
Cretu, A. 110, 115, **133**
customer: affluent 51; brand knowledge 103, 107, 110, 122; complaints 59; concentration **41**; data 61, 62, 114–121, **117–120**; decisions 6; diverse 54; expectations 10; experience 23, 28; feedback 83; friends 86; goodwill 15; groups 30; interactions 49; interviews 51–52, 59, 60; low-income 56; markets

3, **41**; minds of 3, 64; monitoring of 55; needs 6, 24, 52; options 56; perceptions **39**, 45, 48, 64, 66, 85, 86, 144; positioning strategies **71**, **73–78**; preferences 6, 7, 13; relations 9, **12**; relationships with 79, 83, 84–85, 86, 144; satisfaction 30, 111; service 14, 31, 53, 56, 57, 85; service access by 32; and social identification 82; study of 114–115; target 22, 23, 50, 63; trust 110, 124; upper-class 51
customer-focused business 86
customer loyalty 22, 32, 103–104, 105, 107–108; attitudinal 108; behavioral 108; and brand crisis 108–109, *109*, 111–114; and branding 143; and corporate reputation 104, 105–106, 111, 112, 113, 121; data **117–119**; four-item scales for 115; and public relations 145
customer loyalty and corporate reputation 104, 105–106, 110–111, 112, 113, 121, 123; and brand crisis **130–137**; *see also* brand crisis

Dadzie, S. 10
Dalebout, A. 113
Dallas Fort-Worth Metroplex 113
Dall'Olmo Riley, Francesca 8
Dar es Salaam, Tanzania 28
Darley, W. 83, 85
Dawar, N. 107, 115, **133**, **135**
Debrah, Y. A. 35, 48
de Chernatony, L. *see* Chernatony, L. de
Decker, W. 109, 121, **131**
demographics **20**, 26, 31; characteristics 112, **138**
Desarbo, W. 8
Devece, C. 14
Dirks, K. 14
Doherty, A. M. **38**, **42**, 44, 49, 50
domestic firms 23, 24, **39**; customers in **41**; in Ghana 36
domestic markets 23, **42**
domestic retailing 35, 64
Dowling, G. **135**
Dubois, A. 48, 55, 72, 113
Dunn, K. 92

Easingwood, C. J. **20**, 65
Edu-Buandoh, D. 96
education initiatives 15
educational sector 144
Egypt 2
electricity 25
Elnwiller, S. 111

Elsner, S. **43**
entrepreneur, entrepreneurship 29, 30, 31, 81; foreign 51; indigenous 51, 80; micro 82; social networks, influence on 79, 83; women's 80
Ernest Chemist Limited 56
Ertekin, S. 112
Evans, J. **40**

Famiyeh, S. 10
Fante (Ghana) 82
fast food 10, 53, 60, 64, 112
Festervand, T. 96
FIFA World Cup 93, 99
Firestone 106
Fletcher, R. 91
Florence, P. 108
Fombrun, C. J. 105, 106
Food Aid for Ethiopia 90
Ford Motor company 102
France 47, 56
Free Zones Board 95

Gabay, Jonathan 102
Gabon 32
Gadde, L. 48, 55, 61, 113
Galaxy Perfumery 49, 51, 52, 53, 55, 57, 60, **61**, 62, 64
Gambia, The 3
Garg, S. 10
Germany 37, **43**, 94; and BMW 97; pharmaceutical products 56
Ghana 2–3, 10–16, 35, 144; Asantes 82; case study approach **72**; correlation and descriptive statistics of items for 139–140; culture and indigenous entrepreneurship 80; economy 47; marketplace 48; retailers in 36, 50, 51; rural 25, 83, 84; service firms in 31–32; as study setting 46–66; *see also* branding nation-states; United States
Ghana Club 100, 112
Ghana Exports Promotion Authority (GEPA) 95
Ghana Investment Promotion Centre (GIPC) 95
Ghana Telecom 12, 15
Ghana Tourism Authority 95
Ghosh, A. 8
Gillette 13
Godefroit-Winkel, D. 2, 97
Goff, P. 92
Gold Coast 81
Golden Rule 83
Gripsud, G. **41**

Guinness 97
Gupta, S. 10, 11, 24
Gürhan-Canli, Z. 107

Hamzaoui-Essoussi, L. 89
Harman's one-factor test 116
Haunschild, P. 109
Hausa (Nigeria) 82
Herstein, R. 93, 99
Hinson, R. 11, 95
Hooley, G. J. 11, **20**
Huberman, M. 114
Hutchinson, K. **41**, 44

Igbo (Nigeria) 82
India 47, 54, 85, 86
indigenous: brands 29; business 52; firms
    47, 48, 53, 60, **61**, 66, **72**, 144; stores 49;
    wholesalers 56
indigenous retailers 36, 37, 45, 46, 50, 51,
    63, 64, 65; case studies **73–75**
International Monetary Fund (IMF) 47,
    48, 95
Italy 47, 51

Jaffe, E. 93
Japan 94, 106
Johannesburg Stock Exchange (JSE) 53
Johar, G. 111
Johns, R. 11

Kachersky, L. 8
Kalafatis, S. 9, 13, 16, **21**, 45, 53
Kano, Nigeria 81, 82
Kapferer, J. 64
Karnani, A. 1
Keh, H. T. 110, **132**
Kenya 2, 3, 27, 31; mobile phone
    penetration in 28; telecommunications
    market 144; *see also* M-Pesa
Kenya Airways 35
Khojastehpoura, M. 11
Kim, S. 112, 122
Klein, J. 107, 110, **135**
Kluckhohn, F. 80
Koch, C. 7
Kuada, J. 11, 29, 30
Kwahu (Ghana) 82
Kwame Nkrumah University of Science
    and Technology (KNUST) 96
Kwarteng, A. 10

Lagos, Nigeria 53, 91
Lapiedra, R. 14

Leblanc, G. 103, 110, 122
Lei, J. 107, **133**
Lesotho 54
life and health clinic 55–56, **73**
Life Healthcare Clinic 49, 51, 52, 60, **61**,
    62, 64
Lindell, M. 116
Lindestad, B. 108
Lindgreen, A. 10, 11
Liu, M. 10
Lovelock, C. 6, 8, 23, 24
loyalty 103; attitudes 116; brand 103; card
    39; concept 122; and customer care 86;
    see also customer loyalty
Lucozade 13

Ma, B. **132**
Mackey, A. 105
Made-of-Black 2
Mael, F. 82
Mahajan, V. **20**
Mahon, J. 105
Make Poverty History 90
Mandela, Nelson 91, 92–93, 96, 99
man-nature orientation 80
Maon, F. 10, 11
marketing: activities 51, 57, 80, 108, 115;
    communications 48, 65; efforts 90;
    experience 63; and globalization 64, 102;
    improving 14; international 46, 47, 54;
    literature 108, 123, 145; methods 52;
    nation-states 89; practices 86; research 55,
    112, 121, 122; skills 82; strategy 6, 37, 50,
    84, 145; tactics 85; theory 104, 107, 122;
    of tourism 3, 98, 145
marketing mix strategies 22, 33, 144;
    communication 28; and economic
    development 24; for service brands
    30–32
Marks and Spencer 44
Mauritius 54
Mavondo, F. **40**
Mbah, C. 94
Mbiti, J. 80
Mercedes 16
Merchant, A. 111, **130**
Michael Power 2
micro business 79–86, 144–145;
    relationships with customers 84–85;
    relationships with staff 84
micro entrepreneur 82
Middle East 37
Miles, M. 114
Mills, John Evans Atta 94

Mishler, E. 114
mobile: communication 15; money
    transfer 27, 30, 32, 144; phones 15, 28;
    technology 27, 144; *see also* M-Pesa
Möller, K. **20**
money 3; transfer of 27, 28, 31–32; raising
    29, 81; sending 30; *see also* value for
    money
Morocco 3
Mozambique 54
M-Pesa mobile money service 27–28, 30,
    32–33, 143–144
Mpoyi, R. 96, 104
MTN Ghana 12, 23 39, 40
multi-domestic marketing 102
Murphy, G. 15

Namibia 54
Namibia Stock Exchange 53
Nariswari, A. 116
Nelson Mandela Business School 96
Netherlands, the 47, 51
Nguyen, N. 103, 110, 122
Niger Delta militants 91
Nigeria 2, 51, 53, 54, 82, 91
Nike 16
Nkrumah, Kwame 35, 95
non-governmental organizations (NGOs)
    31, 33, 144
nostalgia 97, 99
Nukunya, G. 15

Obeng, B. 114
Odin, N. 108
Odin, Y. 108
Ofei, K. 29
Ofori, D. 11
OK Franchise Division 53
Oman 54
Opare, G. 35
Opoku, R. 95
Overseas Private Investment Corporation
    (OPIC) 46
owner-managers 82–86, 144
Owusu-Frimpong, N. 7, 9, **21**, 31, 51,
    65, 94

Pakistan 54
Papadopoulos, N. 3, 89, 90, 92
Papaye 10
Parasuraman, A. 116
Peterson, R. 115
Pillutla, M. 115
Pinto cars 102

poor, the 1, 2, 3, 4, 26; rural 30, 31, 32; and
    social networks 83; urban 30, 31, 32
Porter, M. 9
positioning 1–4; activities 35–36, 48, 51;
    brand 6; and branding 7–9, 14, 15, 16;
    brand-oriented 7; clear 23; congruence in
    44–45, 46; constructs and concepts **20–21**;
    developing 31, 33; and international retail
    36–44; market-oriented 7; strategic **12**;
    types 8, 9, 13
positioning strategies 6, 64, 79; application of
    71–78; based on consumer perceptions 7;
    marketing and 79–80; summary of **61**;
    typology of **20–21** 54; *see also* branding;
    social networks
poverty 1, 90, 95; alleviation 3
Prahalad, C. 22
price-quality relationship 23, 58, 60
pricing 16, **21**, 31, 32, 33, 144; general 56;
    off- **20**; strategy **39**; value 56
proximity 9, **12**, 14, 32, 33, 144
Pugliese, Michael 25

Qatar 54
quality 3, 6, 9, 10, **20**, 51, 110, 143; controls
    94; of products 52, 53, 56, 59, 86, 97; of
    service **12**, 13, 14, 16, 31, 32, 97, 111,
    131, 133

Rennings, K. 12
reliability 9, 10, **12**, 14, **20, 21**, 52, 94;
    validity and 54–55, 113–114
reliability positioning strategies 57, 58, 60,
    61, 62, 63, 64; case studies **71, 73–78**
"reputation-loyalty" relationship 108
retail **39**; brands 26; malls 46, 52; research
    49, 50; sector 110; shops 27; outlets 32
retailers 26, 60–66; foreign 36, 45, 48,
    76–78, 144; international 36, 37, **38, 40**,
    41, 42, 44, 49; local **43**; upscale 35; *see also*
    indigenous
Rhee, M. 109
Ries, A. 16, **20**
Ritchie, R. 83, 84
Roberts, P. W. **135**
Roehm, M. L. **134**
Rojas-Mendez, J. 89
Romania 37, **43**
Romaniuk, J. 6, 8
Rosa, J. 85, 86
Ryanair 16

Safaricom 27, 28, 31, 32
safe guarantees 9, **12**

Salzer-Mörling, M. 23
Samsung 12
Sanlu 106, 110
scandal 102
Scandinavia 47
"scenario qualifier" 116
Schuiling, I. 64
Segal-Horn, S. 23
selectivity **21**, 60, **61**, 62, 64, 91; positioning strategies **71**, **73–78**
service(s) 3, **20**, **21**, 81, 113, **136**; business 23; clinical 56; economy 15; and emotions toward 93; financial 46; generic 54; "good" 8; goods and 89; industrial 36; industries 110; instant 28; limited 26; medical 52; needs 144; photo 53; pricing 32; products and/or 89, 90, 91, 97, 108, 100, 143, 145; promise 24; provision 31; quality 8, 14, 111, **131**, **133**; recipient 25; *see also* branding services; customer service
service brands 22, 27, 30, 143; successful 33
"service" positioning strategy 56, 57, 58, 59, 60, 94; summary and case studies of **71**, **73**, **74**, **75**, **76**, **77**, **78**
service reliability strategy 9, **12**, 13
Shanley, M. 105
Shansby, J. **20**
Sharma, K. 10
Shi, G. 10
Shoprite 49, 51, 53, 60, 63 65; application of positioning strategies 58–59, **61**, **77**
Sims, J. T. **20**
Singh, J. 3
small- to medium-sized enterprises (SMEs) 10, 11, 14, 16, 29–30
small volumes 33, 144
Smithson, S. 14
snowball techniques 112
Snow Milk 106
social capital 79, 82–85; theory 79, 83, 85
social identity theory 79, 82–85
social networks 32, 79, 80–86
"social responsibility strategy" 15
Sokoya, S. K. 96, 104
solar power 25
South Africa 2, 3, 16, 26–27, 32, 51, 92; branding 89–94, 96, 98–99; origin 60, 63; Pretoria 54; wines 94; *see also* Barcelos; Safaricom; Shoprite; Tshwanes
South America 37
Spain 37, **39**
speed (of service) 10, **12**, 14, 28

Spendstre Photo Store 49, 51, 53, 57, 60, **61**, 62, 64, 65, **76**
Sridharan, S. 83, 84
stability **42**, 107
Standard (brand) 12
Strannegård, L. 23
strategic positioning options **12**
Strodtbeck, F. L. 80
sub-Saharan Africa 14, 47, 53, 90, 95, 96, 97; economies 36, 64; negative perception of 91, 99; overlooking of 46
Sudan 54, 92
susu 83
Sweeney, J. 55, 113
Switzerland 37, **43**
Swoboda, B. 37, **43**, 44

Tanzania 3, 28
Tardits, C. 81
Tarkwa (Gold Coast/Ghana) 81
Tasavori, M. 31
telecommunications 12, 31, 110, 144
Tesar, J. 29, 30
TinMan project, The 24, 25
"top of the range" positioning strategies 60, **61**, 62, 64; case studies **71**, **73–78**
Toroitich, O. 35
Toyota 9, 12, 102
Trout, J. 16, **20**, 63
Tshwanes 26–27
Turkey 47

United Kingdom 13, 16, 37, **39–42**, 44; foreign firms and retailers originating from 47, 51; franchises in 54; sourcing from 56
United Nations Conference on Trade and Development (UNC-TAD) 46
United States 37, **40**; college students in **130**; correlation and descriptive statistics of items for **141–142**; foreign firms and retailers originating from 47; and Ghana, comparative study of 104, 105, 112–122, **117–119**, **138**; product recall in 102, 106, 109
University of Science and Technology (UST) 96
Urde, M. 7

Vallaster, C. 10, 11
value for money **21**; strategy 56, 58, 60, **61**, 62, 63, 64; positioning strategies case studies **71**, **73–78**

Variations in Value Orientation (Kluckhohn and Strodtbeck) 80
Versi, A. 90, 95
"vice versa" relationship 93
Vicdorris 56
Visiting Friends and Relatives (VFR) 95
Viswanathan, M. 83, 84
Vodafone Ghana 12, 15, 31–32
Volkswagen 102, 106, 116
Voltic 12
Volvo 9

Walsh, G. 110
Watatu Company Limited 28–29, 30
Weiner, B. 106–107, 111, 115
West Africa 81, 83
Whetten, D. 105
Wierenga, B. 113
Williams Jr., R. 96
Wind, Y. **20**

Wirtz, J. 6, 8, 23, 24
Wolak, R. 53
Wong, I. A. 10
World Bank 47, 48, 83
World Cup *see* FIFA World Cup

Xie, Y. 110, **132**

Yang, Z. 46, 115
Yannopoulou, N. 108, **131**
Yoruba (Nigeria) 82
Youde, J. 89

Zaefarian, R. 31
Zambia 54
Zambian Stock Exchange 53
Zeithaml, V. 116
Zimbabwe 32, 92
Zins, A. 103, 122
Zumah, Jacob 99